95

# Public Policy and Politics

Series Editors: Colin Fudge and Robin Hambleton

Important shifts in the nature of public policy-making are taking place, particularly at the local level. Increasing financial pressures on local government, the struggle to maintain public services, the emergence of new areas of concern, such as employment and economic development, and increasing partisanship in local politics, are all creating new strains but at the same time opening up new possibilities.

The series is designed to provide up-to-date, comprehensive and authoritative analyses of public policy and politics in practice. Public policy involves the expression of explicit or implicit intentions by government which result in specific consequences for different groups within society. It is used by power-holders to control, regulate, influence or change our lives and therefore has to be located within a political context. Two key themes are stressed throughout the series. First, the books link discussion of the substance of policy to the politics of the policy-making process. Second, each volume aims to bridge theory and practice. The books capture the dynamics of public policy-making but, equally important, aim to increase understanding of practice by locating these discussions within differing theoretical perspectives. Given the complexity of the processes and the issues involved, there is a strong emphasis on inter-disciplinary approaches.

The series is focused on public policy and politics in contemporary Britain. It embraces not only local and central government activity, but also central–local relations, public-sector/private-sector relations and the role of non-governmental agencies. Comparisons with other advanced societies will form an integral part of appropriate volumes. Each book presents and evaluates practice by drawing on relevant theories and applying them to both the *substance* of policy (for example, housing, employment, local government finance) and to the *processes* of policy development and implementation (for example, planning, management, organisational and political bargaining).

Every effort has been made to make the books in the series as readable and usable as possible. Our hope is that it will be of value to all those interested in public policy and politics – whether as students, practitioners or academics. We shall be satisfied if the series helps in a modest way to improve understanding and debate about public policy and politics in Britain during the 1980s.

**Public Policy and Politics**

Series Editors: Colin Fudge and Robin Hambleton

# Urban Economic Development

## New Roles and Relationships

*edited by*

**Ken Young**
*and*
**Charlie Mason**

*First published 1983 by*
THE MACMILLAN PRESS LTD
*London and Basingstoke*
*Companies and representatives throughout the world*

ISBN 0 333 32554 0 (hard cover)
ISBN 0 333 32555 9 (paper cover)

*Typeset in Great Britain by*
WESSEX TYPESETTERS LIMITED

*Printed in Hong Kong*

The authors and publishers are grateful to the Controller of Her Majesty's Stationery Office for permission to include work based on chapter 6, vol. I in *Monitoring Manufacturing Employment Change in London 1976–81: Implications for Local Economic Policy*, by Roger Leigh, Jamie Gough, Karen Escott and David North.

# Contents

# Contents

# Guide to Reading the Book

One of the most striking features of local government in the 1970s was the rapid adoption of an *economic policy role* on the part of many urban authorities. The severity of the recession in the national and international economies and the continuing trends in manufacturing job loss prompted many local policy-makers to initiate new programmes and practices aimed at supporting urban-based industry, a trend which received some reinforcement in the post-1977 policy for the inner cities. Today, almost a decade after these developments were first triggered by the energy crisis, it is worth examining the significance of the new economic policy role of local government. Does it serve welfare needs or those of the market? Are the activities it generates of more than symbolic significance? Can it hope to turn the tide of urban decline?

Concern with these issues need not be narrowly confined to the direct economic consequences of local authority interventions in the local economy. These obviously vary as particular actions interact with local circumstances to provide policy effects that may flow either with or against the trend to urban decentralisation. The complex question of economic consequences can only be answered in its particularities, by a close examination of the ways in which policies impinge on the decision processes and well-being of firms and individuals in specific places.

Our purpose in this book is quite different. We are concerned with the economic development role itself and with its impact on the internal and external relationships of the local authority: relationships between different professions and departments, between neighbouring authorities, between the public and the private sectors and (implicitly) between the older urban centres and the non-urban areas which are now the prime locations for growth.

We have therefore organised this book around three themes. In the first part, *new initiatives*, we deal with the changing relationship between local authorities on the one hand, and firms,

vii

developers and other public agencies on the other. The 1970s saw small but significant shifts towards a closer relationship between local government and the private sector. In comparison with West Germany and the United States, however, public and private decisions in the cities are still made at arms' length.

Our second theme is *organisational processes*. The adoption of an economic development role can affect the pattern of relationships within the authorities themselves, as well as between neighbouring authorities and central and local government. On the other hand, the change may be more apparent than real. Economic planning may attract few resources and routine practices may be almost immune from newly declared goals. Moreover, the declaration of new policies can itself obscure a continuity of intention that has received belated endorsement. The processes of public action require a close examination if we are to distinguish rhetoric from reality.

The third part of the book deals with our final theme: *evaluating* the impact of local authority activities upon firms. Most urban economic development programmes are firm-based rather than people-based. The welfare gains for individuals are supposed to derive from the advantages conferred on firms. Whether or not this assumption is accepted, the ability of local economic policy-makers to bear upon the decision processes of firms is crucial to the evaluation of their activities. Do firms get established, expand, contract, survive, collapse, remain or relocate as a result of local authority action? Can such action have important effects at the margin? These questions lead naturally enough to our concluding section, in which we return to the starting-point of this enquiry and attempt to assess the significance of urban economic development programmes.

*August 1982*                                        KEN YOUNG
                                                     CHARLIE MASON

# 1 Introduction

**KEN YOUNG and CHARLIE MASON**

The nine essays in this book all deal with the involvement of local authorities in the management of their local economies. In common with many other 'innovations' in public policy, urban economic development programmes are not entirely novel. Nevertheless, the great expansion in, for example, the construction of factory premises, in industrial development partnerships with the private sector, or in financial support by grant and loan, is a very recent feature of local government activity. It has bred a new professional creature in the form of the Industrial Development Officer, and heightened the interest in economic issues among planning departments and chief executives' offices across the country.

The five-year period from 1976 to 1981 saw a rapid spread of concern about urban unemployment. The major metropolitan areas in particular were experiencing unexpectedly high levels of population decline and industrial job loss; the continuing recession seemed to hit the older cities with particular force. A few authorities began to develop their own initiatives, which were given increasing attention in the local government press and were gradually imitated elsewhere. 1977 saw a shift of emphasis away from tackling deprivation and towards economic regeneration in the Labour government's White Paper on the inner cities and a DoE circular on *Local Government and the Industrial Strategy*. National and local concerns appeared to converge and, in the Inner Urban Areas Act of 1978, a number of local authorities gained new powers to assist industrial development.

Since 1978 the collapse of Britain's urban industrial base has continued and unemployment has steadily mounted. Already new questions are being asked about the scope and limits of local economic policies. In many cities the rhetoric of economic

1

regeneration has given way to a more prosaic search for palliatives for a tide of dispersal and decline, which few believe it is possible to reverse with conventional measures, if at all. In particular, there is considerable scepticism about the effectiveness of supplying financial aid to firms by 'string-less' loans and grants. Instead, support has grown in some Labour-controlled cities for a more radical and comprehensive approach centred on local equivalents of the National Enterprise Board, on worker co-operatives, on the planned investment of pension funds, on the positive use of purchasing power and on municipal enterprise.

It is far too soon to judge the effects of these versions of a revived municipal socialism. The new central controls over local expenditure may prevent their full development. Whatever their fate, these 'alternative strategies' represent the pinnacle of the belief that local authorities can and do exert influence in their local economies. The essays in this book chart the course towards that pinnacle, the initial, tentative and sometimes misplaced attempts to manage the urban economy.

These various developments in urban economic management brought about a shift of attention among researchers and led, during the late 1970s, to the setting up of the several studies represented here. Each of us, as a researcher, was concerned to explore aspects of this new activity. Independently, largely unaware of one another's interest, yet almost simultaneously, we began work on complementary studies with funding from such diverse sources as the Department of the Environment (Boddy, North and Gough), the Social Science Research Council (Young), the German Marshall Fund (Hart) and the Gatsby Foundation (Storey). In the course of time we contacted one another and exchanged information and experience. From these contacts arose the idea of this book.

During October 1977 and January 1978 the School for Advanced Urban Studies was able to hold two well-subscribed seminars to explore 'the initiatives that local authorities have taken, or can take, to affect, however marginally, the economic situation in their own areas'. The marginality of such action was already apparent; few local policy-makers have been able to point conclusively to substantial achievements in employment terms. Perhaps inevitably, most activity was seen as pump-priming, as demonstrating market opportunities for the private sector or as plugging the gaps between the activities of other public agencies.

Our purpose in this book is then to present a selection of specially commissioned papers from these recent research projects. We hope to cast some light upon a new aspect of local authority activity and to encourage a fuller appraisal of the significance of economic development programmes within the mixed economy of the city. What follows is not, by and large, an economic assessment, but rather a policy commentary and analysis to which our various disciplines – geography, planning, public administration and political science as well as economics – have contributed. Our particular concern is indicated by our subtitle: it is with the *new roles and relationships* which have emerged from the expansion of local economic development programmes.

The current prevalence of local authority economic development activities obscures the very considerable uncertainty that persists as to the local government role, an uncertainty which is reflected in several of the papers which follow. Central departments, on the one hand, may be unconvinced of the net gains to welfare which flow from apparently competitive activities and have increasingly defined the local authority role as a facilitator of whatever developments arise from market forces. Those local politicians and officials who look beyond these limits to a more creative role may none the less nurse lingering doubts as to the effectiveness of the newly devised policies.

Some of the papers illuminate the background to these doubts and may be usefully previewed here. In the paper by North and Gough, the authors see some perhaps surprising conclusions. First, despite the confident assumption of a local authority role in support for small firms, *actual* contacts with private industry are for the most part with the larger enterprises. Notwithstanding the considerable attention given by policy-makers (and, in their turn, by researchers) to the newer and more visible forms of industrial support, it is development control policy – the common bugbear of industrialists – which affects the greater number of firms in the most immediate fashion.

It would be unwise to neglect these more established roles of the local authority, for they may be important determinants of industrial climate. The paper by Young indicates that long-standing land-use policies change more slowly than surface impressions suggest. Similarly, the paper by Stewart and Underwood invites the reader to look beyond the institutional innovations of the inner city partnerships to the continuities in pre-existing roles in relation to economic development. In both cases the rhetoric of innovation can be misleading.

Of all the new relationships which flow from this intensified economic role those with the private sector demand the most fundamental reappraisal. We have deliberately chosen to juxtapose the papers by Hart and by Boddy. The first reviews a range of public, private and joint undertakings in both West Germany and the United States, where the expectations of public–private sector relationships are markedly different from those which have hitherto obtained in Britain. In the second, however, Boddy sets out the highly complex interdependencies which follow from the contemporary UK trend towards adoption of closer forms of public–private partnerships in the industrial development process. The immediate outcome of such partnerships is measured in industrial floorspace and shares of the financial returns; the longer-term effects are the more profound if they leave their mark on the mutual perceptions of public and private actors in the urban development process. Making the mixed economy of the city work to public purposes requires great sophistication in the relationships through which it is achieved.

It is the understandable tendency of policy-makers to justify new or enhanced activities by demonstrable results and in many authorities the recent assumption of a local economic development role will be readily justified to the most casual enquirer with impressive figures of jobs 'created', often at impressively low attributed costs per head. Elected members may be impressed with such confirmation of the success of their policies. Storey's paper, however, counsels extreme caution in the assessment of the true costs and real impact of such strategies. We are clearly a long way from being able to reassure the protagonists of local economic programmes that their real net achievements actually justify their new and often eagerly grasped role.

It would in any case be a mistake to suggest that all the significant decision-makers in all distressed urban areas share a common view of the desirability of a local authority economic role. The willingness to intervene in the local economic situation is highly variable even, as Mawson's contribution shows, among the contiguous authorities of a single (and badly afflicted) metropolitan area. Where there is scepticism or a reluctance to become involved, this will often be attributed to the belief that a host of other agencies already exist to manage the disparate aspects of the local economy; we still hear – if less frequently than before – that 'there is no role for the local authority'.

Two of the papers, in rather different ways, challenge the validity of this assumption. Mason shows that in the relatively unexplored area of labour market policy a new role can be assumed and new relationships forged between the local authority and the other agencies involved. Arguably only the local authority can press the needs of the most disadvantaged groups, for it seems that the target groups of most other agencies are dictated by market needs. Even in the case of more conventional promotional activities the local authority can, as Mawson shows, play a role in orchestrating inter-agency action. Indeed, while experience of local economic initiatives gradually accumulates, there may be a discernible shift from the more straightforward forms of intervention under existing land-use and financial powers towards a more indirect role of brokerage and *concertation*, in which the local authority pursues its goals by influencing and manipulating other statutory and non-statutory bodies. This, perhaps, is the 'lead' role which many feel local government should play in relation to the local economy. It is a far cry from land assembly, infrastructure provision or cosmetic rehabilitation of industrial improvement areas and demands a different skill and will.

The assumption of an economic development role generates new and unfamiliar relationships between local authorities and employers and developers on the one hand, and public sector agencies on the other. Yet, like any new departure in policy, its impact may be felt most acutely within the authority itself; it tends to promote new roles for departments and their associated professions and, in consequence, new relationships between them. The rise of the industrial development officer as (in some cases) a glamorous peripatetic 'networker' is but the most visible of these internal developments. Mawson clearly shows the pattern of divergent professional concerns and conflicting roles in his study of the West Yorkshire districts. Young portrays decisions on industrial land use as the outcome of inter- and intra-departmental struggles to assert the primacy of industry and employment over housing and amenity. To make a role a reality involves some realignment of bureaucratic power. It is apparent that the adoption by local authorities of an economic development role carries with it a number of implications for internal and external relationships. Our collective purpose in the following chapters is to inform the reader about these relationships, using both case study material and more general accounts of recent practice.

# I   NEW INITIATIVES

# 2 Urban Economic Development Measures in West Germany and the United States

D. A. HART

## Introduction

In both West Germany and the United States the last few years have seen a shift in the ways in which city governments deal with firms adversely affected by urban economic change. During the 1950s and 1960s when a general climate of economic growth existed, large urban redevelopment programmes simply demolished a number of existing business premises in the inner city and those who survived were often encouraged to move to the periphery, assisted by public subsidies. While this large-scale approach has not completely ceased it has in many ways been overtaken by events. One of the most significant of these events has been the large increase in oil prices in 1973 and the economic downturn which followed. At the same time public protest against large-scale redevelopment projects also mounted. During the period following 1973 urban authorities in major German and American cities have been increasingly forced to reconsider both the scale and the impact of their activities on the local economy. This paper reviews some of this recent experience, looking first at the general political and economic characteristics which to some extent both countries share, before turning to examine specific examples of promotional activities and public–private relationships.

**The context of local economic development measures**

Cities in the United States and Germany obviously differ from British cities in a host of ways. Two points of difference, for the purposes of this paper, are particularly significant: their geographical scale; and what might be termed their 'economic decentralisation'. Each of these factors will be discussed in turn.

From an American point of view British cities are both compact and well defined. Population densities are high in British urban areas and there is a clear separation of town and country. In the United States, on the other hand, urban sprawl is pronounced. For a variety of reasons including mass automobile usage, relatively cheap petrol, extensive highway systems and the simple availability of land, many major American cities have low population densities and cover several hundred square miles. Because of complex annexation laws most American metropolitan areas are, in fact, clusters of legally separate but physically adjacent cities and surrounding suburbs. Because of the sheer scale of these complexes confusion about terms applied to particular geographical components can result – especially when international comparisons are being made. The phrase 'inner city' for example, has a fairly precise meaning in Britain. A good deal of this precision is lost when this term is used in the United States. Rather than use the term 'inner city' to describe older, decaying sections of urban areas in the United States, we will follow the American convention and use the phrase 'central city'. Although American cities vary widely, the central city is typically the oldest part of the metropolitan area and consequently exhibits a number of environmental and economic problems.[1]

German cities, on the other hand, are in terms of scale roughly comparable with their British counterparts. Because of the damage done to German cities during the Second World War, however, and the consequent large-scale rebuilding programme undertaken after the war, few German cities contain substantial areas of old housing and industrial premises. Urban decay, in terms of obsolete physical plant, is relatively minor by British standards. Nevertheless, problems in terms of structural changes in the economy and the beginning of inner area job loss, as new factories and offices locate in the periphery of cities, are beginning to become evident in the Federal Republic.

Second, both Germany and the United States are organised along federal rather than unitary governmental lines and this has a number of significant fiscal consequences. In terms of the public sector this means that both countries are more economically decentralised than in Britain. A far higher proportion of city funds are raised at the local level in Germany and the United States than they are in Britain, for example. Although it is true that in recent years German and American cities have been provided with an increasing level of federal funds under the Community Financial Reform Act in Germany and the General Revenue Sharing Act in the United States, it is also true that the proportion of central government funds supplied to local authorities in both countries is still a good deal lower than in Britain.[2] The central government block grant in Britain makes a major contribution to the budgets of local authorities and provides them with a level of fiscal uniformity which is unknown in Germany and the United States.

In German cities funds are raised through a local real estate tax which is assessed at 1.4 per cent of the value of land and buildings. In addition, businesses are also required to pay a local trading tax which is based on net assets and includes both a capital and a profit component. The basic rate of the capital tax is 0.2 per cent and the basic rate of the profits tax is five per cent. These rates are then multiplied by differing locally determined amounts so that tax levels on firms can vary significantly from city to city.

If anything the range of financial diversity is even larger in the United States than it is in Germany. A wide variety of revenue-producing devices are employed at the local level. Most cities levy some form of property tax and in addition may also charge a payroll tax, a sales tax and local income tax. The level of taxation differs enormously. Studies have shown that some large American cities have per capital taxation levels which are five times as high as others.[3]

American and German cities are not cushioned from local economic fluctuations to anything like the extent that British cities are. American and German cities are very directly dependent on locally derived revenue. The loss of a major firm, for example, means not only the loss of employment, but, in a very direct way, the loss of tax revenue which allows the local authority to carry out its everyday duties. For these reasons, amongst others, German and American local authorities have, for some considerable period, exhibited a keen interest in the economic health of their cities and in financial measures which could preserve or promote that health. By the same token, it is in the direct interest of these local authorities to both preserve and protect their existing firms and to seek actively to attract new ones, since a good deal of the taxation revenue which they generate is locally spent.

The economic decentralisation in German and American cities referred to earlier also has a private sector element. Most financial institutions – particularly in the United States – are locally based. The financial consequences of this situation are difficult to exaggerate. Following the failure of a number of banks during the Depression in America, federal and state legislation was introduced which limited branch banking. Banks were prevented from setting up branches in states other than the state where they were initially established. In a number of states banks were prevented from setting up branches outside the *city* in which they were initially established. One of the effects of this type of legislation is that financial institutions like banks, and savings and loan associations, develop a lively concern for their local community since their deposits are drawn from this area. A combination of corporate social responsibility and enlightened self-interest means that financial institutions in German and American cities give tangible and often preferential financial support to firms in their areas. By contrast, in Britain the four major banks and the leading building societies are national institutions which adopt a nationwide perspective in allocating their funds. The economy of the local area in which the branches of these institutions are based is often a matter of interest to individual branches but not of overriding concern, since these firms deal with the country as a whole.

Having suggested that there are significant spatial and financial differences between British cities on the one hand, and American and German cities on the other, it is important to establish that there are also a number of similarities. In Germany and the United States, as in Britain, it is possible to find urban decay, continuing job loss and massive disinvestment.[4] These processes are far more advanced in America than they are in Germany, but even in the Federal Republic a number of worrying economic trends of the kind mentioned above are beginning to develop in the inner areas and give rise to public concern.[5]

American cities therefore have had the most experience with continuing decline and decay. Britain occupies some kind of mid-position and the German cities have had the least experience although problems are now beginning to become evident there as well. Something of benefit can be learned in Britain from both other countries in that in the United States remedial measures have been developed to try to combat what has become a chronic condition. In Germany, on the other hand, there is growing concern that unless existing intervention activities – including financial incentives – are at least continued, and possibly even increased, as preventative measures, there is a danger of a gradual urban deterioration over time.

In Germany and the United States there are specific types of financial incentives which share a number of features. In the first place these incentives are highly selective; second, they are spatially 'targeted' on specific development projects which have a demonstrable economic potential; and finally, these incentives are based on the assumption that most of the capital for the project will be supplied by the private sector. Public sector intervention is thus seen as a vehicle for stimulating private investment. This process is called 'leveraging' and it is central to urban economic development thinking in both Germany and the United States. It is not simply assumed that economic regeneration can only take place with the active involvement of the private sector; the much more important assumption is made that *the private sector is the major source of regenerative funding and the principal source of continuing employment and that its performance can be enhanced in the inner city through the selective use of public financial incentives.* The function of the public sector is to catalyse development rather than to carry out the development itself, or leave the development entirely to the private sector.

**Agencies and outlooks**

This section of the paper explores three issues in respect of which the American and German experience contrasts with that of Britain. First, there is the leading role in these two countries of the private sector in urban economic regeneration. Second, there is the concern of local officials there with the promotion of their areas. Third, there is the particular nature of public–private collaboration in the United States and Germany.

*The private sector*

Private business associations at a local level play an active part in economic development both in Germany and the United States. Chambers of Commerce and related organisations composed of local firms have an important role in business promotion. Particularly in Germany, the Chambers of Commerce and Chambers of Craftsmen are powerful bodies who help direct the formation of local economic policy, with large firms becoming members of the Chamber of Commerce and smaller and craft-based firms becoming members of the Chamber of Craftsmen.

By British standards the German Chambers have significant budgets and large staffs. Chamber membership is mandatory and this means that they have substantial revenue and are in the position to develop considerable expertise on economic matters. In Berlin, for example, the Chamber of Commerce employs 200 staff. Individual companies are reluctant to approach the local authorities directly and therefore prefer to work through these trade associations. From an economic point of view, both the Chamber associations perform three functions: first, they operate as a sounding board where an informal and continuous exchange of ideas takes place between Chamber members; second, they regularly consult and are consulted by, a range of outside agencies including the local authorities and the Lander; third, they research and produce written reports of a comprehensive nature on particular problems experienced by member firms.

In certain areas, such as Hamburg, consumer services extend to include financial assistance. In these cases interest relief **on** loans and credit provision is supplied, with the local banks and the

Craftsmen Association sharing the risk. Finally, the Chamber plays a vital part in initially selecting apprentices, finding them employment under the supervision of a qualified master craftsman, then examining their competence during various stages of their vocational training and finally assisting them in finding permanent employment.

Chambers of Commerce are also active in America but it seems that their range of functions is more limited. Two interesting examples of local business associations concerned with economic regeneration are the Old Philadelphia Development Corporation (OPDC) and the Greater Baltimore Committee (GBC). Both organisations began as downtown merchant associations whose principal interest was in helping to arrest central business district (CBD) decline when an increasingly large number of commercial concerns moved from the CBD to suburban shopping centres in the late 1950s. Over a period of two decades, however, both the OPDC and the GBC expanded their concern to include virtually the whole of the central city areas of Philadelphia and Baltimore.[6] It is also interesting to note that in 1978 the Chamber of Commerce of metropolitan Baltimore was merged with, and in effect became part of, the Greater Baltimore Committee.

The membership, and certainly the guiding force, behind these organisations comes largely from private commercial and financial institutions. The OPDC and the GBC have helped the city authorities in conceiving, planning, financing and executing a number of multi-million dollar projects in their respective cities, such as Market Street East in Philadelphia and the Inner Harbour project in Baltimore.[7] Both the OPDC and the GBC have their own planning councils and draw detailed costed development proposals and submit them to the city government for discussion. Additional funds are provided by local banks, savings and loan associations and property development firms. A number of these types of organisations are members of the OPDC and the GBC. The details of financial transactions are then printed, audited and made available for public scrutiny. Initiation of large-scale projects thus, once again, often comes from private sector associations, with approval, land assembly, infrastructure provision and loan support coming from the municipal authority.

The advantages of this type of local business association are obvious. Not only do they have an acute sense of what is financially practical, of what is *good business*, but they are also able to mobilise considerable political and financial support to ensure that proposals actually take place.

Clearly these organisations have achieved a good deal in formerly declining urban areas but there are also potential disadvantages with this type of economic development approach. However powerful these organisations are they are still private groups with limited membership. They are not in the position of being able to speak on behalf of, nor are they responsible to, the citizens of the city as a whole in the way that democratic and effective city government is. Second, and related, because of the nature of these organisations they tend to concentrate their efforts on renewing the CBD although, as we indicated earlier, they are beginning to work in other central city areas as well. Yet they do not seek to take on the role of general urban economic development agencies for the city. Their brief and their area of interest is more limited than that of the local government agencies.

*The public agencies*

In both Germany and the United States city authorities have been increasingly drawn into economic development activities. This involvement takes a rather different form in each case. Many German cities are actively involved in economic promotion as well as preservation and rehabilitation measures. A number of promotional inducements and a wide variety of organisational forms have been created to carry out this work. In general the public sector lead is taken by local authority economic development departments (Amr für Wirtshaftsförderung). Economic development departments which are integral parts of city government are common in Germany.[8] Many have been in existence for a lengthy period of time – some since the end of the Second World War, and were often established at the instigation of the occupying American and British governors. Ironically however, both in Britain and the United States itself this type of department is a good deal less frequent, although interest in many cities is beginning to quicken. Instead, economic promotion as an activity of city government in both countries is usually carried out by a small unit located within the planning or housing departments, or attached to the chief executive's office.

Many of the German economic development departments are extremely effective, with substantial resources. In Dortmund (a city in the Ruhr which had lost 78 000 jobs since 1957 through the closure of surrounding coal mines and the reduced production of its four Hoesch steel plants) the city's economic development department played an active part in attracting new firms. The city had 600 000 square metres of land – often reclaimed coal-mining properties – fully prepared and ready for use and another 800 000 square metres in preparation. As a matter of standard operating procedures the city often subsidised the cost of the land which it sold to private firms. In ten years they have spent 86 million DM for land and site preparation and 'wrote-down' an estimated 1.5 million DM. The annual budget of the economic development department is prepared on a five-year planned projection of expenditure in consultation with the other city departments and they work closely together to develop an economic programme for the city. This type of medium-term budgeting is also supplemented by an attempt to look further ahead and become aware of potential economic difficulties before they become major problems. The economic development director estimated that during the previous ten years 14 000 jobs had been attracted to the city and 18 000 jobs had been retained.

Land is seen as a key resource in economic development in German cities. Both economic development departments and property boards (Liegenschaftsamt), which are largely controlled by the local authority, have established land banks. Land is normally sold to private firms rather than leased. The intention in German cities is not so much to derive income flow from land management or to gain substantial capital appreciation from land sales; it is rather to establish a revolving fund so that additional purchases of land can take place and be sold to private firms, which the local authority believes can provide specific kinds of employment which the area is deficient in and thus achieve a broad economic base.

German city economic officials are particularly concerned to avoid what they call a 'mono-structure' economy: the excessive dependence upon a single firm or industry. As technologies change and patterns of demand alter, large firms engaged in the production of steel, for example, can simply cease to exist. Second, and more subtly, it is known that during a downturn in the trade cycle some firms, such as construction companies, are affected very early in the cycle and other types of industry, such as chemical plants, are not affected until later. By the same token some firms recover from the economic downturn more rapidly than do other types of businesses. The aim of the urban economic development planners is thus to achieve a diversified and balanced local economy so that no single plant closure is too damaging and so that firms can achieve a counter-cyclical balance between them, as they enter and recover from the trade cycle at different points.

In Wiesbaden, for instance, the economic development department carried out a sophisticated microeconomic analysis of its area – a former resort spa – and identified the city's chief economic strengths and weaknesses. After further analysis they identified the kinds of firms which they felt would give the city a stronger, more diversified base. Managing directors of these firms were contacted either personally or by letter from the mayor, with a detailed and costed proposal about the type of advantages Wiesbaden could offer their particular firm. One of the central inducements in these tailored packages was a fully serviced and well-sited plot of land. This microeconomic analysis is regularly brought up to date as the economy of the city changes over time.

American public agencies at the city level have also played an important part in helping to preserve the urban economy of the central city. For example, in keeping with a number of other large American cities located on the north-eastern seaboard, Philadelphia suffered a substantial loss of retail trade and employment in the central area during the 1950s and 1960s. Unusually for American cities, however, it also developed a powerful comprehensive planning process and substantial elements of its 1961 plan, *Center City: Philadelphia*, have been constructed over the past two decades. At least part of the credit for implementing the plan is due to Philadelphia's department of city planning and its retired Executive Director, Edmund Bacon.[9]

Bacon and others in the city government decided to fight the apparently inexorable decay of the central area and the resulting movement of retail shopping to the suburbs, and once again make the city a major shopping centre. The city plan was used as a device to help co-ordinate public investment and the provision of public infrastructure. Although elements of the plan changed over time the key objective of redeveloping the central area in an integrated way remained unaltered.

The phased development of the city centre provided the opportunity to do three things. First, public transport facilities and land use could be more effectively linked. Second, the area could be made more environmentally attractive by extensive pedestrianisation and the siting of different types of activity on various horizontal 'decks' above and below the ground. Finally, because of the improved access and environmental facilities, it was hoped that the sites would become more commercially attractive and this in turn would help arrest the decline of the city centre.

By the beginning of the 1980s the *Center City* plan has been approximately one-third completed. The Philadelphia case provides an interesting example of a city authority which has developed a co-ordinated and integrated planning process without the powerful statutory backing which local authorities in Britain have; and which has used the plan as a device to bring together funds drawn from both the public and the private sector in the joint realisation of their aims. As a result, retail shopping and night-time activities in the central area have increased considerably during the life of the plan with a corresponding increase in both business profits and city property taxes.

The city government of Philadelphia is far from unique in America in seeking ways to respond positively to central city decline and decay. Different cities have, however, adopted different strategies in dealing with the economic and physical problems of their central areas. The city of Boston, for example, has also been troubled for many years with continuing job loss and with the resultant abandonment of physical structures. Instead of undertaking large-scale renewal of the central area as Philadelphia did, Boston decided instead to adopt a different approach which is widely described in America as 'adaptive reuse'.[10]

Adaptive reuse simply means preserving the basic structure of disused buildings and altering their interior so that they can be put to new uses. Thus while redevelopment is about clearance and rebuilding, adaptive reuse is about the rehabilitation and recycling of physical structures. One of the best examples in Boston of reuse is that of the Quincy Market complex which is located in the downtown area of the city.

The Quincy Market complex was initially acquired by the powerful Boston Redevelopment Agency (BRA) as part of their attempts to improve the waterfront area of the city. The BRA has, over time, become interested in reuse as well as redevelopment and the historic market area provided the authorities with a major challenge. The complex consisted of Faneuil Hall and three market buildings, each 500 feet long, which were constructed in the early part of the nineteenth century. The buildings, like Les Halles in Paris and Covent Garden in London, formerly housed the fruit and vegetable wholesale markets for the city, but as their tenants moved out to acquire newer accommodation the market buildings were left idle and became increasingly derelict.

After BRA purchased the market areas the city received a $2.7 million federal preservation grant from the Department of Housing and Urban Development. It was estimated, however, that the total cost of the rehabilitation would amount to more than $20 million. To secure the additional funds the BRA worked closely with the James Rouse Company who acted as the developers and Benjamin Thompson and Associates who became the project architects. After a number of early funding disappointments Rouse – who also developed the private new town of Columbia, Maryland – managed to arrange a financial package which was accepted by the city and the project was launched. The interior service streets have been closed to traffic and extensively pedestrianised; trees have been planted and cobblestones have been laid.[11] Dozens of different types of restaurants and food stores have been opened and the market is visited by hundreds of thousands of people who also enjoy open air entertainment within the complex.[12]

One of the lessons to be learned from both the Philadelphia and the Boston experience is the vital catalytic role which can be played by the public authorities at the city level. The public sector have the unique ability to designate areas for special types of development; to assemble sites; to provide 'priming' grants; to supply infrastructural services; and to co-ordinate transport and land use. The public sector thus typically takes the lead in renewal and redevelopment projects in both conceptual and financial terms. It is extremely unlikely that the private sector, acting alone, would or could have carried out these developments without tangible support from the public sector, and the tangible support often took the form of preservation or infrastructural grants.

Another point which could be drawn from the two different types of strategies employed – large-scale redevelopment in the case of Market Street East, and selective rehabilitation in the case of the Quincy Market – was that neither approach was necessarily superior to the other. Both have their strengths and weaknesses and both need to be carefully related to the social and economic context within which they work.

*Joint ventures*

Finally, there is an important group of economic development organisations in American and German cities which occupy the middle ground, between purely public departments on the one hand, and purely private associations on the other. These organisations, at their most effective, combine the best features of both public and private bodies. They are often incorporated as limited companies in their own right and we will, for the sake of convenience, describe them as joint venture companies (JVC).

In several German cities there are Associations of Economic Assistance (Wirtschaftsförderungsgesellschaften) which, although not part of city government, are partially staffed and largely funded by the public sector and yet retain very close links with the private sector generally and with the Chambers of Commerce and Craftsmen in particular, to provide their member firms with improved premises and prepared sites, normally at an economic rent. A good example of a JVC is a body in Berlin called GSG which is concerned with preserving and promoting small and medium-sized industrial firms.

GSG is a limited company owned by the city-state of Berlin, the Chambers and various local banks. Its board of directors is composed of Senators for Economic Affairs, private sector representatives and federal Ministry of Building representatives. The firm purchases old multi-storey loft buildings (*Gewerbehofe*), modernises them and then rents space on the premises to tenants. The rents are set to cover the real costs of conversion, administration and maintenance under what is called in Germany the 'profit rental' method. The buildings are versatile and tenants include an offset printer, a mirror manufacturer and an engraver.

Typically the tenants pay a rental of from 3.50 to 4.00 DM per square metre.

Another method of promoting the development of small and medium firms is to allow them to expand at their current location. Kreuzberg, an inner area district of Berlin, houses a group of highly specialised, interdependent firms which have taken over closely adjacent residential buildings where historically the owners and workers in the businesses had lived. As people moved out of the area, GSG were instrumental in acquiring these residential properties and converting them to industrial use. This allowed the firms to remain in close proximity to one another and yet increase their productive capacity.

GSG was provided with 55 million DM in operating capital. Of that amount 35 million DM was spent on loft conversion in multi-storey buildings and the remaining 20 million DM was spent in small urban renewal areas, by buying old residential property and then either converting it or demolishing it and building new commercial premises. As property is sold or let, new funds are returned to the operating capital amount. GSG's role in urban renewal was significant since it was estimated that of the firms affected by urban renewal programmes, 40 per cent ceased to exist, 30 per cent found themselves new premises and the final 30 per cent moved into converted lofts of the kind provided by GSG.

American examples of the JVC include the Council for Revitalization of Employment in Industry (CREI) in Philadelphia. Its fifty-person board of directors includes not only a number of business people but also several city political leaders, including the mayor and many top union leaders as well.

CREI was initially oriented towards the local garment industry which, while depressed by low-cost foreign imports, is still one of Philadelphia's largest employers. In addition to providing technical, managerial, marketing, training and financial information to employers, a revolving loan fund has been established to provide low-interest loans for local industrial expansion, often on inner area sites. CREI derives most of its finances from marketing its information and training programmes to private employers (see Table 2.1). Using these funds and the pension funds of a number of local garment unions CREI has also constructed a 700 000 sq.ft 'Garment Center' on a central city site.

A particularly interesting example of a JVC concerned with

**TABLE 2.1  CREI sources of funding**

| | |
|---|---:|
| Federal grants | 9.0 (%) |
| State grants | 13.0 |
| City grants | 13.0 |
| Private donations | 0.7 |
| Programme income | 63.7 |
| Total income (rounded) | 100.0 (%) |

urban economic development overall is to be found in Philadelphia – the Philadelphia Industrial Development Corporation (PIDC). While CREI has tended to concentrate on training programmes relating to the clothing industry, PIDC, established in 1958, was described as the 'grand-daddy' of economic development agencies in the United States, and has developed a complementary working relationship with other JVCs in the city, including, of course, CREI and Old Philadelphia Development Corporation. PIDC has a fifteen-person board of directors which consists of seven senior city officials, including the president of the city council, and eight prominent business people, and meets once every two weeks. Only the board members are allowed to attend the meetings – they may not send alternates. PIDC has a staff of thirty-five which includes financial advisers and real estate experts who work with other agencies to 'package' commercial transactions. In terms of operating strategies PIDC is concerned with 'going after growth' as the city economy changes from being principally industrial-based to being more service oriented. The executive vice-president of PIDC claims that attention is being focused on growing activities such as the health service sector which could then serve as a way of employing people who were made unemployed in declining activities such as textiles. At the same time, a policy-oriented research section constantly attempts to anticipate the economic impact of national and state legislation on the economic structure of Philadelphia and to seek out additional opportunities for development.

Funds for the PIDC's operation come from local banks, such as the Girard Bank, and insurance companies, with roughly half coming from each source, in addition to the initial capital which it was provided with by the city. Staff are of a very high quality, 'production oriented' and are paid on the basis of results. They are expected to provide complete development proposals, including financing, to firms within four weeks from the date the request is received. The organisation's credibility is high and they have conducted transactions approaching one billion dollars in value.

Among other activities PIDC has developed and marketed 1200 acres of land including a 650-acre industrial park. Currently another 1300 acres are being prepared for sale on seven different sites within the city. The land is purchased through a revolving capital improvement fund created in 1961, which provides for the acquisition and development of land for industrial and commercial use. The initial capital was composed of $9 million of city-owned land, plus the proceeds of a $10 million bond issue. As in many German cities when land is sold to a private developer, the accruing funds are returned to the revolving fund and new acreage is purchased by PIDC, so that a range of sites for selection is continuously being prepared and marketed.

One interesting activity currently being conducted by PIDC is the creation of a Foreign Trade Zone (FTZ) in Philadelphia. This 200-acre area is considered to be outside of the United States for customs duty purposes. Merchandise may therefore be moved into this area, stored, manufactured, exhibited or repacked without being subject to American customs duties. Merchandise may also be combined with domestic goods to qualify for a lower duty. If the merchandise is being directly exported to a foreign country no customs duty is levied.

PIDC has a wide range of interests. For example, it manages a 385-acre Food Distribution Center which represents a $100 million public/private capital investment, and provides 900 permanent jobs. In total, during its twenty years of life PIDC has been involved in 1085 property transactions representing over 800 million dollars of private capital investment. It is estimated that 120 000 jobs have been created or retained and over 55 million sq.ft of floor space has been made available to private commerce and industry. The PIDC is a particularly large-scale and successful example of a joint venture company but it is not isolated. JVCs concerned with urban economic development are operating in 200 cities in the United States and a number of German cities as well.

**Urban economic development programmes: two examples**

This section of the chapter takes a closer look at two economic development programmes, each of which exemplifies the *differences* between the American and German approaches. First, we examine the American Urban Development Action Grant scheme (UDAG), a federal programme to stimulate private investment in distressed urban areas. Second, we examine an example of a German city level programme for comprehensive urban renewal, which places particular emphasis on local economic linkages.

*The Urban Development Action Grant*

In order to leverage capital effectively from the private sector, an economically distressed city must demonstrate some potential for recovery. Unless a target area demonstrates some hope of providing a reasonable return on investments made it is unlikely that significant amounts of private capital can be attracted. This means that in the attempt to alleviate social and environmental problems, hard-headed microeconomic profitability calculations need to be made if public/private collaboration is to be anything other than a limited expression of social concern by the private sector.

One interesting example of a financial measure which is specifically aimed at meeting these criteria is UDAG. The purpose of the grant is to help equalise the additional risk and cost imposed on developers who undertake work in the inner and central cities rather than on the periphery, or, as they are called in America, 'green grass' sites. It is very roughly estimated that central city sites are 20 per cent more expensive to develop that are periphery sites. In order to be eligible cities must have a relatively high level of unemployment, an older housing stock and a high proportion of people at or below the official defined poverty level.[13]

The UDAG grants, which are administered by the Department of Housing and Urban Development (HUD), seek to leverage between 4.5 and 6.5 units of private investment for every one unit of public funds which have been committed. A good deal of selective judgement is thus involved on the part of those who evaluate the grant applications. Typically private sources such as local banks would supply 80 per cent of the funds for a project and the remainder would be provided by a combination of the city involved and a UDAG grant. The primary prerequisite is that a high proportion of the funding comes from privately supplied capital which is then backed by public funds. Although it is notoriously difficult to measure the effectiveness of public programmes the UDAG grant appears to be at least a qualified success. The programme has been in existence for a relatively brief period but during its first eighteen months $800 million have been committed in forty-five cities, although the overall grant was initially fixed at $400 million per annum. It is argued that the UDAG leveraging mechanism has been instrumental in creating 80 000 new inner area jobs.

Another interesting feature of the UDAG grant is the way in which grant applications are dealt with. In the first place, the private applicants are those who take the initiatives in putting development projects forward, and are required by law to submit the same information to HUD as they provide to private funding sources and to their local authority. Second, the relatively small federal staff (twenty professionals) based in Washington who process the applications include a substantial proportion of people who have been drawn from the private sector and who have development experience.[14] Finally, since time is at a premium in questions relating to development, HUD must reply to a proposal within sixty days. For each grant made, two applications have been rejected. Once approval has been granted, a legal contract is drawn up and payments are made on the basis of physical progress.

Critics of the initial pattern of UDAG allocations have argued that a very high proportion of the grants were spent on hotels. Defenders of the grant argue that the grant is now being used for an increasingly wide variety of purposes including residential projects. Further, it is argued that the hotels are very labour intensive. To take a specific example from Baltimore, a $10 million grant to build a new hotel to serve the convention centre created 500 permanent jobs in the hotel complex and an equal number of jobs in surrounding service businesses. Most of these jobs are expected to be filled by low or semi-skilled workers. In addition, the hotel will pay the city of Baltimore more than one million dollars each year in taxes of all kinds.

According to a recent statistical analysis of the first two years of operation of the UDAG programme, it is clear that grants are being concentrated on the most 'distressed' American cities and that private investment is taking place in a number of areas where it would probably not have done so otherwise.[15] At least on the face of it, the vitally important goals in urban economic development mentioned earlier – *leveraging* private funds with public grants, and *targeting* that spending on specifically chosen sites in depressed areas – are being achieved. The really vital question surrounding the whole UDAG strategy is: to what extent (if at all) would private investment have taken place in these areas in the absence of the provision of a public grant? Given the complexities of urban economics, this question is extremely difficult to answer precisely and more sustained and systematic analysis is required. Nevertheless, it is already clear that the UDAG approach is a major public policy initiative and that it has already begun to achieve some notable results.

It is important to place the UDAG approach within its wider economic context. UDAG will not, on its own, restore large numbers of manufacturing jobs to declining cities in the north-eastern seaboard, for example. What it might succeed in helping to do, however, is to *ease the transition* between an urban economy which is chiefly based on industrial manufacturing, to one which is chiefly based on service sector employment. Even so, the net result is likely to be an overall reduction in the number of jobs available – particularly in the unskilled end of the market. As one American commentator notes, 'by encouraging shifts in investment among areas, UDAG can speed the transition of distressed areas to new – if reduced – economic functions'.[16] The UDAG approach is therefore initially promising, but it must be seen as a facilitating device rather than an attempt to turn back the economic tide which is affecting older industrial cities in many parts of the world. It is also important to make the point that UDAG is only one of a range of measures currently being employed in the United States to promote economic development.

## Urban Renewal in Small Steps

Among the German cities the positive reaction to urban economic decline of the northern city of Hamburg is particularly interesting. A rolling urban programme called 'Urban Renewal in Small Steps' (Stadterneurung in Kleinen Schritten) has been developed by the city which is concerned with simultaneously renewing both business premises and residential accommodation.

From an economic point of view the overall objective of Urban Renewal in Small Steps is to retain and, if possible, increase the number of jobs available in Hamburg in general, and certain deteriorating areas in inner Hamburg in particular. The importance of existing firms as local suppliers and local employers is paramount. Small industrial plants and small retail outlets are of direct concern since it is recognised the loss of these types of activities can have very severe long-term effects on the economic and social fabric of a neighbourhood, even when the existing housing stock of an area is of adequate quality. The chief advantage of the Hamburg approach is that it identifies a neighbourhood and treats it as a cohesive, functioning economic unit, rather than dividing it into a number of parallel but administratively separate public programmes individually concerned with, for example, housing, urban renewal and environmental improvements.

One of the first tasks of this approach is to select a deteriorating area and examine its microeconomic linkages. Following this microeconomic analysis those businesses which have strong ties with the local community either as suppliers of goods or services or as employers, and whose activities are not residentially disruptive, are encouraged to modernise and remain in their areas. Small firms are valued by the local authorities in Hamburg on the grounds that they are more flexible and innovatory than large firms and also because they – acting as suppliers and retailers – are essential to the production processes of the large firms.

Once this microeconomic analysis is completed plans are drawn up and firms are divided into those who are integrally linked with their local area and whom it would be economically unwise to uproot, and those whose operations would benefit from additional space and newer premises and who could survive being transplanted to a new location. The economic development plans, which are deliberately selective and sensitive, operate on the general principle that firms should not be moved unless there is no other suitable course of action available.

Those firms which are required to move are compensated under the 1971 National Urban Renewal and Town Development Act (Stadtebauforderungsgesetz), which designates certain areas for action and which provides a legal right of substitution of land and compensation for 'unprofitable' moving costs. Landscaped sites are from 2000 to 10 000 square metres and are provided on the periphery of the city by the authorities at subsidised rates. After moving a profitability calculation is made and the economic difference between the old site and the new is made up and the firms are compensated for loss of trade and for removal costs. New premises for firms are also provided within the renewal area itself. If a suitable building can be found it is modernised by the city and floorspace within the building is leased to industrial tenants. Priority for space is given to those firms which have been displaced by urban renewal activity. The firms pay a subsidised rent which goes up in stages over a period of seven years until they are paying an economic rent.

When the small firms stay where they are, there is a modernisation programme operated as part of the Urban Renewal in Small Steps strategy. Firms are encouraged and provided with financial assistance to instal devices, such as noise abatement screens, to improve the quality of their local environment. In addition, collective small goods yards are created so that delivery of materials can be improved. If an owner does modernise his/her firm and the rent increases as a result, (s)he is compensated by the city authority for the difference between the new rent and old rent. Among the major cities of Germany, Hamburg is unique in that renewal compensation is paid to both owners and tenants. Small leaseholders are protected in exactly the same way as are owners. This protection is particularly important for inner area residents since many of them rent rather than own their own property. Hamburg currently spends 30 million DM per year on urban renewal and of that amount between 1.5 and 4 million DM per annum is spent directly on the modernisation of small trade premises. Under the Urban Renewal in Small Steps approach, once a complete neighbourhood size area is improved a new area is selected for renewal and so the process continues in a kind of modular improvement 'patchwork quilt' of development. Because of its ability to deal with a local area as a cohesive economic whole, the limited disruption which it causes and the relatively low cost which it imposes, this approach is currently being discussed in the federal Parliament as a model for development for other German cities.

## Conclusions

It is worth noting that many of the urban areas we visited began economic development programmes precisely because they were experiencing severe economic decline. Boston, Philadelphia and Hamburg, for example, are all examples of waterside cities which have been badly affected by technological changes in shipping and cargo carrying. It is against the background of long-term structural decline that these areas began their economic development activities to fight back actively against growing deterioration. It should also be emphasised that even when these urban economic regeneration measures are working at their best, they cannot be expected completely to reverse long-term economic trends. The worst areas of some of the major cities on the north-eastern seaboard of the United States are far more grim than their British counterparts.

There is, however, a school of thought which suggests that at least some of the major northern cities in the United States may have 'bottomed out', a phrase which means that their population and economic decline is beginning to stabilise and may actually be slowly reviving in a few cities, such as Baltimore. It is far too early to talk about a 'renaissance of urban life' in the central city. Nevertheless, something encouraging is beginning to happen in a few cities and their economic and population base is beginning very slowly to grow. There are obviously a complex variety of factors at work in this limited regeration process including the rising cost of energy and hence the incentive to reduce the distance of the journey to work. Economic development measures on their own are limited tools but they could have an important role to play in helping to arrest urban decay as part of an overall strategy.

In addition, we felt that intangible qualities such as confidence and trust were important and strengthened the working relationships between the public and private sectors. In both German and American cities economic regeneration measures are given strong and sustained political backing. Economic development is not a party political issue and it is supported by Christian Democrats, Democratic Socialists, Democrats and Republicans alike. Over time the range of close contacts between the public and the private sectors has grown as a result of working on well supported projects, and suspicions have been dispelled and uncertainty reduced.

Another intangible quality – the positive attitude towards private profit and public entrepreneurship – was also significant. As a city official in Philadelphia remarked, 'a good deal for us is jobs, property taxes and a fair return on capital'. Many public and private actors are concerned with doing something to help the city; they feel that the most important service that they could perform for their local community is the retention or attraction of secure employment. In this way, what begins as vague feelings of civic pride in distressed areas often ends as concrete and tangible major projects.

This chapter has been concerned almost exclusively with economic considerations. However, we are well aware that the plight of Britain's inner cities is not simply economic and that social and environmental factors are also involved. Even if all of the inner cities' economic problems could be solved at once there would still be a substantial legacy of social and environmental difficulties to be faced which have accumulated over a period of years. Yet, while it is true that the inner city in Britain is not simply an economic construct, unless the economic component is directly addressed the other facets of the problem cannot be satisfactorily resolved. Some form of joint public/private economic intervention would seem to be a *quid pro quo* for the effective management of the complex bundle of issues which is collectively described as the decline of the inner city. There is no guarantee that the inner city problem can be solved purely through economic measures. There is every likelihood that it is insoluble without them.

We would therefore argue that much remains to be done since economic decline is an important part of the inner city problem in Britain; that the public and private sector could fulfil an important role by actively exploring alternative methods of working together to promote economic development; that actual examples of such joint ventures are in operation in Germany, in America, and more recently in some inner areas in Britain; and finally that the relevant empowering legislation already exists to promote such programmes in other British cities. It must be recognised that the economic plight of the inner areas is unlikely to improve spontaneously.

## References

1.  For an overview see B. Berry, 'Inner City Futures: an American Dilemma Revisited', *Institute of British Geographers Transactions*, new series, 5 (1), 1980.
2.  S. Gude *et al.*, 'Urban Policy in the Federal Republic of Germany', in G. Schwartz (ed.), *Advanced Industrialisation and the Inner City* (Lexington Books, 1981) p. 104. See also G. Schwartz, 'Urban Policy and the Inner Cities in the United States' in her *Advanced Industrialisation*, p. 53.
3.  D. Caraley, *City Government and Urban Problems* (Prentice-Hall, 1977) p. 411.
4.  On the American situation see J. Black, 'The Changing Economic Role of Central Cities and Suburbs', in A. Solomon (ed.), *The Prospective City: Economic, Population, Energy and Environmental Developments* (MIT Press, 1980).
5.  For a comparative view of the structure of the relationship between the public and the private sectors in Britain and Germany, see W. Corden and G. Fels (eds), *Public Assistance to Industry: Protection and Subsidies in Britain and Germany* (Macmillan, 1976) p. xxii, cited in N. Johnson and A. Cochrane, *Economic Policy-Making by Local Authorities in Britain and the Federal Republic of Germany* (Allen & Unwin, 1981). See also on the German situation, U. Pfeiffer, 'Market Forces and Urban Change in Germany', in R. Rose (ed.), *The Management of Urban Change in Britain and Germany* (Sage Publications, 1974).
6.  Old Philadelphia Development Corporation, *Twenty-Second Annual Report*, (Philadelphia, Pa.: OPDC, 1978) p. 2.
7.  The Market Street East project, and the role of the public sector, is described in more detail in the next section of this chapter.
8.  Johnson and Cochrane, *Economic Policy-Making by Local Authorities.*
9.  K. Halpern, *Downtown USA* (New York: Whitney Library of Design, 1978) pp. 109–15.
10. On this topic generally, see The Centre for Urban Policy Research, *Adaptive Reuse Handbook* (Piscataway, N.J.: Center for Urban Policy Research, 1980).
11. Halpern, *Downtown USA*, p. 197.
12. Compare the similarity of treatment of the market buildings in Boston and the more recently rehabilitated Covent Garden site in London, and contrast both with the demolition which occurred at Les Halles in Paris.

13. G. Schwartz, *Retrospect and Prospects: Urban Policy Profile for the United States* (Columbus, Ohio: Academy for Contemporary Problems, 1979).
14. For a discussion of the administration of the grant see D. Cordish, 'Overview of UDAG', in R. Nathan and J. Webman (eds), *The Urban Development Action Grant Program* (Princeton, N.J.: Princeton Urban and Regional Research Center, 1980), pp. 11–12.
15. J. Webman, 'UDAG, A Targeted Urban Economic Development Program', in Nathan and Webman (eds), *UDAG*, p. 106.
16. Ibid, p. 109.

# 3 Changing Public–Private Sector Relationships in the Industrial Development Process

MARTIN BODDY

## Introduction

The emphasis in the responses of British local authorities to recent economic decline and rising unemployment has been firmly on providing or facilitating the provision of sites and premises for industry. Loans and grants to industrialists, promotion and advice and labour market policies have played a part in many authorities but the central plank of local economic policy has been industrial development.[1]

The scale of provision and the range of authorities carrying out industrial development expanded dramatically from the early 1970s. In particular there has been an upsurge of local authority involvement in the provision of small factory units. This expansion took place despite increasing pressure upon authorities' dwindling financial resources. Overall local authority expenditure on industrial estates and development rose from £29 million in 1976–7 to £97 million in 1978–9,[2] and a number of individual authorities have funded substantial development programmes. Sunderland Borough Council's capital expenditure on industrial land acquisition, site development and factory construction averaged

34

over £600 000 per year from 1977–8 to 1979–80; Sheffield City Council's 1979–80 capital programme includes industrial development expenditure totalling £3.6 million between 1974 and 1980, including £2.9 million for factory development; and Lewisham London Borough Council's 1979–80 to 1983–4 capital programme includes expenditure of £3.2 million for industrial development.

Local authorities are involved in the industrial development process in a variety of ways: as planning authorities, concerned with plan preparation, development control and processing planning applications; as landowners; as developers of sites and estates for industry; and as developers providing actual premises for industry. Other activities also relate to industrial development including, for example, provision of roads, environmental works and action related to industrial improvement areas, maintaining registers of sites and premises which are available or for sale, and financial assistance to firms acquiring sites and premises.[3] This chapter focuses specifically on local authorities' direct involvement in industrial development as providers of land and premises, and the changing role of authorities in the industrial development process in recent years. In particular, it looks at the way local authority roles in relation to the private sector have changed and evolved. The more active and direct involvement of local authorities in industrial development has drawn them into closer and more complex relationships with developers, financial institutions and other private sector actors. This evolving relationship is explored here by looking in turn at the supply of sites for industry, the provision of industrial premises and, lastly, the crucial issue of funding for industrial development.

Before presenting this analysis, two qualifications need to be made. First, the chapter is concerned with the nature of local government *activity* and no attempt is made to evaluate its immediate *impact* or effectiveness in combating economic decline and unemployment. These issues are, however, crucial and their neglect here neither represents any necessary endorsement of the current emphasis in local economic policy on industrial development nor acceptance of the assumptions behind it. Second, there are problems facing any attempt to generalise about this field of local government activity. On the one hand, there is great variation between local authorities' industrial development activity relating both to the individual characteristics of different authorities and their local economic circumstances. On the other hand, there is a lack of general information covering all authorities and the range of activities and issues discussed in this chapter. Postal surveys carried out in 1971–2 and 1978[4] give some idea but they are partial and not strictly comparable. Much of the detailed analysis is therefore based on case studies of individual local authorities carried out by the author,[5] which are supplemented by a number of secondary sources. Inevitably then, the analysis is largely qualitative and to some extent subjective although one can, I believe, be confident that its main features are essentially correct.

**Industrial sites**

A number of authorities throughout the country have a municipal tradition of industrial trading estate development in the postwar period. Bristol City Council, for example, established the first of a number of estates immediately after the war and made further land acquistions in the early 1960s; Derby City Council have established four major estates totalling almost 200 acres on land acquired from the 1950s through to the early 1970s and have been the main source of serviced sites for industry in the city. Typically a local authority would acquire a freehold site, provide roads and sewers on site in several phases and offer individual plots to industrialists on a long lease. Many authorities have acquired sites through slum clearance which have been subsequently rezoned for industry and made available after clearance and site works; redundant school sites, council depots, and abandoned road schemes have, for example, also yielded sites for industry. Such sites while not specifically acquired as part of a conscious industrial development strategy, have been turned to this purpose. Sheffield City Council, for example, have extensive holdings of slum clearance land rezoned for industry in the Lower Don Valley, the city's traditional industrial area, while Derby's latest estate development utilises slum clearance land.

In the late 1960s, characterised as 'a period of intensive activity' in the industrial development field,[6] local authority development activity was stimulated by the Local Authorities (Land) Act 1963. This gave them powers to acquire and develop land and give loans to developers utilising local authority sites. The exact scale of activity under the 1963 Act is unclear.[7] Industrial site provision seems, however, to have expanded significantly more recently. Survey evidence suggests that in 1971–2 36 per cent of British local authorities had sites available on industrial estates and 42 per cent had industrial land for sale. By 1978, 53 per cent of authorities were developing significant industrial estates.[8]

Local authorities' role in land supply in the late 1970s was stimulated by the Community Land Act 1975 which gave all authorities powers and finance to acquire, compulsorily if necessary, sites for industry and to fund infrastructure works prior to selling leasehold interests to the private sector.[9] The Act was slow to start, remained under strong central government control and only limited funds were made available. It was wound up by the incoming Conservative government in 1979. Nevertheless, 251 sites for industry (646 hectares) were purchased from 1976–7 to 1978–9, 145 (58 per cent) of which were in designated assisted areas. Total expenditure on land acquisition amounted to £16.5 million. Many authorities used the Act to pursue industrial development objectives. Most acquisitions were relatively small individual sites which were disposed of to individual industrialists or developers. Some authorities were, however, able to make more substantial acquisitions: Sunderland Borough Council acquired three sites totalling 87 acres and Gillingham Borough Council bought a 90-acre former barracks site, 37 acres of which are currently being developed by Grosvenor Estate Commercial Developments. Furthermore, the Act undoubtedly encouraged a wide range of authorities towards more active involvement in the industrial field and more sophisticated development practices.

## Changing motives for involvement

Although provision of industrial sites is not a new form of activity for local authorities, their motives for involvement have undoubtedly changed through time. Immediately after the Second World War estate development was seen as a contribution to postwar reconstruction and modernisation. By the late 1950s and throughout the 1960s, authorities were more concerned to provide sites for industry displaced by road schemes, comprehensive redevelopment, slum clearance programmes and planning policies. Securing the local industrial base was the general aim but largely as an adjunct to the primary policies of redevelopment and planning. The main exceptions were authorities in assisted areas where efforts to attract industry, supplementing central government regional policy, became a priority. Generally, however, it was not until the 1970s that the provision of sites for industry was pursued specifically in response to local economic decline and rising unemployment, with a significant expansion in the scale of activities and the range of authorities involved.[10] More authorities sought to acquire sites for industry, and also to turn existing landholdings to industrial use; land not specifically acquired for industrial purposes became increasingly important in terms of industrial development programmes. Much of the emphasis was on economic regeneration and stimulating growth. Mention should, however, be made of authorities in areas of relatively high growth pressure and demand for industrial sites, typically shire counties in the south of the country. A number of such authorities are substantial landowners, involving themselves in the development process in order to control the form and rate of development and to reap the financial rewards of development activity.

The role which local authorities have seen themselves playing in the land market and development process and the specific need or demand they have sought to meet have also changed through time. Until recently many authorities restricted provision to industrial firms seeking sites on which to have premises built for their own occupation. Warehousing and distribution activities were largely excluded on the assumption that they generated less employment and represented an insecure foundation for the local economy, compared with manufacturing industry to which it was thought, therefore, that local authority efforts should be directed. Reappraisal of this assumption against the background of the overall switch in economic activity nationally towards the service sector, and the feeling that any jobs are better than none has led many authorities to relax this policy, though many will still resist retail warehousing on council trading estates.

Similarly, authorities have in the past been reluctant to supply land to private industrial developers as opposed to industrial firms. Authorities saw their role as meeting the immediate needs of industrialists rather than aiding developers to secure profits.

Furthermore, private developers were providing mainly standardised speculative warehouse units suited to the investment market, rather than units tailored to the particular needs of the industrial firms on which local authorities were concentrating their attention. Authorities saw themselves as complementing the private sector providing firms with an alternative to leasing premises on private industrial estates. Since the mid-1970s, however, authorities have been more willing to dispose of sites to private developers and, indeed, to promote development on a joint basis with the private sector. This reflects authorities' concern to ensure the availability of a wide range of types of premises despite their own lack of resources for substantial construction programmes, coupled with a broadening of the type of industrial development which the private sector has been prepared to undertake. Furthermore, the Community Land Act, which intended that development land would eventually pass through the hands of local authorities, led many of them to reassess their role in relation to the private development industry.

**The mechanics of land disposal**

The precise nature of local authorities' involvement in the industrial development process and, in particular, their changing relationship with the private sector is illustrated by the detailed forms of land disposal which are discussed in this and in succeeding sections of the chapter. Authorities' involvement in the development process has broadened considerably as different methods of disposal have evolved. Different forms of disposal have implications both for the financial return received and for the type of industrial development which is to be promoted by the authority. Thus to make an initial distinction, sites may be sold *freehold* to give an immediate financial return but minimal control over development beyond the provisions of the planning Acts. Alternatively, *leasehold* disposal allows much greater control over the development by means of legally binding covenants incorporated in the agreement, and is financially more flexible. Leases may be granted in return for an initial lump sum or 'premium', a stream of rental payments over the period of the lease, or a combination of the two. Periodic reviews of the level of ground rent payable enable a local authority to participate in rental growth, whereas freehold sales or premiums generate a once-for-all estimated market value. Authorities may favour either leasehold or freehold disposal as a matter of principle depending on whether they favour retaining public ownership of assets in land or not. Others may be more flexible or pragmatic depending on the merits of individual cases, though from 1976 to 1980 under the provisions of the Community Land Act authorities were not permitted to dispose of freehold interests in land. Authorities may, however, want immediate capital receipts for financial reasons even though ground rents may be more beneficial in the long term. The choice of disposal mechanism can also affect the type of industrial firm that can be attracted or the type of development a developer is willing or able to carry out. It can therefore have implications which go beyond the narrowly financial to wider issues of economic and employment policy.

Local authorities have tended to favour leasehold rather than freehold disposal, though both have been important. But leasehold disposal has become increasingly important, and more complex in form. Changes in local authority practices reflect in part general changes in the industrial land market and development process. Thus with accelerating inflation rates, fixed ground rents which were common after the last war were replaced by rents reviewed periodically over the term of the lease. Intervals between reviews have dropped from ten or fifteen years in the 1960s and seven to ten years in the early 1970s to currently five or even three years. Lease lengths meanwhile have lengthened from 50 or 75 years after the war, to 99 years and more recently in some cases to 125 years, under pressure in particular from institutional investors.

As landowners, local authorities have also developed more sophisticated forms of leasehold disposal, particularly as their involvement with private developers as opposed to industrial companies has grown. Authorities have been seeking both to improve their share of the financial returns generated, given rising inflation and accelerating rent levels, and to promote the type of development which they want to see built. These changing practices were fostered by the experience and awareness generated by operating the Community Land Scheme and also through the application to the industrial sector of more complex disposal arrangements evolved in town centre redevelopment and major commercial and retail schemes in the 1960s and early 1970s. The fact that the private sector has become more willing to undertake industrial development and investment over the last decade has provided opportunities for these more complex arrangements involving local authorities. Thus changing methods of land disposal by local authorities reflect in part a response to changing market conditions, but they are also the means whereby authorities share in the financial benefits of closer and more complex relationships with the private sector, and can influence the nature of the development which is undertaken. This will be illustrated by looking at three aspects of land disposal: rent sharing and joint development; 'lease-leaseback' agreements; and lastly, development briefs.[11]

*Rent sharing and joint development*

Local authorities disposing of land to industrial developers would, in the past, usually agree a freehold price, premium or ground rent before development started. This would be based on some estimate of what the completed scheme would be worth to the developer but was not tied directly to the actual value of the development or the actual rental income it would generate. Now it is increasingly common for an authority to take part or all of its return on the land, after a development has been completed, in the form of a share of the actual value of the scheme or of the rental income generated. The exact return is less certain at the outset than where the authority simply disposes of land for an agreed amount, but by sharing more of the risk and uncertainty the authority will usually receive a larger share of the rewards.

Rent sharing is one form of joint development: the authority receives over the period of the lease an agreed share of the rent paid by the tenants of the factory units which the developer constructs. The authority's share will reflect the value of the land and any other contributions it makes, such as infrastructure, in relation to the cost of the completed development, and its income will rise as the tenants' rents are periodically increased. Derby City Council, for example, granted a 99-year lease to a development company in return for 10 per cent of the rental income generated by the small factory units which the company were to build, let and manage.

Similarly, Wakefield District Council granted a 125-year lease to a developer and provided infrastructure works for a £2.5 million, 250 000 sq.ft warehouse development in return for a share of rental income.

On completion a development is often sold to an institutional investor rather than held by the development company. In such cases the local authority and the developer will commonly divide up the development value created; that is, the difference between the cost of the development and its sale price. There are many possible bases for this division which will reflect both the value of the respective contributions to the scheme made by the authority and the developer, and also the degree of risk or uncertainty each partner bears. They may simply share the development value on a percentage basis. Alternatively, it may be agreed that the local authority receives a fixed amount first and then a percentage share of the remainder; or the developer may be guaranteed an amount to cover the cost of construction plus a share of the rest. Many variations on the themes of rent sharing and joint development are possible. The general principle, however, remains the same: rather than an authority simply selling land to a developer, it contributes land and possibly infrastructure to the development process and shares the return on the development. The authority shares the risks and rewards of the development process.

*Lease-leaseback agreements*

The rent sharing and joint development arrangements discussed above are essentially alternative ways of generating receipts from land disposal which, while possibly beneficial in financial terms, may have little effect on the actual form of the development that takes place. To overcome this, local authorities have increasingly turned to lease-leaseback agreements which guarantee the return on investment in industrial units. This may enable the authority to influence the type of units the private sector will build and the sort of locations where they will undertake development.

Typically a developer constructs units on a local authority site. The developer sells the completed units to a financial institution to which the authority grants a long lease for a nominal ground rent; the authority then takes a lease back on the units from the institution for which it pays the institution an agreed proportion of their market rental value for the term of the leaseback, the rental value being periodically reviewed. The authority sublets the individual units to occupiers and is responsible for their management. Since the authority pays the agreed proportion of rental value whether or not it actually sublets the units, the institution's investment income is guaranteed. Thus, for example, Hindscourt Properties constructed 60 000 sq.ft of small factory units on a site owned by the London Borough of Greenwich. On completion the Council granted the Property Growth Assurance Company, which purchased the units, a 125-year ground-lease for a nominal rent and took a 125-year leaseback from the insurance company on the units under which it pays 80 per cent of rental value and retains the rest. Most schemes have been funded by insurance companies or pension funds and have been based on 99-year or 125-year leases. The 1980s, however, saw the growth of shorter term schemes funded over 25 years by commercial leasing companies, several of which are offshoots of the main clearing banks. These developed partly to take advantage of tax allowances introduced in 1980 on the financing of factory units up to 2500 sq.ft. Since part of the tax benefit is passed on to local authorities these schemes had obvious financial attractions and expanded rapidly.

Again, there are many variations on the general theme but the principle underlying these schemes is that rents are guaranteed by the local authority.[12] This can enable an authority to secure private sector funds and to promote development where private development interests would not otherwise proceed, and where the authority lacks funds to undertake development itself. Lease-leaseback agreements have thus been used primarily by authorities in order to facilitate development of small industrial units. They may also increase the financial return compared with conventional leasehold disposal of sites since the authority is offering the private sector a risk-free investment. But whereas financial motives largely explain the growth of rent sharing and joint development, in the case of lease-leaseback arrangements they have been largely subordinated to the desire to facilitate the provision of industrial units.

*Development briefs*

With the growth of public–private sector collaboration, local authorities have been playing an increasingly active part in the industrial development process. This has been fostered by the growing practice of using 'development briefs' to initiate, promote and control development in line with authorities' policy aims.[13] These are documents drawn up when leasehold interests in sites are offered for sale, which give information about the site but also indicate what the authority is seeking by way of development. Briefs vary considerably but might typically indicate prevailing planning policies, site characteristics, the intensity, form, layout and design standards of development, the form of leasing and financial arrangements sought and the way the developer is to be selected.

Hampshire County Council, for example, offered 125-year leases on sites on a new industrial estate in the form of a brief restricting occupiers to desirable industrial users, excluding speculative development, warehousing, firms requiring open storage and the motor repair trade and specifying a high standard of physical design, layout and construction in order to enhance the Council's financial return and the local environment. Many authorities have marketed sites with a brief specifying small units: Derby, for example, offered the lease on a nine-acre site with a brief for small units and indicating they wished to receive 10 per cent of the rental income generated by the completed scheme; and Leicestershire offered a 0.8-acre former highway depot with a brief inviting schemes on a lease-leaseback basis. Development briefs in themselves are only indicative. Leasehold disposal, however, enables legally binding conditions or 'covenants' to be incorporated into the lease agreement.

Local authorities as landowners have, as we have seen, become increasingly actively involved in the industrial development process. More complex forms of land disposal have evolved with authorities taking a larger share of the risks and rewards of development. In particular this has involved authorities in collaborating with the private sector, initiating and promoting particular types of development, sharing rental income or development value and underwriting investment risk through guaranteeing rents. Major changes have thus taken place in local authority roles and activity. Here, however, it is important to distinguish between the evolution of more sophisticated land management and disposal practices by local authority estates, valuation and development sections which reflect a desire to participate fully in the *financial* rewards of development, and changing practices which reflect a wider concern for *economic* development and *employment* issues. In terms of the specific forms of land disposal discussed above, the growth of more complex forms of leasehold disposal, rent sharing and joint development has been motivated primarily by financial concerns indicative of an increasingly entrepreneurial approach by local authorities. Lease-leaseback agreements, on the other hand, have enabled authorities to play a more positive role by promoting development schemes which the private sector would not otherwise have been willing to undertake – development of small factory units or in locations considered marginal in commercial terms, which may have benefits in terms of wider economic and employment criteria. Finally, the influence of development briefs will vary. They may be used to suggest, initiate and promote development schemes, such as small factory units, which an authority considers appropriate in economic and employment terms. They may, however, be used to secure schemes or financial arrangements which, it is thought, will maximise an authority's financial return. To the extent that an authority insists on a development which does not generate the maximum return possible on a particular site, its financial return from disposing of the site is likely to suffer. Gains in terms of economic and employment criteria may thus have to be bought at the expense of monetary gain.

**Industrial premises**

Changes in forms of land disposal have brought greater local authority involvement in the actual development process. The 1970s, however, saw also a dramatic expansion of direct development of industrial premises by local authorities themselves. A number of authorities did construct advance factories in the immediate postwar period and, later on, the Local Authorities (Land) Act 1963 promoted some activity.[14] But relatively few authorities had built new industrial units until the early or mid-1970s. According to the 1971–2 survey[15] only 5 per cent of authorities had new factory units available; by contrast, 57 per cent of respondents to the 1978 survey (and 68 per cent of London boroughs and metropolitan districts) had built or were building new units of under 5000 sq.ft and a further 24 per cent were considering doing so.[16] Several authorities have carried out substantial building programmes. Tyne & Wear County Council and the district councils within the county completed 187 units between them in the four years 1976 to 1979 totalling 435 000 sq.ft of which all but eight units were no larger than 5000 sq.ft.[17] Sheffield City Council completed seven factory developments between 1972 and 1979 containing 149 individual units. Major programmes on this scale are mainly confined to authorities in assisted areas and to the more interventionist Labour-controlled authorities. Many more authorities throughout the country have completed one or two developments of small factory units.

As this handful of the many possible examples suggests, local authorities have concentrated almost exclusively on small factory units of less than 5000 sq.ft but including in many cases 'workshop' units of say 500 to 1500 sq.ft. This sector of the market had until recently, been largely neglected by the private sector and to some extent also by other public agencies and authorities have tried to fill the gap. It also reflects the specific concern of many local authorities for small and new businesses.

The majority of small factory developments have used individual sites of around one to three acres. These have often been redevelopment sites acquired, say, through slum clearance, or older industrial sites. However a number of authorities have incorporated small factory unit developments on industrial estates where they are providing primarily serviced sites, the aim being to ensure that a full range of unit sizes are available to industry.

The actual part played by the local authority can vary greatly, the major common factor in direct provision of premises being that the capital cost is met by the authority. An authority may, for example, engage a private developer to provide factory units on a 'design and build' basis, it may put out to tender the building contract for a scheme designed by its own staff or by a private architectural practice, or it may use its own direct labour force for the construction work carrying out all aspects of the development process itself. The degree of expertise required of an authority obviously varies as does the implied political commitment to public or private enterprise.

Factory units are usually let and managed by authorities themselves. Overt letting policies may give priority to industrial activity rather than warehousing or to new and local firms rather than outsiders. In practice, however, the financial imperative of ensuring that units are let and generating income is dominant and choice of tenants on wider economic or employment grounds is only usually exercised when there is excess demand for units. Rents are set initially at commercial, market levels. Some authorities in assisted areas do pass on a Regional Development Grant to their tenants in the form of initial rent concessions, and financial assistance to individual firms may take the form of rent subsidies. But this is kept separate from the initial setting of rent levels which it is not intended should subsidise or assist firms.

Local authorities have successfully expanded the supply of small factory units and responded to demands or needs of firms which were being neglected by the private sector in particular. To some extent this is because they have identified and demonstrated demand of which private developers were unaware or uncertain. But it is also because authorities have been prepared to accept higher risks and lower rates of return than commercial developers, in pursuit of economic development and employment objectives (their success in meeting these objectives is not at issue here).

More recently there has been a marked increase in private sector provision of small units. This has followed on to some extent from the demonstration by local authorities that demand for these units exists and was stimulated also by government tax allowances from 1980. Public sector agencies, including the English Industrial Estates Corporation and the Scottish and Welsh Development Agencies, have also turned their attention to smaller units. Where private sector or other public agency provision has been adequate, local authorities have generally been content to relinquish their own direct involvement in developing units. Although direct provision of premises by local authorities did expand dramatically in the late 1970s and into the 1980s, shortage of capital funds is likely to curtail this, and place the emphasis more on joint development of premises in collaboration with the private sector.

**Development finance**

Industrial development has faced increasing competition from other areas of activity within local authorities for shrinking capital funds, while most recently the Local Government, Planning and Land Act 1980 has constrained and altered the possibilities for capital expenditure. The availability of funds from different sources has varied considerably through time. Furthermore, the financial circumstances of different local authorities, particularly regarding the level of their capital funds and their ability to generate capital receipts or attract private sector finance, differ. The main sources of funds can, however, be summarised.

Until the mid-1970s, industrial development was traditionally funded out of authorities' internal capital funds or by borrowing, allowed by the general 'Locally Determined Sector' allocation. But LDS allocations dried up through the 1970s and pressure on internal funds grew in most authorities. Authorities increasingly relied, therefore, on collaboration with the private sector and on specific initiatives by the central government. Such initiatives as the construction package are discussed further in Chapter 7. In response to the squeeze on their traditional sources of funds and the limited and selective nature of the alternatives offered by central government, local authorities have increasingly sought private sector finance. Lease-leaseback agreements have been used to underwrite risk and thereby encourage pension funds, insurance companies and other institutions to invest in industrial units and to enable developers to obtain finance. Leasing companies have been used to fund the construction of small factory units on an expanding scale since 1980. More generally, local authorities have relaxed their emphasis on supplying sites to industrial firms and become more willing to offer sites which are attractive to private developers and investors, on disposal terms which facilitate and encourage private investment.

Various forms of joint development of local authority landholdings have been employed to fund the provision of both serviced industrial sites and industrial premises. A range of more innovative arrangements has been discussed, but with only limited practical application as yet, including joint public/private sector companies, development trusts, 'covenant schemes', short-term local authority rental guarantees. Local authorities have also in a wider sense attempted to create the confidence necessary to attract private sector development finance by selected use of public funds to improve the physical environment, to demonstrate demand by successfully providing and letting small factory units and to improve infrastructure.

Local authorities have thus come to rely less on their own internal sources of finance or on general borrowing permission and more on specific initiatives by central government – the Community Land Scheme, Inner City Construction Aid money, Inner City Urban Programme funds – and on private sector finance. On the one hand therefore, they are subject to the particular form and direction of specific central government initiatives, and authorities pursuing continuing programmes of factory building, for example, have had to switch pragmatically between sources of funds. On the other hand, to the extent that local authorities come to rely on private sector funds and on joint development, they will become increasingly subject to the commercial financial and investment criteria operated by the private sector and they may find themselves increasingly underwriting risks and providing the preconditions for subsequent private sector profitability. Where authorities have acquired sites which are commercially attractive, collaboration with the private sector may enable them to maximise their financial returns. But where local authorities are promoting forms of development for wider economic or employment objectives, which the private sector is unwilling to undertake on purely commercial criteria, this will inevitably, in many cases, involve authorities in subsidising the private development industry.

**Conclusion**

The major emphasis in local authorities' responses to economic and employment problems has been on providing industrial sites and premises. The scale of provision has expanded dramatically since the early 1970s, in particular the supply of small factory units. Quantitative expansion has, however, been accompanied by qualitative change in the nature of authorities' industrial development activity. The motives for this activity are now, above all, to combat local economic decline and rising unemployment, whereas previously they were more diverse. Also, until recently local authorities saw their role as catering directly and primarily for industrial companies; now they are usually willing to provide on an equal basis for warehouse and service activity and to supply sites to speculative industrial developers as well as industrialists having premises built for their own use. Most significantly, local authorities' more active and direct involvement in the industrial development process has drawn them into closer and more complex relationships with development companies, financial institutions and other private sector development interests.

Forms of land disposal by local authorities have changed considerably in recent years. In part this reflects general changes in the industrial land market and development process. More sophisticated disposal mechanisms have, however, developed particularly as a result of increasing involvement with development companies, as authorities have sought both to improve their share of the financial returns and to facilitate and promote the specific types of development they wish to see built. Local authorities have adopted a more entrepreneurial approach through a variety of joint development arrangements with the private sector, increasing their share of both the risks and rewards of development. Authorities' roles in such joint development schemes commonly involve them in underwriting at least part of the risk which would otherwise be borne by private development interests. The extent to which specific employment or economic regeneration objectives can be met through such arrangements is strictly limited and must often be bought by an authority at the expense of higher risk or lower financial returns.

Major changes in local authorities' relations to private development interests have thus taken place, based on authorities' role as landowners. Local authorities have also moved into the field of direct development on their own account, building small factory units. They have successfully expanded the supply of units on a significant scale, to meet evident demand from industry which had been neglected by the private sector. To some extent authorities may have identified real demand which had not been apparent to private developers. More significant was the fact that they were prepared to accept higher risks and lower rates of return than the private sector, in pursuit of economic policy objectives. By the early 1980s, private sector provision of small units was expanding in many locations while the squeeze on local authorities' financial resources was checking their direct development activity. This shifted the emphasis in small unit provision back towards joint local authority/private sector development or purely private sector activity.

Availability of capital funds has been a key determinant of the scale and nature of local authority involvement in industrial development. Authorities' traditional sources of funds, internal finance and general permission to borrow, were progressively squeezed through the 1970s. Public sector funding was available on only a selective and limited basis through specific central government initiatives, notably in recent years the expanded Urban Programme. In so far as authorities relied on public sector funds, authorities were therefore subject to the scale and direction of central government policies. Consequently, authorities turned increasingly to the private sector as a source of funds, raised through joint development arrangements. This, however, has meant that authorities have become increasingly subject to or constrained by the commercial criteria of private development and financial interests and increasingly involved in underwriting risk as a way of attracting private funding into industrial development activity. This must inevitably inhibit local authorities' ability to pursue wider employment or economic policy objectives where the financial rewards are lower and the risks higher, than in the narrow pursuit of industrial development for its own sake.

## References

1. K. Young, C. Mason and L. Mills, *Urban Governments and Economic Change* (London: Social Science Research Council, 1981); M. Boddy and S. Barrett, *Local Government and the Industrial Development Process,* Working Paper 6 (Bristol: School for Advanced Urban Studies, 1979).
2. *Review of Local Authority Assistance to Industry and Commerce* (London: Department of the Environment, 1981).
3. Boddy and Barrett, *Local Government.*
4. M. M. Camina, 'Local Authorities and the Attraction of Industry', *Progress in Planning*, 3 (2), 1974; N. Falk, 'Local Authorities and Industrial Development – Results of a Survey', paper presented to Association of Industrial Development Officers Conference, 1978.
5. Detailed case studies were conducted in eight English local authorities. Examples of joint local authority/private sector

industrial development were examined in a further eight authorities. This research was funded by the Department of the Environment. See Boddy and Barrett, *Local Government*, and Barrett and Boddy (eds), *Local Authority/Private Sector Industrial Development Partnerships*, Working Paper 18 (Bristol: School for Advanced Urban Studies, 1981). References in the text to individual local authorities are drawn from this research unless otherwise noted.

6. Camina, 'Local Authorities and the Attraction of Industry', p. 84.
7. According to Camina, 'Local Authorities', p. 165, local authorities in England and Wales received loan sanction for land acquisition averaging £3.4 million per annum between 1967 and 1971 and £2.5 million per annum for preliminary development.
8. See note 4.
9. S. Barrett, M. Boddy, M. Stewart, *Implementation of the Community Land Scheme*, Occasional Paper 2 (Bristol: School for Advanced Urban Studies, 1978); S. Barrett and G. Whitting, *Local Authorities and the Supply of Land to the Private Sector*, Working Paper 19 (Bristol: School for Advanced Urban Studies, 1981); M. Boddy, 'Community Land Scheme is Dying of Neglect', *Roof*, May 1978, pp. 78–80.
10. Evidence from studies of individual local authorities, see note 5.
11. Joint development and lease-leaseback agreements are examined in detail, together with case studies of development schemes in Barrett and Boddy, *Local Authority/Private Sector*. See also J. Ratcliffe, *An Introduction to Urban Land Management* (Estates Gazette, 1978) ch. 13, 'Joint development'; and M. Boddy, 'Partnership – the Way Forward?', *Estates Gazette*, 257 (1981) pp. 667–80.
12. The principle may in fact be applied even where an authority does not actually own the development site. Where a development company is proposing to construct premises on a site which the company owns an authority may agree to purchase a lease on the completed units which it is then responsible for letting and managing. This guarantees the developer's return and helps the company to raise development finance. See M. Boddy, 'Partnerships in Practice', in Barrett and Body, *Local Authority/Private Sector*.
13. See J. Ratcliffe, 'Development Briefs: a Basis for Agreement', *Estates Gazette*, 251, September 1979, pp. 1260–2.
14. Camina, 'Local Authorities', p. 165, indicates that the Department of the Environment on average issued loan sanction to English local authorities for the erection of factories of £2.4 million per year between 1967 and 1971.
15. Camina, 'Local Authorities'.
16. Falk, 'Local Authorities and Industrial Development'.
17. G. Dabinett and P. Whisker, 'The Declaration of Industrial Improvement Areas and the Provision of Advance Factories, Loans and Grants by Local Authorities in Tyne and Wear 1974–1979', Inner City Employment Project Working Paper 2 (Department of Town and Country Planning, University of Newcastle upon Tyne, 1981).

# 4 Labour Market Policy

CHARLIE MASON

## Introduction

This chapter deals with the preoccupation of public agencies with unemployment, and attempts to explain it by looking at the nature of the relationships between organisations, and between departments within local authorities. The first section introduces labour market policy with a brief description of the most important characteristics of the national labour market. This backcloth is followed by an account and explanation of the narrow view of unemployment which characterises the priorities and preoccupations of most local authority departments. By way of contrast, the penultimate section provides examples of broader and more interventionist responses which involve the initiation of links between agencies and these are analysed in order to draw some conclusions about the nature and limits of the relationships. In the concluding section, some general comments are made about local government response to unemployment and some suggestions made regarding more appropriate and sensitive action.

## The national labour market

The major preoccupation of central government in recent years has been the concern to reduce inflation. Commentators have observed that since 1965 inflation has displaced unemployment from the top of the political agenda.[1] However, more recently the monetarist policies of the present Conservative government have accentuated trends in the economy, the most notable being the extent of job loss in the manufacturing sector which is considered by many to be the backbone of the economy; meanwhile alarm has intensified as restructuring has failed to improve productivity and maintain output.

In the twenty years from 1960–80 the number of people employed in manufacturing in Britain fell by almost 2 million. This trend, whereby an economy shifts from a manufacturing base to a service base and where high technology further reduces the workforce in both sectors, is known as 'de-industrialisation'.[2] Faith in the capacity of the service sector to compensate for this reduction in manufacturing jobs has been undermined. While the numbers employed in the service sector have increased they have not done so at the same rate as the decline in manufacturing. Furthermore, the shortfall does not account for the total number of unemployed, for while these trends have been occurring the number of people entering or re-entering the labour market has been increasing, notably among school leavers and women.[3]

With the decline of manufacturing jobs the ability of the service sector to accommodate ex-manufacturing workers has been put to the test. However, by its very nature the service sector tends to be an employer of women rather than men; it offers lower earnings and has a propensity towards part-time employment. While 1.4 million 'male' jobs were lost in manufacturing between 1966–76, 1 million 'female' jobs were created in the public service sector and new job opportunities for men in the public service sector were outweighed by the loss of male jobs in the private service sector.[4]

This situation, whereby the structure of the labour market changes so that demand for labour decreases while output is maintained, has recently been described as 'jobless prosperity'.[5] This is expressed in the rate of turnover vacancies: every month people both leave and enter the labour market but as more people join the unemployment register (the inflow) than leave the register (the outflow) the number of unemployed will rise. Not only is the rate of flow between these two categories slowing down but also the queue is not an orderly one. In this situation some individuals, for a whole variety of reasons, become misplaced or sent to the back of the queue and may never become part of the outflow.[6] Such is the situation of the long-term unemployed. Obviously the rate of outflow is influenced by the level of vacancies which, judging by Job Centre statistics, have dropped dramatically.[7]

This description of the labour market and the mechanics of

inflow and outflow, although highlighting the dynamics of unemployment, fails to present another and equally disturbing trend in the structure of unemployment. Detailed analysis of the distribution of unemployment shows that certain groups, principally the young school leaver and the older worker, are more likely to suffer than others. In both cases the effect is intensified for certain occupational groups. In June 1979 general labourers accounted for 43 per cent of males registered unemployed, while non-manual occupations accounted for less than 20 per cent. While the incidence of unemployment among ethnic minority groups cannot be deduced from the register, we do know from information gathered by the 1971 census, the Great Britain Labour Force Surveys of 1973, 1975 and 1977, and from the National Dwelling and Housing Survey of England 1977, which include registered unemployed, that 'rates of unemployment tend to be substantially higher among minority groups than among whites'.[8] Official figures for the year ending February 1981 reinforce these findings by showing that unemployment among this group has risen by 82 per cent to twice the national average of one in ten.[9]

Race discrimination accounts in part for this effect. From 1971– 5 a survey was carried out in Yorkshire with results which support the claim that discrimination took place against black youths as they applied for jobs, identified by Shirley Dex as the 'Gateway Effect'.[10] More recently a study of unemployment in Manchester, Liverpool and Wolverhampton concluded that racial discrimination was certainly a factor in the high unemployment rates among young blacks.[11] The Manpower Services Commission (MSC) acknowledge that the disadvantage of ethnic minorities is due in part to discrimination and are in agreement with the Commission for Racial Equality when they state that specific measures to improve language skills and overcome discrimination and educational disadvantage are required.[12]

Women face similar problems to blacks in the operation of the 'dual labour market'.[13] The disadvantaged position of women in the labour market was presented in a joint report by the Equal Opportunities Commission (EOC) and MSC in December 1979, which acknowledged that equality of opportunity, although promoted and protected by legislation, is not yet a reality.[14] As was pointed out by the chairman of the EOC, knowledge of equal opportunity legislation among managers, trades unions and women is negligible and equal opportunity is not seen as an issue.[15] The result is that women are placed in a limited number of jobs at the bottom of the pile, usually in clothing, footwear and textiles, and with the recession opportunities have been further reduced. The MSC response was to extend its experimental 'wider opportunities for women' initiative from two locations in 1978 to eleven in autumn in 1979. The courses are aimed at women wanting to return to paid employment and are designed to enable women to make realistic plans and to develop the confidence and skills to put the plans into action. This initiative has faded in the face of MSC expenditure cuts so that women are no longer included in MSC's list of 'possible priority groups'.[16]

The most important conclusion to draw from this section is that the 'secondary' labour market is increasing in size while, at the same time, unskilled job opportunities are declining. Furthermore, training facilities are not only inadequate but may not be flexible enough to accommodate technological change. Although measures to increase labour demand in both the manufacturing and service sectors are crucial they will not be enough to accommodate the growing secondary sector. Latest estimates predict 500 000 unemployed school leavers by 1983, many of them long term, and 700 000 long-term unemployed.[17] Consequently, restructuring the nature of the labour force through increased investment in education, training and retraining is essential.

### The local government role

*The prominence of economic development*

In both the inner city and the shire authorities unemployment is frequently identified as one of the major problems and prominence is given to economic development rather than labour market policy.[18] The reinforcement of this orientation in recent years is due to a number of factors. The statutory powers available to local authorities have been restricted by central government to assistance for the manufacturing sector, an emphasis which was particularly pronounced in Circular 71/77 which outlined local government's role within the industrial strategy. This trend has reinforced local government's traditional response to economic problems and has been refined to relate specifically to a concern for small firms, where local government is seen by central government to play a particularly useful role in constructing small factory units.[19] The strength of this bias towards economic development is reflected in local government's response to two inner city initiatives. First, the well documented case of local authorities' failure to 'bend' main programmes in favour of disadvantaged groups or localities as part of the Comprehensive Community Programme.[20] Second, the allocation of resources under the Inner Urban Areas Act 1978, whereby partnership and programme authorities are spending by far the greater proportion of their funds on regenerating the industrial infrastructure,[21] an activity which is fully in accordance with the priorities of the Secretary of State for the Environment.[22]

In the shire counties the appreciation of the importance of economic development has been reinforced and perhaps prompted by central government in the form of English Industrial Estates (EIE) which, under the Industry Act 1980, are committed to attracting private capital and adopting a more commercial approach. The counties are typically most concerned to improve their communication links and such basic services as water supply, in an attempt to become more attractive to industrialists. However, a survey of shire county activity to promote rural generation indicates that activity is gradually extending to include the direct provision of land and buildings.[23]

The dominant assumption behind this activity is that the resulting growth in industry will eventually benefit the whole community and that those benefits will filter down and eventually provide jobs for the unemployed. There are local authorities who have adopted an economic growth-oriented strategy and have succeeded in attracting a large number of firms. However, this strategy does not guarantee a match between incoming jobs and the existing unemployed either in terms of numbers or skills. In fact, due to the rapid change in product cycles more and more skills are becoming redundant. Furthermore, this preoccupation to attract firms and provide sites and buildings is often accompanied by a relaxation of concern for working conditions and wage rates. Much of this concern to attract industrial development at all costs is found in recent government circulars which have asked local authorities to positively discriminate in favour of industrial planning applications, both in terms of the speed at which the authority processes the application and in regard to relaxing its interpretation of nonconforming uses.[24]


## The organisational imperative

The responses of both inner city authorities and shire counties not only emphasise industrial development within the economic development policy but also reveal a similar 'market' preoccupation of the more socially oriented functions within a local authority: the careers service and further education. This section develops this concept of the 'preoccupation' or 'imperative' of agencies and departments and draws upon Allison's 'conceptual lenses . . . which lead one to see, emphasize and worry about quite different aspects of events';[25] put more simply, 'what you see depends on where you stand'.

Members of an organisation or department identify certain functions, roles or activities to be specific or peculiar to their own organisation. This assertion is supported by the tendency of many local authority economic policy documents to define the limits to their activity by using the phrase 'to fill the gaps between the activities of the other agencies'. This phrase is used both to describe the limits to action and to justify activity. This also serves as a 'catch all' phrase which indicates that a department of the local authority, or one particular individual within it, also has a perception of the specific role or organisational imperative of some of the other organisations acting on the local labour market. Such perceptions may, of course, either invite or preclude a local authority role.[26]

Interviews with industrial development officers (IDOs) suggest that they commonly subscribe to the following perceptions. They will see the Manpower Services Commission as the agency concerned to improve the efficiency of the labour market by providing an employment placement service, training facilities, and by implementing policies for vulnerable groups through training schemes, job creation schemes and advice services for the disabled and long-term unemployed. They will see voluntary groups as either lobbying for rather worrying or uncomfortable lost causes or doing small fringe projects which are innovative but uneconomic or even dangerous politically, for example, 'stop the cuts' campaigns.

Trades unions, being concerned with workers' rights, working conditions, wages, job security and redundancy schemes, will not be seen as being in the same 'league' as policy-makers and implementers. The IDO will have little knowledge or contact with education departments and the careers service, and may consider them irrelevant. This generalised view of the world as seen by an IDO will do much to reinforce the existing concern of the local authority with alleviating unemployment via industrial development.

This perception of the world can be compared with a more objective appraisal of the role of the agencies. The MSC is concerned with manpower management and its priority is to meet the demands of industry and the employer. This emphasis has always existed within MSC but now, in a period of recession and with its own credibility at stake, its concern for the efficiency of the labour market is heightened. Voluntary groups are inhibited in the impact they can have due to their lack of power and resources. Trades unions are often a barrier to job creation, especially the civil service and local authority unions. Furthermore, they are not heavily involved in policies for 'vulnerable' groups but are heavily involved in restructuring local labour markets. The careers service gives priority to dealing with those youngsters who have good qualifications and who meet the needs of the labour market. This activity takes priority over a concern for 'low achievers' who require a disproportionate amount of time. Education departments' further education courses have to be justified on the grounds of demand but little money is available for demand generation (marketing); therefore, courses are unlikely to be provided which meet the needs of special groups such as long-term unemployed.

The main conclusion to draw from this more objective review is that all the agencies concerned directly with the local labour market have as their major concern the needs of the industry and employers. Those agencies having policies concerned with 'mopping up' those adversely affected by restructuring and with aiding vulnerable groups find that the overwhelming market orientation accords such activity low priority and comparatively few resources. Those local authority functions which appear to be best placed to deal with social problems caused by restructuring of a local economy are unable to do so simply because their concern is to meet the demands of the market; they are reactive agencies. Whatever the level of resources available the more vulnerable members of the labour market will always be a second rather than first priority. Once again it is commonly assumed that the benefits derived from adopting a market orientation will eventually filter down to the vulnerable groups.

## Labour market initiatives

The picture presented so far suggests that local authorities, in common with other agencies concerned with unemployment, either facilitate the restructuring of the manufacturing sector by direct provision of sites and buildings or meet the demands of the employers through job placement, training, further education and the careers service. *In either case they act at the expense of the more vulnerable and disadvantaged in the labour market.*

This section will present examples of local authority activity which involve developing links with other agencies concerned with the labour market in order to pursue more positive policies. This alternative approach might be described as 'interventionist' or 'thrusting' rather than 'reactive' or 'sleeping'. The intention is not to argue that these are examples of good practice, but to indicate the breadth of local authority activity concerned with both labour supply and demand, and to raise some issues about the development of relationships between agencies and to consider the barriers to the development of more 'socially' oriented initiatives. We will consider three areas relating to the mobility of labour, the relationship between education and industry, and the role of the voluntary sector.

### Facilitating labour mobility

The present government has argued quite strongly that the unemployed should be prepared to move in order to find work.[27] The extent to which local authority housing policy can have an impact on the labour market is difficult to assess; however, within the last year central government has formulated two initiatives which aim to improve the availability of housing in order to aid the mobility of labour.

In September 1980 a General Consent for the Sale of Council Houses was introduced which aimed to help mobility in two ways. First, by allowing tenants who had purchased from the local authority to resell their homes at the current market value rather than at the original purchase price, as was the previous arrangement. Second, a council has the discretion to sell a vacant dwelling to someone who wants to move into the area for employment reasons and to give them a discount of up to 30 per cent. Not only is this seen as helping councils to sell off empty and difficult-to-let dwellings but also to help those moving into high-cost areas.

More recently, in March 1981, the National Mobility Scheme was introduced which aimed to extend and formalise the existing mobility schemes between authorities, for example, key-worker and mutual exchange agreements. This scheme is available to tenants, people on waiting lists and other people with a pressing need to move. In order to apply a person has to have obtained permanent employment beyond reasonable travelling distance, or have social reasons.

Both these schemes are dependent on the discretionary judgements of the local authority. They must perceive employment criteria to be important enough to allocate part of their building stock to incoming workers. In addition, initiatives can be taken by local authorities in response to local circumstances, two of which are described below. The first, a key-worker scheme – in this case operated by the London Borough of Ealing – is not uncommon. The second, a development scheme involving Poole District Council, is quite unique.

In January 1978 the London Borough of Ealing's employment working party decided to run an experimental key-worker scheme. This was in response to the claim by a number of large manufacturing employers that they were having great difficulty in finding skilled workers due to the lack of suitable housing at moderate prices. The scheme involved thirty dwellings and the definition of a key worker was left to the individual employer, although if there was any doubt the decision was made by the chairman of the housing committee.

At the start of the scheme the authority advertised through the local press and by letters to the major employers. However, the best channel of communication was found to be through the local Job Centres who knew the needs of the particular employers and could identify those having particular recruitment problems.

This link with the Job Centre also gave the authority information on recruitment trends generally and particularly the extent to which employers had tried to recruit locally. Although the allocation of thirty dwellings was used up it did take more than a year: this was held to be due to the inadequate supply of skilled labour nationally and the relatively low wages available to skilled workers when compared to the alternative sources of well-paid employment for unskilled and semi-skilled work, notably at Heathrow Airport.

A more collaborative scheme has been implemented at Poole, Dorset. Since the early 1960s the District Council has been sympathetic to the housing needs of skilled workers, initially in response to the location of the Plessey organisation. More recently in 1976, the key-worker subcommittee of the Housing Committee, which contained representatives of the Dorset Chamber of Commerce and Industry and the Poole Trades Council, formulated a housing development scheme specifically for key workers recruited from other parts of the country. The local authority, Hamworthy Engineering (one of Dorset's largest engineering firms) and the Dorset Chamber of Commerce, jointly sponsored a £1.4 million low-rent housing scheme through the Knightstone Housing Association. Under the provisions of the Housing Act 1974 non-profit-making housing associations are able to obtain government grants and borrow public money to build 'fair rent' accommodation. The 104-dwelling estate was entirely funded (80 per cent by grant and 20 per cent by loans) by the Housing Corporation, who bought the land from the local authority. Half the homes have been allocated to the public sector which includes statutory undertakers, social services, education, health and the post office, and half to the private sector. The houses are not tied to the employing company and only if the tenant actually leaves the area does the house go back into the pool of accommodation.

Since the scheme's inception the definition of a 'key worker' has altered. Initially a key worker was defined as a worker whose employment should lead to the provision of ten–fifteen semi-skilled jobs. In June 1979 this was altered to a condition that the key worker has to be essential to either the maintenance of a firm's current production, or provide an increase and/or to provide employment for additional semi-skilled or unskilled workers. In order to protect the local labour force the district manager of the Employment Services Division has to certify that this category of person cannot be recruited locally. A final clause is that consideration will be given to companies who have consistently operated a recognised training scheme and that the employer can certify that the person has received appropriate and adequate training.

Both these examples indicate the close links between the local authority and the large manufacturing employers and both schemes were initiated in response to need expressed by this particular interest group. The Poole examples show a longer history of collaboration with large manufacturing companies to the extent that the scheme discriminates in favour of companies having a recognised training scheme which would tend to discriminate against small companies. One should also note that, in sympathy with trends in manufacturing and particularly the restructuring of larger concerns, the definition of a key worker emphasises the maintenance or improvement of levels of production rather than job creation. In addition, both local authorities developed links with the MSC's Employment Services Division and in doing so developed a greater understanding of the nature of the local labour market.

*Education–industry links*

The statutory basis for education–industry links in the form of work experience for local school pupils has existed since 1973, with the Education (Work Experience) Act. More recently, the nature of the links have expanded and intensified, with increasing youth unemployment and the claims by industry of a shortage of scientific and technical skills and public failure to appreciate the importance of industry in society.

Following James Callaghan's Ruskin College speech in 1977, the Green Paper, *Education in Schools*, suggested that local education authorities (LEAs), schools and industry should work more closely together, primarily to be concerned with curriculum development both nationally and locally. Subsequently the Department of

Education and Science (DES), in Circular 14/77, asked local authorities to report on the steps taken to promote contact between pupils and teachers in individual schools and local industry, commerce and trades unions.[28]

The primary aim of LEAs has been to develop the curriculum in order to influence the appreciation of industry and thereby improve the status of industry-oriented careers in the eyes of highly qualified pupils. Concerned primarily with the curriculum and the application of principles, LEAs have little or no concern for the nature of the local labour market or for the need to relate vocational guidance directly to it. Obviously the degree to which this narrow perspective exists will depend on the attitude of the LEA and, equally if not more important, the head teachers. The autonomy of each of the educational institutions is recognised by central government, in the form of the Department of Industry's Education Unit, who aim to promote national initiatives but refrain from imposing on the local level.[29]

The other main agency which has a more obvious but less well defined link between education and industry is the careers service whose functions are to offer information and guidance to pupils, to carry out a counselling and placement service for young people whether in work or unemployed, and to identify sponsors for the Manpower Services Commission's Youth Opportunities Programme (YOP). With the recent rise in youth unemployment and the debate on education and training, the careers service has been trying to identify its most appropriate role. According to the Central Policy Review Staff (CPRS) 'the role of the Careers Service is dependent to some extent on the local labour market and the level of the unemployment'. The CPRS felt that the careers services remit could not be met given its limited resources and it therefore should reduce its interview work, leaving the inidividual to choose his/her own vocation or job, and concentrate on difficult cases.[30] This proposal can be interpreted as 'don't waste time trying to place school leavers when there aren't enough jobs available'. However, local careers officers may well argue that it is in such a situation that more advice, not just on vacancies, is crucial to enable school leavers to appreciate the tightness of the labour market.

This situation has led some careers service departments to give more time to negotiate work experience opportunities under YOP, which has led to some duplication in nature with work experience schemes set up by individual schools, and the possibility of duplication in terms of demands made on employers. Whereas in the mid-1970s careers officers would attempt to make heavy demands on employers, in the present climate with sponsorship being difficult to find, especially in the more depressed regions of the country, the careers service is negotiating short work experience programmes which duplicate the role of the some schools.

Obviously the nature of the careers service–school relationship depends on the nature of the local labour market and the traditions of the respective institutions. In Manchester and Salford there are only twelve Young Enterprise sponsors simply because, for the individual schools, sponsors are hard to find and enthusiastic teachers are required as much of the work has to be carried out outside school hours. For some schools there is great difficulty in finding the resources which are required to forge a link with industry. Perhaps it is indicative that of the three main initiatives proposed as a result of three forums devoted to a discussion of youth employment in one small area of Salford – improving school–industry links, setting up a Community Service Agency, and a Community Workshop under the new Community Enterprise Programme – the school–industry link initiative failed to develop due to lack of resources and enthusiasm on both sides.[31] The careers service has identified this gap and is taking steps to set up work experience courses for school pupils.

One might expect that the more prosperous regions of the country allow the careers service and schools more scope for independent action. However, here, just as in the less prosperous regions, there is a need to consider both the quality and the quantity of the links. To negotiate a large number of schemes with industry creates the opportunity for a dialogue but often there is little feedback or monitoring. It is also important to avoid duplication, although to do so successfully the parochialism of some schools must be overcome. Finally, there is a growing opinion within the careers service that because of the changing nature of the labour market, school pupils should be educated in order to develop their resilience, and that rather than inheriting wisdom learned at school they should acquire self-knowledge. There is some doubt that schools are changing sufficiently to prepare young people for life after school. To quote a past President of the Institute of Careers Officers:

> There is now a need for the Careers Service to make the case for its educational role (vocational guidance) . . . the principal careers officer is too often seen as the manager of a function divorced from the central policy of the Education Department . . . he should 'act as adviser' to the Chief Education Officer on employment policy, unemployment policy and careers guidance and education.[32]

In Bedfordshire County Council this appreciation appears to have developed. There are a number of initiatives which are the responsibility of the education department, notably work experience for final-year students, teachers' secondment to industry and a Young Enterprise Scheme; the careers service, however, initiates and co-ordinates the schemes in close co-operation with the further and higher education sectors. This close relationship is expressed in the form of an Industry and Education Liaison Group which brings together teachers, advisers and inspectors, representatives of the careers service and further education representatives, trade unionists, industrialists, and county councillors, and reports to the County Education Committee. The careers service produces a directory of facilities available within industry in the county in the field of education–industry links. At present this totals 350 firms who are prepared to accommodate work experience placements, accept teachers on secondment, provide speakers for careers education programmes and to provide materials for use in the curriculum. In addition, a Users Guide has been set up which monitors the frequency with which each company is used in order to avoid overload.

The justification for the careers service playing this central co-ordinating role is based on its regular day-to-day contact with local industry. In this particular county the careers service made over 2000 industrial visits in one year in the process of carrying out its three functions, a figure far in excess of the product of all the other sectors of education. In addition to the number of visits the careers service argues that it is well placed to consider the quality as well as the quantity of contacts within industry by its involvement in the secondment of teachers to industry, setting up discussion groups of head teachers and employers and through the placement and work experience function.

This section has presented the polarisation of interests within the school–industry context. On the one hand, the educationalists are concerned with curriculum development rather than the vocational aspects of education and the labour market. On the other, the careers service are having to reassess their own role in the light of the present recession's impact on job opportunities for school leavers, and feel that careers guidance and work experience are more and more important.

*Voluntary sector initiative*

In the organisational imperatives section above, voluntary organisations were presented as seen by local government as marginal to the concerns of the local labour market and as more of a threat to the local authority than a positive force. Even with the overtures to the voluntary and community sectors present in the Inner Area Partnership and Programme initiative the opportunities for them to voice their opinions and the extent of the financial aid they have received has been considered minimal. In the opinion of an officer of the National Council for Voluntary Organisations: 'whilst a few local authorities have encouraged community initiatives and involvement in the Inner Cities Programme, the general pattern has been for voluntary groups to make the running, often in the face of discouragement (and even hostility) from government'.[33] In the main, the activities carried out by the voluntary groups which have been financed by Inner Area Partnership or Programme money are limited to the provision of space and salaries for the setting up of cultural, recreational, educational and advisory services. The legitimacy for involving voluntary groups in projects specifically oriented to provide permanent jobs and for the development of production has been minimal.

However, there are exceptions to this general rule which owe as much to the resilience and resourcefulness of the voluntary groups as to the sympathy of the statutory agencies with which they have to relate. In fact the example of the setting up of the Notting Dale Urban Studies Centre in Hammersmith highlights the problems which have to be overcome.

The Centre considered setting up a technology centre. This idea developed from an appreciation that not only did job loss and skill mismatch exist side by side within the borough, but also at the macro level fundamental changes were taking place in the structure of industry. The intention was to offer the young unemployed in the borough the opportunity to train in the computer sciences, but also for the Centre to develop both research and development and a production function, thereby creating permanent jobs.

For the MSC Special Programmes Division the Centre's proposal proved too complicated and created a good deal of disagreement. The MSC's criteria could not accommodate the separation of training from production, for the training element at the centre aimed to use the characteristics of high technology as a learning/educational tool which was very different from the more traditional training in order to develop manufacturing skills. Finally, the association of low status–low achievers with high-status technology was difficult for the administrators to accommodate due to the assumptions made about the educational attainment required in order to engage in certain activities. Essentially the complexity of the enterprise created mismatch with the MSC financial and budgeting system, whose conditions and criteria were not met.

These difficulties were finally avoided upon the realisation by the director of the Notting Dale Centre that although MSC may fund training workshops they do not accept liability for financial losses. This stance would obviously adversely influence MSC's approach to the management of the centre. An alternative approach was sought, and found, in the form of a limited company. This allowed the Centre to manage its own affairs and also to achieve Educational Charity status which gives relief and/or exemption from certain taxes and rates.

The first year's budget of £250 000 was drawn mainly from the local authority's Inner Area Programme allocation and from the Department of Industry. The London Borough of Hammersmith and Fulham covered running costs for the first year and the rehabilitation of the building. The Department of Industry funded the setting up of the Research and Development Unit from its Microprocessors Awareness Programme. Obviously the interest of both these institutions was aroused through the high networking skills of the Centre who were able to draw on resources from such 'interested parties'. Imperial College and North-East London

Polytechnic were prepared to offer their expertise and time free of charge in order that the case for support could be well presented.

Although the variety of funders inhibited the co-ordination of all the activities in the centre, this was the price to be paid for managerial autonomy. By the second year (1981-2) the funding profile had changed dramatically. The DoI was no longer involved, and the MSC had agreed to fund the forty trainees, and made some contribution to the Workshop. Furthermore, due to its status as a charity the Centre attracted funds from numerous trusts, banks and the Silver Jubilee Fund, which, together with continued support from Hammersmith, contributed to the limited company and to a co-operative.

The director of the Centre gave high praise to the local authority for its financial support and praised particularly the responsiveness of the officers. However, at least of equal importance would be the priority given to the Notting Dale scheme and the administration of the Programme from the chief executive's department.

This example represents the importance of the perseverance and resourcefulness required in order to set up a community-based initiative and particularly the need to approach the reactive agency, in this case the MSC, with an urgent and well argued request for support and action which can touch a nerve. It also indicates the diversity of aid and support available to people proposing such an initiative. Perhaps the greatest problem is actually identifying the sources of the aid and support available. In this respect the Community Business Ventures Unit offers a great deal of experience and has recently been producing proposals and recommendations for schemes which could draw on the resources allocated to the MSC's new Community Enterprise Programme (CEP). CEP replaces STEP and will have a budget of £77 million for 1981-2, of which approximately £2-3 million will be allocated to schemes intended to create new enterprises through partnerships involving the private sector, public and community bodies.

The advantages of such initiatives as the Notting Dale Centre and those advocated by the Community Business Ventures Unit are that they are community based and aim to create permanent jobs rather than the temporary schemes available under other MSC initiatives. Furthermore, the jobs created will not just be for the unemployed but for the more vulnerable groups amongst the unemployed. This social objective provides the justification for public support and subsidy, and ensures that the loans and grants provided are not manipulated for undue private gain.

Untimately the question which faces the initiators of such a community-based initiative is how far the initiative should be both community based and controlled, and how far autonomy may be undermined by support from other institutions and agencies. For the Notting Dale initiative, managerial autonomy is a high priority and has been maintained due to the nature of the support from the local authority and charitable trusts. At present the conditions attached to the MSC under the new initiative are not available, but if this initiative is to be anything more than a symbolic gesture the MSC will have to think seriously about its conventional attitude towards the investment of public funds in 'private' initiatives.

*Appraisal*

The introduction to this section stated that agencies gave greatest priority to those functions meeting the demands of the 'market' rather than vulnerable groups. These examples can now be considered in order to assess the strength of the market, particularly its influence in the formation of relationships between actors.

In the case of key-worker housing the market consisted of both the private and public sector, for there was insufficient suitable housing stock to attract key workers for both sectors. In fact, it was the strength of this market concern that brought about its collaborative initiative. It was in the interests of industry, the local housing department and the Job Centre (plus numerous other public agencies) to overcome market constraints. Furthermore, the initiative was in the interest of the manufacturing sector and the least vulnerable group in the labour market, i.e. skilled workers. One can therefore identify a situation of mutual reinforcement.

In the second example the polarised interests of the education department and careers service arose from their conflicting views of the market although neither market was obvious; in fact there may only be a subtle difference. The careers service is concerned with the relatively short-term needs of industry and developing a youngster's appreciation of the changing nature of the local labour market. The education authority has in view a more 'distant' and therefore uncertain market, namely the demands likely to be made by all sectors of industry in the future, and consequently tends to be preoccupied with the prospects of the higher achievers. It is worth noting that this division of interest reflects the segmentation of the labour market mentioned earlier. The outcome is a compromise of professional interest in response to the uncertainty of the market (in terms of the opportunities it holds for the future) in which both professional groups have a committed interest. Anything other than compromise may have undermined relationships with industry in terms of both quality and quantity. So one can identify the maintenance of self-interest by compromise and collaboration.

In the final example, the inter-organisational and inter-departmental links are non-existent and the market is difficult to define due to the close association of community interest, training and production. With a voluntary organisation acting as a catalyst, each agency was simply asked to respond to a request for support without being able to identify an obvious client or market outside the Centre itself. The Centre drew on resources from a number of the sources but there was no formal negotiative or professional link between them; in fact the technical expertise came from within the Centre. The only real conflict to emerge was within the MSC as it found a complex and unconventional request difficult to respond to.

The main conclusion one can draw from this appraisal is the influence of the magic of the market in generating relationships. In the case of the key workers the market was particularly strong in that it was common to all the actors and there were no conflicts of interest, professional or departmental. In the education–industry example there were quite strong conflicts of professional interests and different client groups but both were committed to an uncertain market; as a result compromise and collaboration were expedient. The voluntary initiative had no specific or easily identifiable 'market' orientation and included a strong commitment to social objectives. Neither was there a request for professional skills. Thus in order to secure resources a great deal of resourcefulness and resilience was required. Initiatives which do not have the credibility of a market orientation will find it difficult to secure resources from public agencies which do, as the Centre's dialogue with the MSC shows.

**Conclusions**

This contribution has been critical of the narrow and market-oriented response of agencies involved in implementing labour market policies. The nature of the response is determined by a view of the role of other actors in the field, the expressed demands of the market, and by the cursory nature of the labour market analysis. As a result factories are built, key-worker housing provided, and labour placed on the assumption that the benefits arising will eventually filter down to the more vulnerable and disadvantaged groups in the labour market. It is worth noting that such policies often increase their legitimacy and secure resources by making this claim.[34]

The point has also been made that the public agencies are reactive rather than proactive. Where examples of local authority actively illustrated a much more interventionist role there was no doubting the strength and influence of the market. Little mention was made of the importance of visibility in the choice of a response, nor of any distinction between direct and indirect action. No doubt visibility is a very important criterion, if only to maintain the local authority's credibility. The importance of 'being seen to be doing something' should not be underestimated. A concern for visibility will no doubt reinforce initiatives such as promotion in the local area and factory building, and undermine equal opportunity policy or investment in voluntary organisations.

It has been suggested that some initiatives have a more direct impact upon the labour market than others.[35] The important variable here is the assumptions made about the nature and dynamic of causal factors in the labour market. To suggest, for example, that housing policy to assist mobility has an indirect effect on the labour market and that a job creation scheme has a direct effect implies that the concern of labour market policy is simply to get people off the unemployment register. In fact, if the aim is to provide permanent jobs then housing mobility (although involving some degree of 'poaching' in relation to key-worker policy) is more direct than a job creation scheme which only supplies temporary jobs. The difficulty here is that unless initiatives are monitored (and it is a very difficult task to establish direct cause and effect) then their implementation is simply a question of faith and the choice of initiatives a matter of politics. Perhaps certainty of impact, of whatever sort, is a more exact interpretation of the term 'directness', in which case it means little more than visibility and confirms the 'market' orientation which emphasises responding to 'expressed' need. In this case indirectness would relate to labour supply policy and particularly those policies relevant to the vulnerable and disadvantaged groups.

The general conclusion that policies aimed at influencing the labour market concern themselves with the needs of the market applies not only to Britain.[36] Moreover, with the recession and the associated public expenditure cuts this emphasis has increased. This is particularly obvious in respect of the MSC who are having to reduce their activities and have jettisoned many social policies,[37] and are withdrawing services from some localities particularly hard hit by the recession.[38]

Policies and actions concerned with facilitating the restructuring of industry contrast with the low legitimacy attached to social policies intended to 'mop up' those adversely affected by restructuring and to help the vulnerable and disadvantaged. Although such polarisation may itself help to get social policies on to the political agenda and increase their legitimacy, this will not be possible unless the prerequisites for their formulation and implementation are made quite clear. These prerequisites have been suggested in the previous section: a more vigorous analysis of the labour market; a move away from the preoccupation of responding to 'market' demand; a questioning of conventions regarding eligibility criteria; and a questioning of the values which maintain the private–public distinction. It should also be anticipated that, due to the greater uncertainty of the nature of the market when developing socially oriented labour supply employment policies, local authorities need to forge relationships between agencies and actions.

These socially oriented initiatives will not be comparable to industrial development in terms of prestige, given the present climate of values and preoccupations. However, no doubt they will involve local authorities in a much wider network of relationships, including voluntary and community groups, charitable trusts and all levels of education. The aim should be to create permanent jobs for the members of the secondary labour market and to improve their prospects.

**References**

1.  K. Middlemas, *Politics in Industrial Society* (André Deutsch, 1979);
    J. E. Alt, *The Politics of Economic Decline* (Cambridge University
    Press, 1979).
2.  F. T. Blackaby, *De-Industrialisation* (Heinemann, 1979).
3.  T. Mallier and M. Rosser, 'The Changing Role of Women in the
    British Economy', *National Westminster Bank Review*, November
    1979, pp. 54–6.
4.  F. Cairncross, 'Where Have all the Jobs Gone?', *The Guardian*, 6
    April 1981, p. 6.
5.  S. Brittan, 'The Spectre of Jobless Prosperity', *The Financial Times*,
    30 April 1981, p. 25.
6.  W. W. Daniel, 'Why is High Employment Still Acceptable?', *New
    Society*, 55 (957), 19 March 1981, pp. 495–7; W. W. Daniel, *The
    Unemployed Flow*, Stage 1 Interim Report (Policy Studies Institute,
    May 1981).
7.  'The Flow of Unemployment', *New Society*, 54 (938), 6 November
    1980, p. 281.
8.  D. J. Smith, *Unemployment and Racial Minorities* (Policy Studies
    Institute, February 1981) p. 5.
9.  'Job Toll Hits Ethnic Groups Hard', *The Guardian*, 6 April 1981,
    p. 1.
10. S. Dex, 'A Note on Discrimination in Employment and its Effect on
    Black Youths', *Journal of Social Policy*, 8 (3), July 1979, pp. 357–69.
11. *The Times*, 11 August 1980; K. Roberts *et al.*, 'Ignoring the Sign:
    Young, Unemployed and Unregistered', *Employment Gazette*,
    August 1981, pp. 353–6.
12. Manpower Services Commission, *Review of Services for the
    Unemployed*, March 1981, p. 13, para. 3.22.
13. C. Pond, 'What is Full Employment? The Structure of
    Unemployment', a paper presented at a Social Science Research
    Council workshop, 14 March 1981; N. Bosanquet and P. B.
    Doeringer, 'Is There a Dual Labour Market in Great Britain?',
    *Economic Journal*, June 1973; A. Giddens, *The Class Structure of the
    Advanced Capitalist Societies* (Hutchinson, 1973).
14. Manpower Services Commission, Special Programmes Division,
    *Opportunities for Girls and Women in MSC Special Programmes for
    the Unemployed*, December 1979, p. 6.
15. Baroness Seear, 'Where Do We Go from Here? Equal Pay and Equal
    Opportunity', *Department of Employment Gazette*, 87 (9),
    September 1979, pp. 836–66.
16. Manpower Services Commission, *Review of Services for the
    Unemployed*, March 1981, p. 26, para. 5.15.
17. Manpower Services Commission, *Manpower Review 1981*, p. 17,
    paras 3.8 and 3.9.
18. K. Young, C. Mason and E. Mills, *Urban Governments and*

*Economic Change*, Social Science Research Council Inner City in Context No. 11 (SSRC, 1980).

19. Department of the Environment, 'Planning Relaxations for Small Industrial Premises', a consultation document, 10 July 1980.

20. M. Dean, 'The Challenge of the Heart of Britain's Cities', *The Guardian*, 1 April 1981, p. 22; R. Hambleton, *Inner Cities: Management and Resources*, Working Paper 13 (Bristol: School for Advanced Urban Studies, 1980).

21. A. Shearer, 'Neglecting the Inner Man', *The Guardian*, 20 May 1981, p. 15.

22. *The Financial Times*, a report of a speech M. Heseltine, Environment Secretary, gave to the Manchester Chamber of Commerce when he emphasised the need for more modern buildings for manufacturing industry, 7 April 1981.

23. County Planning Officers' Society, *Economic/Employment Initiatives in Counties*, May 1978.

24. Department of the Environment, 'Development Control – Policy and Practice', Circular 22/80, 28 November 1980.

25. G. T. Allison, *Essence of Decision*, (Little, Brown & Co., 1971).

26. Young, Mason and Mills, *Urban Governments and Economic Change*.

27. See Mrs Thatcher's speech to the Conservative Party in Wales, 19 July 1980, *House of Commons Debates*, 22 July 1980, col. 251, and 24 July 1980, cols 762 and 763.

28. Department of Education and Science, 'Local Education Authority Arrangements for the School Curriculum', Circular 14/77, 29 November 1977.

29. Department of Industry, Industry/Education Unit, *Information Sheet*, 1 September 1980, paras 5, 6 (v), 7 and 11; Department of Industry, Industry/Education Liaison, *A Review of the Initiatives, 1977–80*, June 1980, p. 5.

30. Central Policy Review Staff, *Education, Training and Industrial Performance* (HMSO 1980) p. 37, para. 69.

31. Personal communication with researchers at the William Temple Foundation who organised The Forums as part of a Department of Environment Inner City Research Project, 'Young People and the Labour Market: The Ordsall Project, 1979–80'.

32. D. Peck, 'Local Authorities and the Manpower Services Commission – A Framework for Co-operation in the 1980s', *Local Government Studies*, 6 (3), May/June 1980, pp. 3–19.

33. R. Davies, 'Community Involvement in the Inner Cities Programme', in *Inner Cities and Black Minorities*, report of a workshop organised by the National Council for Voluntary Organisations and the Runnymede Trust, Birmingham, 8 December 1979, (NVCO, July 1980) p. 1.

34. T. Davies and C. Mason, 'Manpower Policy and Economic Goals: the Role of the Manpower Services Commission', unpublished project working paper, 1980.

35. N. Boaden, 'Review Symposium', *Town Planning Review*, 52 (1), January 1981, p. 97.
36. C. Ackermann and W. Steinmann, 'The Representation of Private Actors in the Policy Implementation Process and the Implementation Structure', a paper presented at the Planning Session in 'Implementation Seen from the Bottom Up', European Consortium for Political Research, Joint Workshop Sessions, Lancaster, 30 March–4 April 1981.
37. Davies and Mason, 'Manpower Policy and Economic Goals'.
38. *The Financial Times*, 14 May 1981, a report on the MSC (Scotland) Annual Review, announcing a cut in training services due to a lack of demand by industry.

# II ORGANISATIONAL PROCESSES

# 5 Organising for Economic Development: the Formulation of Local Authority Economic Policies in West Yorkshire

JOHN MAWSON

## Introduction

This chapter presents the results of a study of the development of local authority economic policies in the main industrial areas of West Yorkshire where textiles, clothing and related industries predominate. The focus is on the interplay of political, professional and organisational factors in the process of policy formulation.[1] The study was based on an examination of background documents and a series of structured interviews with local authority officers who were concerned with economic development matters.[2]

It should be borne in mind that the period under investigation – mid-1974 to mid-1977 – was a comparatively short one in terms of the evolution of policy. The authorities which came into being at the beginning of the period needed new policies. Moreover, the recession which followed the 1973 oil crisis resulted in a steep rise in unemployment and prompted a number of local authorities outside the traditional assisted areas to devise local economic programmes for the first time. This study, therefore, records a 'first wave' of activity. Since that time the economy has continued to deteriorate and local authorities throughout the country have become involved in the task of economic regeneration. There is now a greater awareness of the issues and many local authorities (including those described in this chapter) have developed more sophisticated approaches to policy formulation. Nevertheless, the findings of this study point to a number of key organisational problems which remain central to the process of local economic development, in West Yorkshire and elsewhere.

The chapter begins by describing the economic problems of the study area and the approach adopted by central government. It proceeds to examine the manner in which the metropolitan districts developed their local economic policies following the reorganisation of local government; particular attention is given to internal organisation structures and the process of policy formulation. The discussion then turns to consider the significance of inter-organisational relationships in economic development at both county and district levels. Finally, an account is presented of the efforts of one district authority to secure a wider community involvement in economic regeneration.

**Economic problems and policies in West Yorkshire**

West Yorkshire Metropolitan County (WYMCC) has a population of over 2 million and comprises five metropolitan districts (MDs): Bradford, Calderdale (including Halifax), Kirklees (including Huddersfield), Leeds and Wakefield, the last of which was not included in this study because its economic problems and prospects were significantly different from those of the other districts in the county. Unlike other metropolitan areas West Yorkshire does not have a single urban focus but rather comprises a series of linked cities, towns and smaller settlements (see the map). The county is diverse, including agricultural lowlands, major urban centres, commuter settlements and sparsely populated Pennine upland.

Historically, West Yorkshire has not been regarded by central government as a problem area even though it has long displayed many of the outward signs of industrial decay. By the mid 1970s, however, it was apparent that the county was experiencing serious economic difficulties brought about by the rapid rundown of the traditional manufacturing base.[3] Between 1971 and 1975 over 30 000 manufacturing jobs disappeared in West Yorkshire, of which approximately 22 000 jobs were in wool textiles, 7000 in

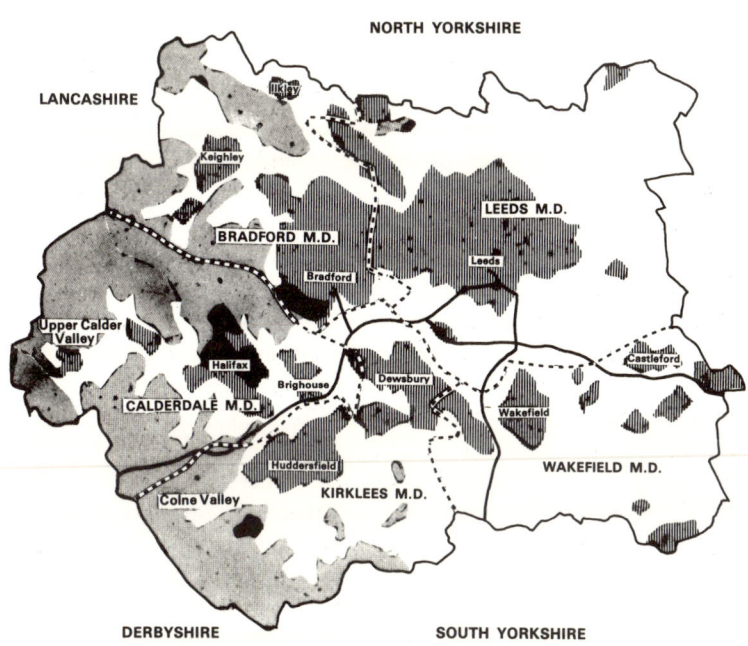

NORTH YORKSHIRE

LANCASHIRE

Keighley

BRADFORD M.D.

Bradford

LEEDS M.D.

Leeds

Upper Calder
Valley

Halifax

Brighouse

Dewsbury

Castleford

CALDERDALE M.D.

Wakefield

Huddersfield

WAKEFIELD M.D.

Colne Valley

KIRKLEES M.D.

DERBYSHIRE

SOUTH YORKSHIRE

**West Yorkshire**
Source: Taken from various West Yorkshire
County Council documents, *Structure Plan
Report of Survey: Part 1*, December 1978, and
WYMCC, *Second Annual Statement*, July 1976.

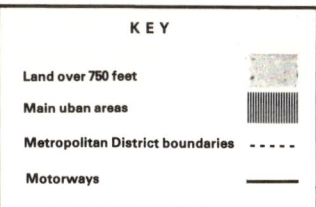

KEY

Land over 750 feet

Main uban areas

Metropolitan District boundaries - - - - -

Motorways ————

clothing and 3400 in parts of the engineering industry. Despite this scale of job loss the county remained heavily dependent on the manufacturing sector (40 per cent of total employment compared with 32.2 per cent nationally). The significance of this dependence lay not simply in the continuing decline of manufacturing employment – a feature of national industrial change – but also in the prominence of wool textiles and clothing, which were vulnerable to further decline and were also the lowest paying industries in the manufacturing sector.

Associated with industrial decline there was a problem of obsolescence of much of the industrial stock and a low level of investment in new buildings. The physical constraints on industrial land availability in the west of the county and the difficulties of re-using derelict and degraded land and premises presented further difficulties. Unfortunately, the collapse of the industrial base took place at the time when the labour force was expanding due to demographic factors; consequently there was a fall in activity rates and an increase in unemployment and outmigration.

Within the county there were variations in the nature and intensity of economic problems. Excluding the coalfield zone in Wakefield, the major difficulties were to be found in the inner areas of Bradford and Leeds and in the western textile region, particularly in the physically restricted Upper Calder and Colne valleys.[4] A survey of metropolitan districts in South and West Yorkshire, undertaken by the Association of Metropolitan Authorities (AMA) in 1976 concluded that Calderdale appeared to be 'suffering from the effects of environmental decay, decline in population and general rundown of its manufacturing industries to the greatest extent'.[5] Other districts in West Yorkshire experienced similar difficulties, but the problems had been partly offset by a compensating expansion in service sector employment, particularly in the case of Leeds which had developed as a regional service centre.

Following the energy crisis in 1973, the UK experienced a major slump reflected in falling industrial output and rising unemployment. In the prevailing climate the government attached great importance to the need to improve productivity and consequently launched the Wool Textile Industry scheme, which was to herald a significant new approach in industrial policy. Based on the wool textile 'Mini-Neddy', it was designed to bring about the modernisation of the industry by closing inefficient firms and concentrating new investment in well-managed companies. Regrettably, no provision was made to deal with the economic and social consequences of the scheme on local communities. By 1976, there had been no fewer than seventy-six mill closures and 4500 notified redundancies in West Yorkshire with no apparent improvement in the prospects of the industry.[6]

There was little evidence to suggest that other aspects of government intervention were having any more positive impact on the area. In the early 1970s, the region was designated an Intermediate Area, thereby entitling it to regional development grants, advance factories, selective regional assistance and, latterly, support from the European Regional Development Fund (ERDF). Monitoring of the policy, in comparison with other assisted areas, indicated that relatively little money was being spent and there was scepticism about the benefits accruing to West Yorkshire.[7] The government's own plan for the region, the *Regional Strategy Review*, produced by the Yorkshire and Humberside Economic Planning Council in 1975, was widely regarded as adopting too complacent an attitude towards local economic problems.[8] Moreover, there was opposition from Calderdale and Kirklees to the policy of supporting growth in the east of the county, particularly in the major cities.[9] In summary, it was felt that not only was central government failing to give adequate recognition to the problems of the county, but also that the broad-brush regional policies were insufficiently sensitive to the needs of specific areas.

Faced with worsening economic prospects and with insensitive government policies, the local authorities launched their own economic initiatives. By the summer of 1977, Leeds, Bradford and Calderdale had all established rolling budgets for land acquisition, infrastructure development and the provision of industrial premises. They had also recently appointed industrial development officers (IDOs), whose function was to liaise with local firms and attract mobile industry to the area. Other initiatives included the development of industrial improvement areas in Bradford and Kirklees, and the use of job creation schemes in Calderdale and Kirklees to undertake environmental improvements.

Leeds, the largest of the metropolitan districts, had only recently become concerned with economic regeneration largely as the result of the closure of a number of major companies, including Burton's clothing factory. Pressure, first from the junior and later senior officers, together with the dramatic worsening of the economic situation brought home the seriousness of the situation to the Council. Bradford's local economic problems had been apparent for a good deal longer and the new metropolitan district had identified industrial and employment matters as a key element in the corporate strategy. A corporate planning team was established in mid-1976 to develop a policy for industry and employment. The momentum for the development of this policy appears to have come from a background of industrial promotion prior to 1974, commitment from the Conservative Council, very forceful chief officers and a strong corporate management system.

In Calderdale, work on industrial problems started almost immediately after reorganisation and the programme evolved continuously thereafter. Industrial development was given high priority in the authority's corporate plan, reflecting the seriousness of the situation. Active policy development was achieved by highly motivated middle-ranking officers, an active IDO and the support of perceptive and concerned local press and key members of the Council. Kirklees had initially placed some emphasis on economic regeneration; however, following the election of the Conservatives, economic development was downgraded in the priorities of the Council. It was the sudden worsening of the economic situation which had prompted the authority to embark on a major programme towards the end of 1976.

**The organisational background to the development of local economic policies**

While there had been limited involvement in certain aspects of economic development prior to 1974, it is nevertheless true to say that industrial and employment policy as a whole represented a new field of operation in all the authorities. The major organisational difficulties arose because this policy field spanned the work of several departments. In a typical local authority the following departments and/or units are likely to have responsibilities which impinge on industry and employment matters: *town planning*, concerned with policy and development control functions; *estates*, involved in the purchase and disposal of sites; *engineering*, dealing with site servicing and reclamation; *industrial development officer*, dealing with promotion; *treasury*, handling finance and loans; *education*, responsible for careers advice and FE colleges. Clearly where there are a number of departments involved, policy development can easily be hindered by the opposition of one or two key officers and time has to be devoted to securing agreement between the parties concerned.

In the case of Bradford, for example, there had been no overall policy framework and the various functions had been pursued in isolation. Following a corporate plan review on industry and employment policy in 1976, it was decided to establish a permanent officer working party with overall responsibility for co-ordination, review and development of an industrial strategy. By the summer of 1977 this group, chaired by the director of the development services, had begun to meet regularly in order to bring together the strands of activity undertaken by the various divisions. One question of particular concern in the organisational review was the role of the IDO. The Bradford IDO was located in a separate unit reporting directly to the director of technical services and chief executive.[10] The IDO commented that he found certain advantages in this relationship as he could play a 'maverick' trouble-shooting role in regard to bureaucratic obstacles within the authority.

In Calderdale the economic policy function was undertaken by the planning department, while site acquisition and development was carried out by the estates department. The bulk of economic policy matters went to the development services committee which in turn reported to the powerful policy and resources committee of the Council. The Calderdale IDO was located in the planning department and since this department was primarily responsible for economic development the IDO was centrally involved in the formulation and implementation of the programme.[11] One other important organisational feature of Calderdale was the establishment of the Calderdale Economic Regeneration Advisory Committee (CERAC) a body which we consider in greater detail below.

After reorganisation in 1974, the (Labour) Council in Kirklees established a simple organisation structure with one committee (economic and employment) to deal with the development programme. A substantial budget for economic development was created and an IDO was appointed to work within the planning department. By all accounts this simplified structure was beginning to achieve results. With the return of the Conservatives in May 1976, the industrial budget was withdrawn, the IDO sacked and a more complex committee structure established. In order to overcome the resultant organisational difficulties, the Council appointed a steering group of officers, called the Local Economic Service Team, to co-ordinate policy. It was suggested that this system did not operate as efficiently as the previous one. Indeed, one officer commented there was now no one person in the authority an industrialist could speak to if faced with a problem.

In Leeds, the authority had a management team of chief officers covering all policy areas. The work of the planning department was overseen by two committees (land committee, and planning and development), which in turn reported to a policy and resources committee. The estates and industrial development officer was not formally involved in this structure as he operated within and reported directly to the chief executive's unit. Again, a steering group of officers from different departments had recently been established to co-ordinate policies and programmes.

*Professional attitudes and rivalries*

Aside from the question of formal organisation structures, it is also necessary to take into account the significance of professional attitudes when examining the development of economic programmes. One issue around which conflicts appeared to arise concerned the tendency for some officers to stick inflexibly to existing procedures. Examples which were cited included: legal officers arguing that section 137 of the Local Government Act could not be used to support local industry; treasurers/finance officers reluctant to lend money or provide industrial mortgages even when this was possible under Local Acts; county highway engineers concerned about grandiose road schemes rather than small-scale site access provisions; estates officers hesitant to offer subsidies on council property or rent-free periods.

Further difficulties arose from arguments about the degree to which a local authority could subsidise or intervene in the local economy. A closely related debate focused on how economic development ought to be accomplished. Alternatives which were discussed included environmental improvements, an emphasis on housing policy, boosting tourism, the attraction of mobile industry and stimulating indigenous-based firms. In Calderdale, the middle-ranking officers spent a great deal of time convincing chief officers and elected members that strategies based on major highway projects and the attraction of mobile industry were not likely to be cost effective. In Bradford, there were similar debates within the directorate of development services.

Such debates reflect not only party politics but also inter-departmental differences which may arise for a number of reasons. For example, the position adopted by officers may express battles between departments over responsibility for the formulation and implementation of policy. In some authorities there is a clear 'pecking order' of officers and departments; this order is jealously guarded, especially in relation to the emergence of a new policy field. There may also be divisions within a department between senior staff and middle-tier officers who are engaged more immediately in policy formulation and implementation. Finally, we need to bear in mind that professional training itself can lead to different perspectives on such questions as local economic development.

Significantly, planning officers played a leading role in the development of policy in all four authorities, reflecting the particular responsibilities and research capabilities of the planning departments. However, only a small number of planning staff – between one and three – were engaged in this activity on a full-time basis. These local economic teams were required to produce policies quickly without an overall policy framework or previous economic research background on which to draw. The planners, then, while they had a key responsibility in this area, often lacked the authority, resources or organisational power to overcome the conflicts of view among their colleagues.

*The policy formulation process*

In order to examine the manner in which local economic policies were developed it was decided to set the work within the context of a rational procedure framework.[12] This decision did not in any way reflect a feeling that this was how planning officers ought to undertake their work, nor that this was how policies were formulated in the 'real world.' Nevertheless, it was felt that without the benefit of previous studies in this area such assumptions might prove a useful device for making comparisons between authorities.

The questionaire survey, therefore, sought to establish the extent to which policy formulation conformed to the following rational procedure: the identification of goals and objectives; the identification of problems and possible solutions; the development of alternative packages; the selection of strategy after evaluation on political, technical and resource grounds; the monitoring and review of policies. Surprisingly, policy formulation approximated to this process more closely than had been expected.

Taking the first stage, it was apparent that of the four authorities Bradford and Calderdale had a more explicit commitment to corporate planning and consequently the two authorities had clear mandates after reorganisation to regard local industrial and employment planning as an important priority. In both authorities, goals of economic prosperity were spelt out by the politicians. In the case of Bradford, the corporate planning team involved the politicians in discussions about the development of policy from which clear operational objectives emerged. Calderdale politicians were not involved to the same extent: in this case, operational objectives emerged from discussions between the planning officers and CERAC in which the officers played a leading role. In Kirklees and Leeds, officers were unaware of any clear political mandate about economic development, and so it was the officers who shaped goals and objectives, which were then presented to the councillors in the hope that they would be accepted.

In respect of the *identification of problems*, economic analysis played a part in each of the metropolitan districts. However, each authority developed its analysis and presented its findings in a distinctive manner. While research into labour market trends was undertaken on a fairly consistent basis, examination of the industrial and commercial structure of the local economy was more variable. In practice there was little evidence of any regular and formalised system of gathering information about local industry. Several of the more detailed economic studies undertaken by the planners provided important insights; they could, however, in no sense be seen as part of a systematic and well-thought-out research programme. Rather, they represented a series of *ad hoc* studies undertaken for a variety of reasons which had been brought together for the purpose of preparing an economic policy report.[13]

The Leeds local economy team was able to draw on a number of research studies stretching back to the late 1960s. These studies included work undertaken for the *Development Plan Review*, a report on the obsolescence of industrial premises and a review of the local economy undertaken in 1975. Based on these studies and the team's own research, it was suggested that three major problems could be identified, namely: the difficulties faced by small firms, the availability of land and premises and the existence of physical obsolescence. The policy document did not present evidence to support the assertion that these were key problems facing the local economy. It would seem they were identified because they could be tackled within the context of the local authority's existing statutory responsibilities.

In the case of Bradford, there had been no previous background of research into the problems of the local economy upon which the corporate planning team could draw. Thus, while the corporate structure of the authority meant that it was possible to take advantage of the expertise of a number of departments, the six months given to the team to produce an analysis and policy was hardly sufficient. The analysis was variable in quality, with some issues considered in great detail, while other issues were not considered at all. In no sense could it be claimed that the policy document presented a comprehensive picture of the problems faced by local firms and the labour force.

Officers in Kirklees had produced a very thorough desk analysis of the census of population and data series from the Department of Employment. Nevertheless, the interpretation of the problems of the local economy was limited by the information contained within these sources. The planners had also produced a joint submission with Calderdale on the problems of the wool textile area which had been prepared for the Department of Industry.[14] The impetus and work for this report had come from the Calderdale planning department.

Indeed, of the four authorities, Calderdale had made the most progress in developing an understanding of the local economy. Their work had commenced almost immediately after the reorganisation of local government, and so by 1977 a series of detailed research reports and papers had been prepared. The work drew not only from published sources but also from direct contact with local industry via the IDO and through CERAC.

In summary, it is apparent from the research undertaken by the four authorities that the identification of local economic problems was of a very low order of resolution. Because of the shortage of staff resources, it was necessary to make use of the most easily accessible official data sources and draw on studies which had been undertaken for other purposes. The interpretation of economic problems was inevitably biased by the quality of information at hand. Much effort was devoted to employment forecasts and the structure of the land and property market. While it was logical to focus on such issues, it was of course difficult to gauge the significance and effectiveness of local authority intervention without a more comprehensive understanding of the local economy. Only Calderdale, with three continuous years of work in this field, gave the impression of possessing a considered view about local economic difficulties.

As far as the question of *the development of alternative strategies* is concerned, it is interesting to note that there was little clear relationship between the problems identified and solutions proposed. Bradford, for example, identified five alternatives: the status quo; minimum involvement; an outward-looking approach with external promotion; an inward-looking approach to local regeneration; and a 'composite' approach. The strategies were not really drawn up in relation to the problems identified but rather in terms of the degree to which existing statutory functions could be developed. The choice was presented in terms of the future state of the economy and alternative political philosophies. In the case of Leeds, the proposals again related to the definition of the area within which the council could operate. The policy document asked for clarification as to how far the Council wished to proceed: (i) as an investor, through direct action via the capital programme (land acquisition, building construction, etc.); (ii) as a planning authority, through the revision of planning procedures; (iii) as a promoter, through internal and external advocacy. Calderdale, in contrast, considered five areas in which action could be based on the problems faced by local firms. The scope of the strategy was widened to include other organisations in the area with an interest in local economic regeneration.

It is clear that with the exception of Calderdale, the policy proposals of the authorities bore little relationship to the research which had been undertaken. Instead the documents stated what were perceived to be the boundaries of statutory local authority action and then asked councillors for clarification as to the degree and form of action which should be taken. Apart from reference to the possibility of providing loans, the majority of the proposals erred on the side of caution and had an extremely restricted view of the scope of local authority action. The proposals were breaking new ground in suggesting that significant resources should be devoted to an essentially new area of local government activity. The cautious approach undoubtedly reflected uncertainty as to the degree of political commitment which would be forthcoming.

In *the selection of strategy*, only Bradford and Calderdale attempted a serious evaluation of the alternatives. The Calderdale proposals were examined in CERAC and then presented to the policy and resources committee for a final political decision. The Bradford corporate planning team considered the alternatives on both technical and resource grounds using quite rigorous methods of appraisal.

There was little evidence of any serious attempt to *monitor the programmes* once they had been selected. Of course, the programmes were in their infancy, but only Calderdale had made any efforts to initiate mechanisms for monitoring trends in the local economy and the success of the initiatives taken. This was achieved through the publication of a quarterly economic review and the preparation of an economic input into the corporate plan review.[15]

Having considered the various stages through which the economic programmes were developed, it was useful to consider the reasons for the differences in approach. In the case of Bradford, the policy was produced in a hurry without the depth of work over a period of time. The corporate planning approach was able to draw on significant manpower resources and thus the policy document gave a superficial impression of a clear, well worked and rationally based programme. The policy was imposed from above through a strong corporate planning system and the commitment of members rather than being based on the initiative of individual departments.

Calderdale's policy, in contrast, while presented in a logical manner, had developed slowly without producing a 'grand design'. The officers had deliberately set out to keep the objectives as vague as possible in order to build up political support gradually. It was suggested that the approach was based on a general educative exercise for the Council. The officers pushed forward particular aspects of the strategy when the opportunity arose. One case in point was the visit of a junior minister to the area, to consider complaints from industrialists about the absence of training facilities and shortage of skilled labour. The officers had used this situation to press for manpower planning initiatives by the authority. The local economic forum was also used by the officers to put forward ideas which, if accepted by CERAC, would have greater credibility when presented to councillors.

In the case of Kirklees, the development of the programme had been handicapped by a complacent attitude amongst politicians about the economic situation. The worsening economic prospects forced them to reconsider their *laissez-faire* position. Unfortunately, at the time of the interview the planners still did not have the political support or the resources to develop a successful economic programme. The situation in Leeds mirrored to some extent the problems faced by planners in Kirklees. It had taken the politicians some time to appreciate that the city was experiencing serious economic difficulties. Once senior officers and a key politician had been convinced, then staff resources and political support began to be provided.

In summarising the situation reached by the four authorities, three and a half years after local government reorganisation, one might conclude that comparatively little had been achieved. It is necessary to bear in mind that the planners were required to produce a policy quickly in response to the pressures resulting from rising unemployment. These were new authorities without a previous research base, with uncertainties about the degree of political commitment, and with a small number of staff who had little experience of the development of local economic policies. Nevertheless, it is clear from the example of Calderdale that progress *could* be made, given motivated and politically skilled officers, and the support of one or two key politicians.

The position adopted by local politicians was, of course, a very significant factor in accounting for variations in the development of economic programmes. However, the distinction between Labour and Conservative parties appeared to be less significant than philosophies within the party groups and the calibre of individual councillors.

## External agencies and local economic policies

While the foregoing discussion of the development of economic programmes has focused on internal organisational issues, a whole range of other public sector agencies impinge on the local economy. The Department of Industry, for example, is responsible for national industrial policy and regional economic planning. The Department of the Environment is concerned with regional strategies, land-use planning, and inner city policy. The Department of Employment and the Manpower Services Commission deal with the labour market and manpower planning. There are also other public sector bodies whose activities have an impact at the local level, including nationalised industries and the statutory undertakings. A local authority programme may then seek to monitor the effects of these policies and where possible influence their application. There are, moreover, other external factors which need to be taken into account (see Figures 5.1 and 5.2*): e.g. the actions of neighbouring local authorities which, where there are common problems, may suggest a need for collaborative action. Trade union organisations and the business community also have a fundamental stake in the well-being of the local community and may be involved in the development of a local programme. How far had the significance of these connections been appreciated and how far had efforts been made to maximise the opportunities available? In exploring these wider inter-organisational issues, it was decided to examine the role of the metropolitan county as well as the districts since the county was particularly concerned with this aspect of economic development.

### Inter-organisational relationships at the county level

Aside from transportation and limited planning and infrastructure responsibilities, the county possessed few of the executive functions necessary to implement strategic policies in the economic sphere.

* These diagrams illustrate some of the organisations and actors to be taken into account in the formulation of a local authority economic development strategy.

## DIAGRAM 5.1    Inter-agency relations at the local level

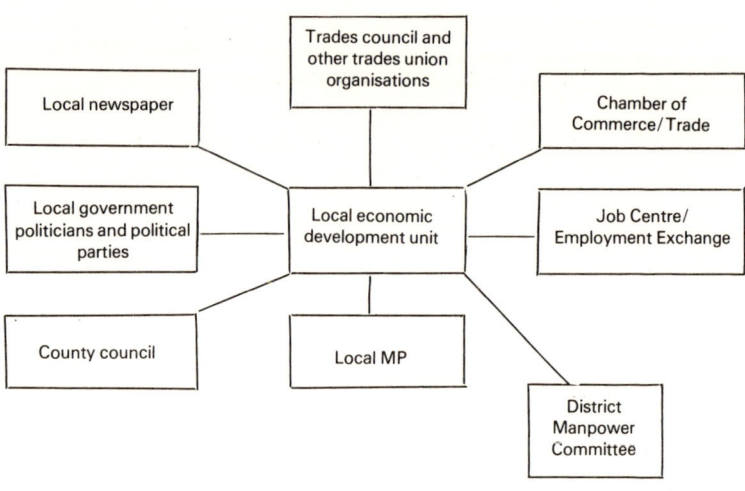

## DIAGRAM 5.2    Inter-agency relationships at the regional level

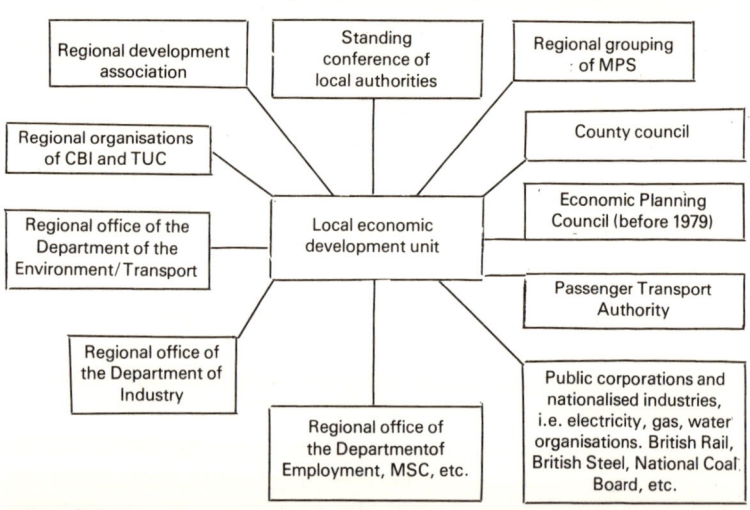

Much of its effort was therefore devoted to co-ordination and lobbying in order to influence the policies and programmes of central government and other agencies and authorities. At the time of reorganisation of local government in 1974, economic development was one of the fields of activity in which there was confusion concerning the division of responsibilities between county and districts. Following a series of meetings, agreement was reached that the implementation of economic development policies would be carried out by the districts, leaving the county to fulfil an advocacy role and undertake external promotion via the county IDO unit.[16]

As the employment situation worsened and economic regeneration became more central to the preparation of the Structure Plan, the county's strategic and intelligence functions were adjusted accordingly. In January 1977, an employment and economic development subcommittee was established to promote employment and economic development, to liaise with outside bodies and to lobby and make representations to government on economic issues. It was served by a corporate unit, the economic development programme team (EDPAT). The team's reports on the local economy were prepared by the research and intelligence unit of the planning department, and were summarised in a quarterly bulletin which was widely circulated in commercial, financial and business circles.

The research and intelligence function provided an important input into the lobbying activities of the county. Attempts to influence central government policy toward a more sensitive application of measures were made via the AMA, through the medium of the Structure Plan and by direct submission to ministers and to the EEC. It was felt, for example, that most of the traditional instruments of regional policy operated by the Department of Industry were ineffective in a period when there was little mobile industry and inappropriate to the needs of the economic regeneration strategy which was emerging from the structure planning exercise.[17]

Contacts with the DoE were primarily concerned to influence the form of the newly emerging inner city policy. The county organised a visit by Secretary of State, Peter Shore, to West Yorkshire, to demonstrate that industrial decline was not restricted to inner city areas. West Yorkshire provided the chairman of the AMA inner city working party, and secured a shift in the emphasis of the AMA's own inner city proposals towards a recognition of the problems of urban industrial areas outside the major conurbations.[18]

County efforts to widen the scope of local authority involvement in the industrial development field included the preparation of a report for the Secretary of State on *Industrial General Improvement Areas*.[19] Powers to declare industrial improvement areas as well as to provide loans and grants were later included in the West Yorkshire Parliamentary Bill, sponsored by the county and districts.

In respect of inter-agency co-ordination, the county was especially concerned with manpower issues. Arising from research for the Structure Plan which suggested a shortage of skilled labour in the county, a joint survey was launched with the Chamber of Commerce, the Employment Services Agency (ESA), the Training Services Agency (TSA) and the regional office of the Department of Employment. The county also acted as a catalyst in bringing together the various manpower agencies, enabling some ESA and TSA officials to meet for the first time.[20]

Turning to the relationships between the county and districts, it was apparent that apart from limited co-operation in, for example, research matters and external promotion there was little joint work in the economic development field. This could be explained, on the one hand, by the tensions resulting from local government reorganisation and on the other, by changing political control in the county and districts.[21] However, at an informal level county planners maintained a dialogue with their district colleagues.

### Inter-organisational relationships of the district authorities

Despite regular meetings of the chief executives, formal political relationships between the districts were not harmonious. This situation reflected the traditional rivalry between the former West Riding County Boroughs. Bradford and Leeds regarded themselves as competing industrial and commercial centres; hence there had been little joint working either at a political or officer level in the field of economic development. In 1975 officers from Bradford had worked with their counterparts in Calderdale and Kirklees on a response to the *Regional Strategy Review*. However, Bradford subsequently withdrew from the exercise due to disagreements over the type of alternative policy that should be proposed.[22]

Relationships between the regional offices of government departments and the districts were uneasy in the sphere of economic development. There were complaints from local authority officers about a reluctance to release data and to discuss policy. In the case of Calderdale and Kirklees, problems had arisen with the Department of Environment in regard to the policies proposed in the *Regional Strategy Review*. These problems were compounded by what was perceived to be a less than supportive attitude towards the handling of applications for infrastructure assistance from the European Regional Development Fund.[23]

There was still less contact with other departments. The Department of Industry had shown little interest in the economic regeneration activities of the district authorities. In the field of manpower planning there was no collaboration between the DoE and local authorities in connection with labour market statistics and their analysis. Moreover, the district manpower committees set up by the MSC were regarded by the local planners as 'talking shops' in which there was little attempt to achieve a co-ordination of the various labour market agencies.

Turning to relationships outside the public sector, it was clear that the trade union movement had little involvement with local authorities in the field of economic development. The regional TUC organisation had only recently begun to take an interest in local economic problems and trade union representatives on the Economic Planning Council (EPC) commented that they were unsure about the issues and were dependent on civil servants for background reports and advice. As far as the private sector was concerned, Bradford, Calderdale and Kirklees had established contacts with the local Chambers of Trade and Commerce through the work of their industrial development officers. These organisations were on the whole hostile to local government intervention and in one instance had refused to lend support to a survey of local firms.

This review of external relationships and inter-agency co-operation indicates that opportunities for joint action were hampered by institutional and political constraints as well as the problem of personal relationships between officers. Of the four district authorities only Calderdale had succeeded in involving outside bodies in their economic programme, primarily through the work of the Calderdale Economic Regeneration Advisory Committee, and this merits a fuller discussion.

## *The Calderdale Economic Regeneration Advisory Committee (CERAC)*

After the reorganisation of local government in 1974, there was increasing concern in Calderdale about the worsening economic prospects for the area. Both Conservative and Labour members were uncertain about the way forward but a small number of councillors, the Chamber of Commerce and Trades Council members argued for a community-based approach. CERAC was established early in 1976 after the publication of the Town Planning Department's document, 'Calderdale: the Case for Economic Regeneration'.[24] From an initial membership of the Trades Council, Chamber of Commerce and local authority, the Committee was expanded to include local MPs, county councillors and members of the EPC, as well as representatives from the Department of Employment. The functions of the organisation were: to work together to create a common consensus of problems; to promote economic regeneration; to share knowledge and experience; to co-operate in pressing a jointly agreed case with government and other external bodies; and to take effective action at short notice to deal with problems of redundancy.

The first stage in the development of the organisation involved the preparation of an action plan based upon the analysis of the problem of the local economy by the planning department. Four main objectives were defined: encouraging new employment, to offset losses in industries with declining labour requirements and to maintain the overall level of employment; improving job opportunities and prospects and working conditions; remedying basic problems of age, obsolescence and poor environment; promoting the full utilisation of the public and private resources of the area in terms of land, buildings, and the labour force skills.

The plan systematically reviewed the obstacles to economic regeneration as they affected local firms and the action to be taken by each member of CERAC was indicated. As the strategy developed, a regular review of initiatives was undertaken in the form of a report to the forum, together with the production of a quarterly bulletin on economic trends in the local economy. In addition to this research support, the Council launched a series of initiatives in association with CERAC, including the establishment of a technical library and business information service (CALDIS), in the local further education college. Another significant development was the establishment of a subcommittee to consider labour market problems which included representatives from the Industrial Training Boards, the local education authority, the FE college, and the Chambers of Commerce and Trade.

A great deal of the work of CERAC was concerned with lobbying to change the policies of various external agencies. The local authority in association with CERAC, had made twenty-eight submissions to outside bodies between the beginning of 1976 and the middle of 1977.[25] This had included five ministerial visits or meetings. It is difficult to measure the success of these activities, particularly over such a short period of time. Nevertheless, it is clear that Whitehall departments had been made aware of the problems of this 'less well-known' part of the country and it was hoped they would adopt a more sympathetic attitude in the future administration of major programmes such as regional policy. At a local level the results of lobbying were more apparent. While little progress had been made in shifting the focus of the Regional Strategy, there can be little doubt that Calderdale had made a significant impact on the final outcome of the structure plan which as part of its package of policies gave priority to economic regeneration in the west of the county.

Local MPs, Shirley Summerskill and Max Madden, made their contributions to CERAC by lobbying ministers and Whitehall departments. Max Madden, in particular, played an active role in arranging visits of junior ministers from the Departments of Industry and Employment to the area. He had also organised the Yorkshire MPs' opposition to the *Regional Strategy Review* in the House of Commons and pressed the TUC to develop an alternative strategy for the region. Powerful additional support for the activities of CERAC came from the local newspaper, the *Halifax Courier*. The editor of the paper was acutely aware of the economic plight of the area and had ensured maximum coverage of the efforts of CERAC and the local authority in order to raise public consciousness. There was evidence that local civil servants and politicians were both aware and influenced by this press reporting as they felt it was a good indicator of the strength of local opinion.

The Chamber of Commerce had also made a positive contribution to local economic regeneration. It had lobbied through CERAC for the provision of additional engineering training courses. This activity had resulted in the visit to Calderdale of a junior minister and the regional director of the TSA and the eventual establishment of a new course in the local FE college.[26] The Chamber had been partly responsible for organising a series of business management courses on accountancy, finance and exporting problems, and prepared a number of papers on the problems faced by small firms.[27] Its survey of local employers provided a basis for a CERAC report on local employment trends.

Finally, the Trades Council had played a leading role in the discussions which led to the establishment of CERAC and made a number of suggestions about initiatives which could be taken at the local level. Its most significant contribution was a paper, *Alternative Employment: the Need for Action*, which pointed to the dangers of rising unemployment resulting from the introduction of new technologies and the capital intensification of manufacturing industry.[28] The Trades Council argued that there was a need for a radical rethink of policy at both national and local levels. In particular it proposed the establishment of a local enterprise board to facilitate economic regeneration and the formulation of a community task force of young jobless people who would be concerned with social and environmental jobs supported by public funds. It also suggested that the various bodies involved with CERAC should press for a consideration of schemes such as earlier retirement, education sabbaticals and work sharing at the national level. The local MPs forwarded the proposals to the Ministers of Industry and Employment and follow-up studies were undertaken by the planning department and the Chamber of Commerce.

In conclusion, it is clear that Calderdale, through the establishment of CERAC, had gone some way to overcoming the problems of inter-departmental and inter-agency co-operation in local economic development. As it built up wider political support for economic regeneration initiatives it became more difficult for any one party to obstruct developments. A measure of the success of CERAC was the way in which an increasing number of organisations had wished to become involved. There were complaints that CERAC was unwieldy and local Conservative politicians were concerned that Labour MPs were getting too much 'good press'. Despite these difficulties CERAC had succeeded in building up an awareness of common problems and a commitment to work together where possible. In the words of a local journalist:

> CERAC's strength is undoubtedly its blanket approach and the broad cross-section of its members. On the surface, putting members of the Chamber of Commerce, Trades Council, Calderdale Councillors and MPs round the same table would seem to spell out a certain formula for political disaster. Possibly because of a lurking informality this is not always so.

**Conclusion**

This chapter has sought to illustrate some of the isses which arise in the formulation of local authority economic programmes. Despite common problems there were noticeable variations in the manner in which local authorities approached the task of developing an economic regeneration strategy. These variations could be explained by the interaction of three factors: differing organisation structures; the role of individual officers and elected members; and the attitude of local political parties.

Unlike many other local authority functions, economic development is *ipso facto* a highly corporate activity and as such is vulnerable to inter-departmental frictions. Three out of the four district authorities set up steering groups of officers to undertake a co-ordination of activities, yet problems of departmental co-operation and professional rivalries remained.

Policy development evolved in different ways within the four authorities. Bradford had a very formalised approach based on a corporate planning system and the commitment of elected members. In Calderdale, in contrast, the policy was built up gradually against a background of potential political hostility. A major role was played by middle-ranking officers, the IDO and key politicians. In Leeds and Kirklees initial efforts by officers to push for an economic regeneration strategy were frustrated by chief officers and politicians who felt that the economic situation did not require such a response. At a wider level the County Council played an active role in promoting the interests of West Yorkshire nationally and also took several initiatives to secure greater inter-agency co-ordination. While the county and districts were pursuing similar economic objectives, co-operation was limited by political and institutional tensions, although in certain cases officers had succeeded in working together on an informal basis.

Overall there was little involvement by the industrial and commercial sector, or trades unions, in the economic regeneration activities of the local authorities. CERAC provided the one example of an attempt to involve the wider community in a local authority economic development programme. The establishment of CERAC had a number of advantages for Calderdale. First, it resulted in a common awareness of problems within the community and hence widened the scope of the local authority strategy; second, it increased the amount of information available on trends in the local economy; third, it presented a mechanism for securing inter-agency co-ordination; fourth, it provided powerful support for lobbying activities by the Council; finally, it created overwhelming pressure for economic development initiatives which could be channelled in such a way as to overcome bureaucratic and political obstacles.

In organisational terms, Calderdale had made considerable progress in developing its economic strategy. Undoubtedly this was a reflection of the serious economic difficulties facing the area and the fact that as a small authority much greater efforts had to be made to overcome the problems. However, those most closely involved in Calderdale's policies were acutely aware that an appropriate organisation could not in itself overcome fundamental economic problems which reflect not only local circumstances but broader trends in the national and international economy.

## References

1.  The author acknowledges that the analysis presented is only partial in the sense that it does not fully take into account the wider economic and political forces at play nor the way they interacted at the local level to shape local authority policies. For an excellent account of these issues see N. Moor and P. Waddington, *From Rags to Ruins:*

*Batley, Woollen Textiles and Industrial Change* (Newcastle-upon-Tyne Community Development Project Political Economy Collective, 1980). See also R. Wiener, *The Economic Base of Leeds* (Leeds Workers' Educational Association, Yorkshire North District, 1976).

2. For a lengthier description of the findings of this study and the methodological background see J. Mawson, *Local Authority Economic Policies in West Yorkshire 1974–1977: an Organisational Perspective,* Occasional Paper 6 (new series) (Birmingham: Centre for Urban and Regional Studies, 1982).

3. B. A. Briscoe, *The Implementation of Economic Policies in the West Yorkshire Structure Plan*, Planning and Transport Research and Computation Annual Summer Meeting 1978, University of Warwick, 10–13 July, p. 2.

4. West Yorkshire County Council, *Structure Plan, Report of Survey, Part 1* (WYCC, December 1978) paras 9.3 and 9.4.

5. Association of Metropolitan Authorities, Employment and Industry Study Group, *The Role and Effect of New and Expanded Towns on Employment and Industrial Development in the Metropolitan Areas: Industry and Employment in Yorkshire* (AMA, 1976) p. 5.

6. Moor and Waddington, *Rags to Ruins*, p. 58. Redundancies may well have been much higher due to women failing to register as unemployed.

7. Moor and Waddington, *Rags to Ruins*, p. 56.

8. Yorkshire and Humberside Economic Planning Council, *Yorkshire and Humberside Regional Strategy Review* (HMSO, 1975). For a critique of the strategy see Town and Country Planning Association, South and West Yorkshire Planning Forum, *Towards Effective Regional Planning in Yorkshire and Humberside* (London: TCPA, 1978); South Yorkshire County Council, *Comments of SYCC on the Regional Strategy Review*, sent to the Secretaries of State for Industry and for the Environment, and to the Minister for Planning and Local Government, 8 January 1976; West Yorkshire County Council Strategic Planning Sub-Committee, *Draft Statement of the View of the County Council on the Government's Response to the Regional Strategy Review, 1975*, 20 June 1977.

9. Metropolitan Borough of Calderdale, *Review of the Regional Strategy: the Case for Supporting a Policy of Economic Regeneration in Calderdale*, June 1975.

10. City of Bradford Metropolitan Council, 'Industrial Development and Promotion – a Comparison of Bradford with Other Metropolitan Authorities', internal report, 1976.

11. P. W. Burton, 'The Developing Role of the Industrial Development Function in Local Government: Case History from Calderdale', Metropolitan Borough of Calderdale, Association of Industrial Development Officers National Conference, 17 November 1978.

12. The research methodology is described in greater detail in Centre for Urban and Regional Studies Occasional Paper 6. For a discussion of

the application of the rational method in planning practice, see N. Litchfield, P. Kettle and M. Whitbread, *Evaluation in the Planning Process* (Pergamon Press, 1974).

13. Research and policy documents examined in the study included: City of Bradford Metropolitan Council, *Local Economy Profile 1976*, Key Issue Team Report, August 1976; City of Bradford Metropolitan Council, *Industry and Employment, First Report*, Key Issue Team Report, December 1976; Metropolitan Borough of Calderdale, *Local Authority Involvement in Industrial Progress and Change*, Development Services Committee, 22 May 1974; Metropolitan Borough of Calderdale, *Land Availability, Industrial Estates, Existing Premises and Office Development*, Development Services Committee, 19 June 1974; Metropolitan Borough of Calderdale, *Review of the Regional Strategy: the Case for Supporting a Policy of Economic Regeneration in Calderdale*, June 1975; Calderdale Economic Regeneration Advisory Committee, *Discussion Document, Economic Regeneration Action Plan*, 25 June 1976; Metropolitan District of Kirklees, *A Profile of Kirklees*, 1975; Metropolitan District of Kirklees, *Steps in the Development of Policy for Economic Development*, Policy and Resources Committee, Economic Development Sub-Committee, 11 March 1976; City of Leeds, *Report on Industrial Renewal and Rehabilitation 1972–1991*, August 1972; Leeds City Council, *Short Term Appraisal of the Local Economy*, Planning and Development Committee, 3 December 1975; Leeds City Council, *Leeds Policy for Industry: Small Firms*, Planning and Development Committee, 21 September 1977; Leeds City Council, *Leeds Policy for Industry: Land and Premises*, Planning and Development Committee, 2 November 1977.

14. Metropolitan Councils of Calderdale and Kirklees, *Statement to the Secretary of State for the Environment on the Yorkshire and Humberside Regional Strategy Review, 1975, as it relates to the textile area of West Yorkshire*, 19 June 1976.

15. Metropolitan Borough of Calderdale, *Corporate Plan Review: Economic Regeneration*, August 1977.

16. Briscoe, *Implementation of Economic Policies*, p. 4.

17. West Yorkshire County Council, *The Operation of Regional and Industrial Policy in West Yorkshire*, Policy and Finance Committee, Employment and Economic Development Sub-Committee, 5 September 1977; West Yorkshire County Council, *Meeting with the Department of Industry 29 September 1977*, Employment and Economic Development Sub-Committee, 17 October 1977.

18. West Yorkshire County Council, *Inner Urban Areas,* Report of EDPAT Employment and Economic Development Sub-Committee, 28 March 1977.

19. West Yorkshire County Council, *Industrial General Improvement Areas,* December 1976.

20. Briscoe, *Implementation of Economic Policies*, p. 13.

21. See E. S. Dixon, 'Management in Local Government in West

Yorkshire April 1974–March 1977', M.Sc. thesis, University of
Bradford, 1978, appendix B, correspondence between Chief
Executives concerning 'County and District relationships in West
Yorkshire'.

22. Metropolitan Councils of Calderdale and Kirklees, *Statement to the Secretary of State*, 1976.
23. Correspondence between the Department of the Environment, Yorkshire and Humberside Region and the Chief Executives of Calderdale and Kirklees, 27 August 1976, reproduced in joint Calderdale and Kirklees *Briefing Paper for Members of Parliament for meeting with the Rt Hon. John Silkin, Minister for Planning and Local Government*, 20 September 1976.
24. Calderdale Economic Regeneration Advisory Committee, *Discussion Document*; Calderdale Economic Regeneration Advisory Committee, up-dated *Regeneration Action Plan*, 30 June 1978.
25. Metropolitan Borough of Calderdale, *Corporate Plan Review, Advocacy, External Promotion and Community Involvement, Assessment of Performance*, 1977, p. 35.
26. Calderdale Economic Regeneration Advisory Committee, *Industrial Training: Follow up to the Visits to Calderdale by John Golding, MP, Under Secretary of State, Department of Employment*, 1977.
27. Calderdale Economic Regeneration Advisory Committee, *Submission to the Calderdale Chamber of Commerce and Industry: the Small Firm in 1977*, 1 April 1977.
28. Calderdale Economic Regeneration Advisory Committee, *Submission by the Halifax and District Trades Council, Alternative Employment – the Need for Action*, 6 January 1978.

# 6 The Problems of Economic Strategy

KEN YOUNG

## Introduction

Local authority involvement in the promotion of economic development has grown rapidly if unevenly during the last few years. Explicit encouragement came in 1977 with the central government circular, *Local Government and the Industrial Strategy* which, until superseded by Circular 22/80, provided local authorities with a rationale for a closer and more positive relationship with industry.[1] Some authorities had already gone beyond the somewhat anodyne phrases of the circular. Others are today still ambivalent about their economic role. Between these two poles lie a number of urban authorities where the concept of local 'industrial strategy' struck a chord and where steps were taken to give industrial issues parity with or even precedence over more familiar concerns with housing or environmental questions.

This chapter recounts the experience of one such authority. Its particular situation and recent history are of course unique to that authority. The intention of this case study is to illuminate certain common features which are widely found in the generation of strategies for local economic development. First, the often rhetorical or symbolic nature of such policies; second, the sharp disparities between the consensual nature of policy formulation and the more conflictual processes of its implementation.

The brief case study which follows highlights first the contrast between the rhetoric and the reality of economic 'strategy'. The rhetoric of corporate planning and rational decision-making emphasises the identification of goals by organisational leaders and their pursuit through optimal programmes to final implementation by a subordinate and undifferentiated bureaucracy. The reality is one of inchoate and conflicting purposes pursued by distinct and sometimes competitive departments (or sections within them), each of which lobbies and manoeuvres to establish the precedence of *its* interests and clients on the agenda of policy-making. This 'administrative politics' perspective sees executive acts – policies – as the ultimate outcomes of such conflict and competition.[2] It also suggests that attempts to frame overarching strategies can themselves be interpreted as moves by central decision-makers to transform the rules and procedures within which this competition occurs.[3] Despite its rational trappings 'strategy' is a political move; despite its apparent concern with 'transitive goals' (preferred states of the operating environment) it is necessarily equally concerned with 'reflexive goals' (preferred states of the internal organisation).[4]

The structure of this chapter is therefore as follows. In the first section I introduce the authority itself, briefly describe the recent economic changes within its area, and outline the pattern of administrative politics at the point when strategy was first mooted. In the second section, the adoption of a local industrial strategy and its subsequent revision and elaboration are described. The third section discusses the impact of these conflicts – endemic in 'administrative politics' – upon the subsequent case decisions through which 'strategy' was to be implemented.

## The context of strategy

Westborough is an outer London borough, an industrial and residential suburb on the relatively well-favoured western fringe of the metropolis.[5] With its 'ribbon' industrial development along arterial roads it is the quintessence of interwar London. Its interwar growth was rapid, and was characterised by progressive tube railway extension, speculative house building and land transactions, and the development of new forms of quick-build (and foreseeably transient) factory construction.[6]

Arguably, Westborough, in common with the rest of industrial Middlesex, has since 1945 become the victim of its own success. The industrial growth of the area by firms migrating from inner London between the wars has been followed by decline in the postwar decades as successive firms have encountered ceilings to growth and have relocated in order to expand.[7] The area has also been hard hit by the restructuring of the manufacturing sector, in particular in the locally prominent categories of electrical and mechanical engineering and chemicals. Thus, between 1966–74, ninety manufacturing establishments closed in the borough, of which about half were complete closures and half outward migrations. Since 1974 this process has continued, with some of the largest manufacturing employers ceasing production there.

During the 1960s and 1970s Westborough was experiencing a process of 'de-industrialisation'.[8] Manufacturing employment fell from over 62 000 in 1961 to 38 000 in 1975; from almost two-thirds to around one-third of the employed population. Within the manufacturing sector itself there was a marked shift from blue- to white-collar employment. Unemployment, however, remained low – as low as 0.5 per cent in 1966 – while 'outer west' London generally has the lowest unemployment rate in the entire metropolis. Despite the rapid and continuing collapse of the manufacturing base, the locality has enjoyed a fairly painless transformation to a predominantly service-based economy in a space of very few years. Office development and commercial growth has been marked, while the international airport at Heathrow has continued to generate employment at fairly high earnings levels (much to the chagrin of local engineering employers). Moreover, the growth of Heathrow and the development of the motorway network created an enormous pressure for warehouse development while industrial sites continued to remain empty.

Westborough's policy framework, on the other hand, stressed the need to maintain past functions. The interim industrial policy adopted in 1966 emphasised the need to resite 'nonconforming' industry, to relieve congestion by decentralisation from London and to resist warehouse development on vacant industrial land.

During the next five years applications to convert and extend manufacturing premises for storage purposes were repeatedly refused as 'contrary to the provisions of the [GLC's] Initial Development Plan' and these decisions were generally upheld on appeal.

By 1971 the pressures were becoming irresistible. *Ad hoc* departures from policy were being made and the planning department feared that refusals of permission for warehouse development were no longer sustainable. The migration of industry was becoming more noticeable and the local press attacked the Council's inflexibility in refusing 'applications from newcomers who were prepared to take over [factory] buildings for offices, warehousing and transport depots'. Several of the larger local manufacturers succeeded in gaining planning permission to convert their premises for warehousing and offices; the planning department, while concerned about possibly encouraging such a trend, recognised the 'expediency' of permitting changes which were nevertheless 'contrary to policy on virtually every conceivable count'.

The department's officers were particularly concerned about the vulnerability of their own position at inquiries and in 1971 advised a policy change to 'accommodate the present demand for warehousing'. The planning committee were less enthusiastic, although during the next twelve months the view that 'any type of use was to be welcomed' in the interests of the ratepayers and amenity began to gain ground. The planners themselves moved still further towards accepting this steady transformation of their economic base as, during the early 1970s, unemployment began to pose an increasing threat. It 'was better to have some employment generation' than empty sites, although this was a reluctant acceptance of 'the apparently inevitable'.

One consequence of these changes was the steady contraction of skilled job opportunities and the fall-off in engineering apprenticeships in particular. These trends began to alarm the education committee and the careers service officials. Their criticism of the planning department for not initiating the attraction of new manufacturing enterprise became gradually more tart. Under their pressure, the focus of attention shifted from the overall level of employment to its structure. Joint meetings with neighbouring boroughs were instituted and deputations dispatched to ministers, all in hope of retaining a manufacturing role for the borough. The planning department were, however, far from sanguine that the education committee's demands could be met.

After 1975 a new factor entered the debate. The property market was enjoying a boom and the valuer's department was keen to take advantage of the opportunities for office development. The newly appointed chief executive advocated the development of municipal land for offices in the interests of fiscal health and employment diversity. It seemed as though a positive acceptance of the transformation of the local economy might meet the interests of all the disparate elements in the internal debates over economic issues.

Some of the planning professionals retained their scepticism about the wisdom of promoting office development, arguing that the jobs created would be filled by commuters and not by displaced local workers. Yet the main constraint on policy change was the Council itself. Safely Labour-controlled, the Council's decisions and debates often displayed a suspicion of the social (and perhaps political) implications of a further shift from blue collar to white. Engineering employment and trade unionism was strongly represented on the Council, and reinforced on the employers' side by a joint consultative committee with the local organisation of the CBI. The links between education and industry were also strong and these factors combined to retain a symbolic commitment to a continued manufacturing role.

That symbol and substance bore a tenuous relationship to one another was largely due to the lack of any mechanism for implementing such a vision. Decision-making was largely *ad hoc*. The organisation of the policy process was characterised as 'a federal system with strong, professionally orientated departments'. The leader's policy group was for the most part a forum for resolving inter-departmental and inter-committee disputes, and the former chief executive had been unassertive. Meanwhile, the planning department itself, small and self-consciously vulnerable, complained of lack of policy guidance while its junior officers noted with resignation that the director of planning and his deputy were happy to respond to *ad hoc* instructions from councillors.

After 1975 some of these factors changed. A new, young and energetic chief executive was appointed. He had a recognised commitment to corporate policy-making and immediately instituted inter-departmental topic groups to deal with difficult or neglected issues. The more restless planners saw an intelligence and strategy role for themselves under this new regime. During the following year the director of planning retired and was replaced by a younger and more professionally orientated planner in the chief executive's mould. Together, these two new officals reviewed the need for a greater policy orientation within the planning department and an increased involvement of a smaller number of councillors in policy discussion. Thus, by 1977, the prospects for a more strategic approach to planning seemed to have improved. It was the natural inclination of the incoming officials to put these new structures into effect: the director of planning needed to rehabilitate his vulnerable department; the chief executive sought cross-cutting or corporate issues to give reality to his notional power. An *industrial strategy* could meet their mutual needs.

**Towards an industrial strategy**

In July 1977 the Departments of the Environment and Transport published a joint circular, *Local Government and the Industrial Strategy*, in which they sought to persuade local authorities to 'develop and maintain a close awareness of the problems and difficulties that industrial undertakings face, to give help whenever it is practicable to do so, to deal speedily with applications and requests for information and to ensure that full account is taken of industrial needs in reaching decisions'.[9]

Circular 71/77 contained novel features of considerable importance for local authorities. In the first place, it defined their local industrial situations as complonents of the national economic problem – it sought to redefine the local issues as macro issues. In the second place, it stressed the significance of a broad range of local powers – in planning, transport and housing – for industrial well-being and implied that co-ordinated policies were essential. It advocated the appointment of identifiable liaison officers for industry.

This was an appropriate moment for the chief executive to press for action. Two weeks after Circular 71/77 was received in Westborough he formally urged the departmental directors 'to examine the operations' of their departments 'to ensure that the maximum assistance is given to industry'. The borough valuer and director of planning were quick to respond, for the circular came at a useful time for them. The valuer's department had been preparing schemes for the development of small industrial units and the circular's emphasis on small firms and 'seed-bed' factories gave the schemes fresh impetus. Moreover, the valuer's and planning departments were already skirmishing with the housing department over a number of industrial sites on which eventual residential development was scheduled. The circular then provided a counterbalance to the momentum of Westborough's housing programme, which depended in part on the relocation of existing small firms from proposed housing sites.

The chief executive, valuer, and director of planning now effectively had the initiative and were able to provide an impetus towards a jointly agreed position for all departments in the nominally corporate chief officers' meetings. In this respect they went far beyond the education department's recurrent demands for action on industrial employment. In particular, they resurrected an earlier suggestion that a seminar on employment problems be sponsored by the Council as a follow-up to a meeting convened two years before. The prime purpose of the seminar would be to give local employers the opportunity to explain what type of assistance they would seek from the authority and for the Council to explain its policies regarding assistance to industry.

These proposals were agreed by the chief officers' meeting and subsequently endorsed by the planning committee. Within four months of the publication of Circular 71/77, Westborough had formally adopted its suggestions *largely verbatim* to provide the explicit policy base that had been sought by the planning department. The keystone of the industrial strategy was the commitment that 'every effort will be made to encourage the maintenance of existing firms and the establishment of new industries through development control measures. Changes of use from industrial purposes will be resisted.' Moreover, vacant industrial floorspace would be developed, developers would be supported by the Council in applying for Industrial Development Certificates and there would be wider contact and consultation with industry.

Two new internal arrangements were proposed: the appointment of an industrial liaison officer (ILO); and the establishment of an inter-departmental officer group 'to discuss the problems of local industry and formulate detailed proposals for their solution'. The appointment of an ILO was entirely in accordance with the DoE's advice and although the first moves towards preparing a policy paper had come from the chief executive's office, the director of planning had successfully nominated one of his own senior staff to the post, apparently establishing the primacy of the planning department in the industrial field. Formally, then, planning now had the major responsibility for industrial matters. However, this appearance was deceptive. The chief executive continued to develop and expand his own contacts with industrialists, engaging in a continuing series of meetings with local managing directors. He continued to intervene personally whenever relations with other major agencies or higher levels of government were involved. More significant still was his insistence that while detailed matters might be taken up with the ILO, *'policy issues relating to industrial matters will continue to be addressed to the chief executive'*.

The chief executive had a strong personal commitment to the new economic policy. Yet there was considerable scepticism among the other officials. The 'strategy' itself was regarded cynically in some quarters; one senior planner remarked that the Council was 'trying to adopt an approach like the inner boroughs ... we must be being laughed at [it's] a waste of time and money'. It was also well known that the ILO himself, being a traditional 'local plans man' with a strong orientation to the physical rather than the economic environment, shared this scepticism. He did not subscribe to the reasoning behind the 'industrial strategy'; he had accepted the ILO responsibility almost under duress; and he had secured written agreement that it was a temporary responsibility. He left it with relief when the planning department underwent re-organisation in the autumn of 1978. His replacement, recruited especially for the post, brought rather more conviction to it. The new commitment of the Council had, however, failed to impress local industrialists. One commented that 'what's being presented is a very big change indeed and we'll take some convincing'. Local CBI members claimed they 'would rather have someone with business experience' as ILO, for it was important 'to be able to talk the language and understand the problems'.

Despite the internal and external scepticism, the initial corporate commitment to an industrial strategy established a definite planning policy context for the first time in Westborough. The ILO was now able to define the borough's position for potential developers:

> the Council's policy towards industry is in principle, one of support for expansion and renewal of the manufacturing base and it aims to support industrialists and developers wishing to build within the area. Industries which would be most welcome are those providing jobs for men and school leavers across a wide skill band. Generally speaking, that attitude to speculative industrial development is conditioned by the supply of space, and development which could be readily let for industrial use and in small units are likely to be viewed favourably.

The initial priorities of the new Industrial Strategy Working Group (ISWG), set up to report to the environmental planning committee and comprising officers of the planning, valuer's, finance, education and engineer's departments, precisely reflected this concern. The topics agreed as demanding attention at the first meeting of ISWG in February 1978 included the shortages and training of skilled workers; the lack of vacancies for unskilled workers; the amount and obsolescence of vacant industrial premises; the extent of demand for industrial sites for expansion; the problems of small firms; the problem of industrial movement; the constraints posed by IDC and nonconforming use controls; and the labour market aspects of housing and education.

The ISWG had no independent budget of their own over and above a slim allocation for publicity. Accordingly, their attention came to focus on those tangible projects that lay within their resources: a guide to borough services, aimed at prospective developers; a register of vacant industrial and commercial sites, available to enquirers; and a survey of the preferences of employers recruiting from among school leavers. The first of these was almost two years in preparation, and generated a series of discussions about how best to communicate the Council's services to developers; the final product stressed the need for 'a joint approach' to the industrial welfare of the borough.

The survey of employers saw the re-emergence of Westborough's education department in developing corporate policy. The establishment of the 'industrial strategy' had enabled the planning and valuation departments to seize the initiative in Westborough, and to consolidate their advantage by staging a seminar for local industrialists. The seminar proposal had initially excluded the education department but they were able to insist on a prominent place in the eventual programme. With their long record of concern about the changing employment structure, the education department were able to claim reinstatement in the mainstream of developments easily enough. Moreover, they continued to be heavily represented on the working group, and their particular interests, far from being subsidiary to the group's main work, gradually came to the forefront of collective concern.

Indeed, in terms of 'giving a factual account' of the borough's *employment* problems there was no one better placed than the principal careers officer in the education department. He worked closely with local Employment Services Division managers and regularly fed lengthy tabulations of the local employment situation into the ISWG. On questions of employment, the education and careers officials had a clear advantage. The principal careers officer held information on major employers' staffing practices and on the training schemes operating in the borough. His primary responsibility was to the careers subcommittee, a body on which industrial and commercial co-optees were a majority of the membership. He had regularly monitored employment trends and his subcommittee had (through the education committee) been the source of pressure on the planning department for some years. As long as the focus of concern was on the employment consequences of industrial change the careers service and the education department had a virtual monopoly of intelligence.

Apart from the planning department, who were represented by the openly sceptical ILO, and the education representatives, who were in effect gaining corporate endorsement for their pre-existing concerns, there were few obvious stakes for the ISWG members. An officer from another department, recollecting the early days of the group openly wondered why he had bothered to attend. The work of the group tended to be *ad hoc*, considering a thin stream of issues whose substance derived largely from the enthusiasm of the diverse individuals who promoted them. Thus one education department official brought considerable energy to the employers' survey. A member of the social services department occupied the group for most of two meetings with pleas of support in a campaign to establish crèche facilities at major employment centres. At the behest of the Council Leader, prolonged consideration was given to the possibility of establishing workers' co-operatives in the borough.

The discussions in the group seemed to neutralise rather than extend the issues of change in the local economy. The industrial strategy group was becoming a forum in which particular departmental concerns could receive an airing and gain a more general status and, thereby, a more direct access to the corporate processes – the Chief Officers' meeting and the Labour Party policy group.

The group was at risk of losing its notional role as the definer of local problems, for it remained open to any other department to independently bid for that role by providing a cogent account of 'what was going on' in Westborough. The challenge came at the end of 1978 from the planning department as the fruition of one of the new director of planning's first departmental initiatives: an 'employment topic paper' reviewing the state of the local economy and discussing its policy implications. Topic papers were a deliberate device to give focus to the department's own work, and to place strategic issues directly before the councillors. Under the new director of planning the younger members of the department were assigned to preparing these papers, which covered such topics as noise in the environment and the impact of micro-technology as well as the employment situation of Westborough.

The young planner who produced the topic paper had earlier written the script of the industrial seminar's tape/slide show and was now working as the research arm of the industrial development interest in his department. His work ran in parallel to the ISWG, which he did not attend. The topic paper was seen as an important statement of the planning department's authority in the industrial field. Something more specific than the Council's anodyne 'industrial strategy' was required if definite policies were to be realised through development control decisions, and planning appeals not lost for the want of a well-argued policy base. Moreover, the internal standing of the department was itself at stake. Not only had the education committee been consistently critical over the years, but the chief executive's department were suspected of harbouring ambitions to wrest the formulation of local plans away from planning and into their own hands on the grounds of its centrality to corporate and community planning needs. The department had been, as one member put it, 'very much on the defensive'; their launch of a closely argued topic paper, supported by appropriate data, strengthened their own position and regained the initiative that an uninterested ILO had let slip.

The thrust of the paper was to portray the problem for the Council as one of 'coming to terms with an enormous structural change in the economy'. The problem for the local economy was not to be found in the overall employment consequences of the 'transformation' – indeed, it was argued that the growth of the service sector accounted for the buoyancy of the local labour market. The problem was rather one of 'imbalances' – mismatches within the pattern and conditions of employment and between the opportunities available in the eastern end of the borough and those available in the western end. The position of 'vulnerable groups' – women, the disabled, young people and unskilled workers – should feature in the development of a new *strategy for employment*.

Meanwhile, the ISWG had prepared their own 'progress report' on the industrial strategy. This was ready for consideration in October 1978. The report began with the premise that Westborough was not ' crisis area' although 'the problems of maintaining a healthy industrial climate are considerable'. It sought to identify areas where 'a corporate approach to industrial problems would be helpful'. Its only substantive recommendation, beyond continuing its investigation of schools–industry links, the provision of information to firms and other projects, was that the Council should consider a deputation to London Transport to press for improved bus facilities in the borough.

As several members of the ISWG recognised, the planning department's topic paper upstaged their own efforts, and raised the issue of whether industry and employment matters were really a key corporate concern or simply part of the proper remit of the planning department. The question was one of who would claim the proper authority for policy initiatives. The chief executive's policy co-ordinator immediately saw the issue and challenged the status of the paper, questioning if it were 'a statement of *this* group's view'. If the paper were simply taken on board, he wondered, what would be left for the corporate group to do? Anxious to maintain their position, the ISWG simply adopted this latest expression of view; the ISWG report was rewritten so as to reflect the new appreciation of Westborough's situation which the topic paper had achieved.

The ISWG's main points of departure from their first draft report came in their conclusions, where it was conceded that:

> whilst the group recognises the importance of maintaining an industrial presence in the borough of the smaller and successful larger firms, the transition of employment trends towards the service sector is recognised. It is considered that in the future, the group should, therefore, be addressing itself to employment in the broader perspective and include consideration of the special problems of certain groups.

Accordingly, the environmental planning committee was asked to extend the group's terms of reference 'to cover the problems of employment in the borough as a whole, not just industrial problems' and rename the group the *Employment* Strategy Working Group 'to reflect this transition'.

The revision of the ISWG's terms of reference was approved with no difficulty, but the director of planning continued to press for firm policy guidelines in the industrial field. To this end, the topic paper was rewritten in more decisive terms and similarly submitted for approval. There was no prior smoothing out of what was recognised to be 'a complete reversal' of existing policy in the version submitted for approval to the new planning policy subcommittee. Yet in the event discussion ran on familiar lines, focusing in particular on recent closures and emphasising the physical and fiscal effects of industrial dereliction.

More generally, the discussion exemplified the difficulties of achieving any firm strategic commitment in Westborough. Intervening to close the discussion on the dilemma of refusing warehouse development to protect industrial sites, the chairman commented that: 'We are talking here about very broad policy. But individual cases are handled on their merits, as they always are.' No one disagreed; this was indeed the familiar decision style of Westborough. The test of the ''industrial strategy' could not therefore lie in the terms of the topic paper or any similar report. It was to be found in the ways in which particular decisions were handled over time, in the light of the ambiguities as to Westborough's industrial character, and the inevitable conflicts with other policy objectives, conflicts which were embodied in the different committees, departments and professional interests.

## Implementing the strategy

The development of Westborough's strategy revealed a temporary resolution of organisational conflicts. Historically, the education department had been the most sensitive to an industrial clientele and concerned both to maintain industrial employment and to gear 'the education product' to industrial needs. The valuer's department were concerned to maximise the returns on land but were interested in providing, where appropriate, small factory units. The bouyant state of the local land market inclined the valuers to favour commercial or industrial users. The planning department's greatest need was for a coherent, consistent and well-supported 'policy base' within which land-use decisions could be taken. Existing interests, however, militated against this consensus. For example, the housing department sought to maintain as large a housing programme as possible, in which they could count on some support from the borough architect. Moreover, the increased attention given to industrial retention was counter to long-standing policies to improve the physical environment.

Thus while it was possible to agree on a declaratory strategy, implementing its intentions proved more difficult. Particular decisions evoked different responses according to particular concerns of the departments or even of distinct groups of officials within them. While 'strategy' claimed to harmonise action, actual decisions became the focus of conflicts; where 'strategy' proclaimed new priorities, actual decisions often reflected existing priorities. Moreover, these clashes between corporate and departmental interests, between the new and the old, had to be resolved by councillors whose predominant orientations were to the separate service committees and to pre-existing commitments. Two examples illustrate the difficulties of implementing policy change.

### *Departmental conflicts: the Wetfield Works case*

The first case of policy conflict in the implementation of the industrial strategy initially arose during mid-1977 when the Council had yet to adopt a formal strategy but when the new director of planning was pushing for a definite policy towards industry. The need to resolve it made the declaration of the industrial strategy a useful objective for the 'industry lobby' in Westborough.

Wetfield Works is a small industrial site in central Westborough, occupying a little under two acres in an area zoned under the Initial Development Plan for residential use. Approximately twenty small firms, mostly engaged in light engineering or special process operations, were located on the site and employed an average of between ten and eleven workers each. The site represented a 'nonconforming use' under the development plan, but by the mid-1970s concern about Westborough's manufacturing base was sufficient to protect the firms there from the threat of relocation. Two factors, however, bore upon their future security. In the first place, the lease on the council-owned site was to expire in December 1980 and the local firms were uncertain as to whether it would be renewed. Second, there had been a long-term intention to include the site in Westborough's housing programme as the second stage of an adjacent development. The decision to carry out the development in two stages and to include the Wetfield Works site in the second had been taken in 1968. The housing department brought the site into its 1979 housing programme on the expectation that the expiry of the leases would free the site for housing.

The valuer's department were the first to challenge this expectation. Traditionally concerned with land acquisition and disposal for all the Council's activities, the department was becoming increasingly aligned with the industrial lobby in the planning department. In particular, securing the provision of small, profitable industrial premises in the redevelopment of larger sites had become a major theme in the department's dealing with developers. The extinction of Wetfield Works as a site seemed to the valuers to vitiate their efforts to maximise the returns to land through profitable industrial uses.

Recognising that the housing department's plans for Wetfield Works would gain momentum as the opportunity to redevelop the site drew near, the valuer's department attempted to head off that prospect. Reporting to the housing (programme sites) subcommittee in June 1977, the valuers deplored 'the displacement of the industrial occupiers and the consequent loss of employment opportunities which would result . . . the borough is singularly short of industrial complexes of this size . . . the prospects of relocation within the borough are low and in consequence the risk of total extinguishment is high.' The report advocated abandoning the plan to redevelop the site for housing. The architect's and housing departments responded stiffly to this suggestion, demanding that alternative sites be identified and depreciating the difficulties of relocating the firms. The site, being contiguous to the phase one development, was 'particularly well suited to housing' and could represent a clear housing gain of fifty dwellings. At the same time, more suitable sites for industry existed elsewhere, and a nonconforming use could be ended by redeveloping the Wetfield Works site.

At this point the planning department came overtly into the discussions. The assistant director had strong arguments to hand in favour of continuing an industrial use. The individual firms were small and there was a shortage of industrial premises of under 3000 square feet. The firms were unlikely to receive favourable treatment in the capital market and would probably lose their local markets if relocated. These were issues on which housing could hardly but concede. Accordingly, the department suggested that the question should, 'due to its controversial nature', be considered by the chief officers' meeting.

The chief executive now intervened on the side of the industry lobby, taking the issue to the policy group, who asked for a joint report from the planning and valuation departments on the 'consequences in estate management and industrial strategy terms' of the retention of industry on the site. This was the point at which the chief executive was advocating a positive response to the government's industrial strategy circular. The policy group accordingly accepted the need 'to encourage the establishment of small and potentially valuable employment opportunities' such as were present at Wetfield Works.

In supporting the proposed industrial strategy the director of planning pointed out that the Wetfield Works dispute illustrated the need for such a corporate policy. His joint report with the valuer stressed 'the acknowledged need to retain skilled employment opportunities in the borough' and the probability that many of the firms concerned would not survive relocation. The report advocated the retention of the existing firms with the erection of a boundary fence to separate out the residential and industrial uses. The political climate for such a proposal could not have been better, and on the advice that 'the maximum retention of employment opportunities should be a priority' the Wetfield Works site was withdrawn from the housing programme.

In October 1977, therefore, the Wetfield Works case appeared to be one of complete and simultaneous implementation of a strategic decision. The expiry of the leases, however, ensured that some further decision would eventually have to be taken. Within twelve months the firms on site were looking to the Council for just such a decision in advance of the end of their leases, while the valuers were advocating the modernisation of Wetfield Works as an industrial site. However, pressures from the housing department to recapture the site were also beginning to mount.

In July 1979 an inter-departmental meeting was held to consider future action. The housing interests were strongly represented by the housing and architect's departments and the possibility of industrial development brought the valuation, engineering and treasury departments to the meeting. The result was to overturn the previous decision. Recognising that employment losses would follow, the various officers nevertheless agreed that 'there was no possibility' of redevelopment for industry, that a loss of employment 'would have to be accepted as an unavoidable consequence of environmental improvement' and this despite their view that 'relocation on a Westborough site could not be guaranteed'. Their report recommended that the site be reinstated in the housing programme. The recently appointed ILO (the second occupant of the post) protested. He reminded the valuer's department that 'it is part of the Council's industrial strategy to assist small businesses'.

The situation, however, suddenly changed. The Wetfield Works employers themselves entered the dispute. The ILO met the representatives of the firms on the site in September 1979 when they 'expressed their strong desire to stay on the site'. The local press, alerted by the employers, began to feature the case. The ILO was heatedly attacked over the delay on deciding Wetfield Works' future at a meeting of the local Chamber of Commerce. The Council was accused of 'intransigence' and the local press recorded that 'businessmen are angry that the Labour-controlled Council has steadfastly refused to say what will happen to the firms'. A prominent local industrialist cast doubt on the reality of the industrial strategy in claiming that 'no small industrial firms have ever got a fair deal from the Council and they never will. We have been promised meetings that never came about and help that has never materialised.'

The Wetfield Works employers accepted the ILO's earlier advice to petition the chief executive. A revised report to the policy group was able to mention these 'increased pressures' from the firms as precipitating the need for an early decision on the site. The chief executive held an urgent meeting of the chief officers, pointing to the bad press which Westborough was now receiving. Yet another version of the report on Wetfield Works was prepared, setting out the planning department's views on industrial damage and employment loss. The housing department now began to retreat. Recognising that 'circumstances have changed somewhat' with the participation of the employers, they changed their ground to emphasise the need for new sites for the housing programme. The director of planning pressed his advantage and made a forceful statement claiming sole prerogative to advise the Council on land use. His colleagues gave ground. Outside the Civic Centre stood the staff of the Wetfield Works firms, displaying their protest placards to the press and photographers.

The result was a satisfactory outcome for the supporters of the industrial strategy. The policy group accepted the now agreed chief officers' view that 'the maintenance of employment and future job opportunities should be the Council's primary objective on this site . . . It may well be that in the current economic climate the preservation of small businesses will from time to time have to be achieved at the expense of the high environmental and traffic standards exacted in the past.'

*Problems of commitment: the Beacon case*

The second case of 'implementation problems' in Westborough's industrial strategy cast severe doubt on the reality of the Council's commitment to the strategy. Once again, a conflict of policies was involved, but in this case the Council's strategic objectives in the industrial field conflicted within the possibility of making some small future gain for amenity. The issue turned then on the resolution of a choice between new and existing commitments within the planning department, under the conditions where the councillors had a strong commitment to environmental improvement. The 'industry lobby' were in this instance isolated, finding themselves both undermined and overruled. The eventual outcome went in their favour but the industrial strategy was severely tested.

Beacon Engineering was a small but successful company located on a riverside site in the declining inner area of the borough. The rundown and decaying air of the local area notwithstanding, Beacon was a thriving company manufacturing equipment for lighthouses, beacons, buoys and channel markers. They had an excellent export record, were considered to be market leaders in this specialised field and in 1978 gained a Queens Award for export achievement. Their labour force was largely skilled and the company had a good training record. They were also a long-standing local firm having occupied the same site on the river since 1913. It would be difficult to conceive of an enterprise that more closely fitted the Westborough image of the ideal local firm, to be nourished by the sympathetic consideration of any planning problems.

Beacon, moreover, were expanding, largely in response to their successes in the export markets. In the four years to 1978 their workforce had increased by 35 per cent to 141, while their turnover had increased from £1.44 million to an estimated £3 million. Their expansion needs could be met on site by the clearance of their existing storage areas to expand their assembly area and office accommodation. The existing buildings were old and inconvenient and with the growth of their workforce more space for car parking was required. In short, Beacon needed to modernise their site, and accordingly engaged architects to prepare plans and submit an application for planning consent.

The chief executive heard of the firm's plans incidentally at the very point when an application was about to be made. He referred the firm to the ILO who followed up the chief executive's visit with his own. The application was a straightforward affair, and the chief executive and ILO looked forward to demonstrating the efficacy of the industrial strategy through this 'model' case. They knew that a quick and helpful resolution of the issue would enhance the Council's reputation and improve relations with local industry. As the ILO commented after his visit:

> this seems to me to be exactly the sort of firm that we should be helping as it is medium sized, expanding and eager to stay in the borough and employ local people. I don't foresee any great difficulties arising but I feel every effort should be made to meet Beacon's requirements by granting permission as quickly as possible.

The application was duly lodged in mid-December 1978. Ironically, it was the *former* ILO, now in charge of local planning for that area, who pointed out that Beacon's plans were in conflict with the Council's long-standing aim of securing a riverside walk, a goal that would be pre-empted at this point on the river by the proposed rearrangement of the site. The former ILO persuaded the director of planning of the importance of the question. He 'wanted to make an issue of it' and the firm were told by telephone that their application would not have a smooth passage.

Beacon's architects secured a meeting with the director of planning and other members of the planning department and expressed their alarm. The outcome of the discussion was that the architects offered to secure a strip of land for possible future use as a footpath. But Beacon's managing director was less accommodating. The very nature of the firm's operations involved them in use of the river frontage for the launching, by mobile cranes, of their buoys and miniature lightships. His objection was one of principle and 'any proposal which will obstruct the access to this river is unacceptable'. However, the director of planning had warned that the riverside walk 'is currently a topical issue of great importance to the Council'.

Certainly the issue *became* topical with the submission of a report to the planning committee in March 1979, pointing out the provision of a riverside footpath would accord with the Council's riverside policy 'which seeks to extend public riverside access wherever possible and, particularly, upon redevelopment of sites'. At the same time, the ILO's influence was noticeable in a passage which extolled the merits of the firm and its need for modernisation. But the committee accepted the recommendation that decision be deferred pending discussions with the firm to secure the riverside walk, and hopes of an early and demonstrative decision were dashed.

The ILO and his colleagues had the unenviable task of negotiating a solution with the firm. As one of the planners later commented, 'we were dead against the bloody footpath'. Not the least of their difficulties was their private belief that the footpath requirement could not be forced upon Beacon as a condition of planning consent. The firm responded furiously to the suggestion that they should enter into a prior legal agreement to secure a public right of way along the riverside. The chief executive now intervened. He asked the director of planning to have further top-level meetings with Beacon, commenting that the planning department's insistence on the riverside walk 'will greatly impede the Company's riverside operations which they have enjoyed since 1913'. Meanwhile the amenity pressure groups who had formerly supported the department's line began to back off, the local Riverside Association indicating that they 'understood the problems facing Beacon'.

The director of planning intended, however, to support his subordinates' manoeuvres to secure the riverside walk and took no action over the chief executive's note. The firm were told once again that 'permission would only be forthcoming if public footpaths could be created'. Beacon meanwhile had rallied their defences. The riverside access was 'of paramount importance' to their own operations. There were issues of public safety involved in their use of mobile cranes. an increased amount of construction was soon to begin 'and two lightships would have to be moored along the wharf's end'. Finally, Beacon's production was 'of national as well as local importance'. The delays involved were holding up the firm's production and the managing director intimated that he was prepared to abandon the site for new premises in Plymouth 'if the matter cannot be satisfactorily resolved'.

The auspices for Beacon were not good. The planning advisory committee for the area, a body with heavy local councillor representation, were supporting the footpath proposal. The GLC planning department took the view that Beacon's plans were visually unsatisfactory. In the GLC's eyes 'the site forms a major part of the view from the bridge giving access across Fordbridge Lock to the Fordbridge Dock Housing Site [a high-income residential scheme]. At the very least, the car part should be set back from the dock by approximately 3 metres to coincide with the south-east facade of the new building . . . The riverside area should be distinguished from the car parking area by distinctive and high quality landscaping.' Fortunately for the firm, the GLC planning department were persuaded not to issue a directive on the matter; their comments therefore had only advisory status.

Beacon's next move was to make written representations to the director of planning, elaborating their earlier remarks about safety and access, and raising again the possibility of the firm relocating altogether. Further, 'the company's operation is of profound international importance and a source of trade for this country . . . Any lack of space will result in either the loss of future orders or work being transferred out of this country or elsewhere within the UK.' The managing director complained that six months had now elapsed since the submission of Beacon's application and his plea that the footpath requirement was 'unreasonable' suggested that a refusal would lead to a successful appeal by the firm. No more damaging outcome could be imagined for the planning department and for relations with local industry.

In late May 1979 the case went back to the committee. Those councillors who spoke were 'entirely in favour of the riverside walk'. The planning-conscious leader of the Council was adamant that the walk was a matter of top priority. The planning chairman took a neutral line, simply opening up the discussion and listening to the views expressed. The committee's concern, guided by the borough solicitor, was to 'safeguard' a *future* walkway by preventing the full development of the site.

Negotiations with Beacon were reopened, but the firm became steadily more intransigent; they had plans for a new product, an unmanned lightship 70 feet in length, 'a new product which looks like taking off in terms of demand both domestically and for export'. While some compromise might have been possible if production were restricted to the smaller buoys, the firm now definitely needed full use of the river frontage. One of the planners handling the negotiations commented miserably, 'it was unclear . . . where to go from here'. Indeed, the next round of proposals indicated the strength of Beacon's position: the planning department were now suggesting the erection of gates at each end of the site to limit public access whenever wharfside manoeuvres were in operation. It was an obviously costly and cumbersome proposal.

The chief executive was meanwhile becoming increasingly anxious about the long delays in what he had hoped would be an exemplary case decision. His hopes for a successful resolution were, however, revived when the borough solicitor and the ILO each independently reported to him on the complex legal foundations of 'planning gain'. Their papers revealed little support in law for the types of condition which the Council sought to impose on the firm.

With these arguments to hand, the chief executive attended the June meeting of the planning committee, the third such to consider the Beacon case. His tone was 'matter of fact' as he advised the committee that 'a condition which purported to require the applicants to provide a public right of way was *ultra vires . . .* was probably bad as it sought to deprive the applicants of a right of access to the river which they currently enjoyed and was one which could not be sustained on appeal.' This last point reflected the department's acceptance that the firm had a very strong case: 'Beacon would have won', commented one planner later.

The fate of the riverside walk at this point was effectively sealed by the leader's disavowal of his earlier support for it. He took over the discussion and argued that Beacon's needs had to be considered. The committee, so emphatic previously, backtracked in the face of the leader's apostasy and the chief executive took the opportunity to 'remind . . . the committee of the Council's industrial strategy which sought to encourage local firms to remain and to expand'. It was a reluctant and hard-won endorsement of 'strategy' attributable as much to *force majeure* as to conviction.


**Conclusions**

The first part of this chapter described the changing economic climate in a prosperous outer London borough, and outlined the responses of the various local authority departments. The second part portrayed the formulation and subsequent revision of the local industrial strategy as a reflection of the shifting pattern of administrative politics. The third part dealt with the impact of these divergent interests upon two case decisions, each of which typified the negotiation of decision outcomes by bargaining and manoeuvre, and each of which was non-typical only in its length and complexity.

The main conclusion to be drawn is that local authorities are not monoliths. Rather, the decisions announced in their name represent the outcomes of an internal process of administrative politics in which departmental or sectional actors not only pursue conflicting interests but translate those interests into the language of policy and principle. Westborough, of course, is not a 'typical' urban authority, least of all in its local economic circumstances. Yet in several senses the experience related here has evident parallels elsewhere. First, the 'federal' or 'concertative' nature of the policy process which tends to maintain existing relations of internal power and influence. Second, the zero-sum nature of the competition between housing and industrial development over scarce land. Third, the tenacity of political commitments to improve standards of amenity which predate the more recent concern to maintain the industrial base at hitherto unacceptable environmental costs. That these factors impeded the implementation more than the formulation of a strategy for economic development is also a conclusion of wider applicability. Conflicts – whether of bureaux, of resource claims or of policies – are readily glossing over when 'strategy' is not expected to affect their outcomes.

The general drift of Westborough's planning decisions through 1977–80 was none the less towards a more sympathetic treatment of industry, while the education department has continued to extend its school–industry links. The social aspects of policy there may well be unsophisticated, yet there has been some reorientation of priorities and some redirection of practice. These shifts are in part accounted for by changing relationships within and between departments. The planning department, under pressure from education, under threat from the chief executive's office and demoralised by unfavourable appeal decisions, was able to regain authority through the industrial strategy while its reformation as an *employment* strategy had the advantage of making planning goals more realistic. The chief executive was able to revise and extend his own sphere of action by the sequential definition of intrinsically 'corporate' issues. Doubtless this development would have come more readily had he enjoyed the support of his own policy planning unit, had one of his own staff chaired the ISWG, or had the ILO appointment been made to his own office.

Administrative politics are a game played by accepted rules. These rules delimit the policy space of each actor. To radically extend this space the rules have to be revised; the identification of such cross-cutting issues as economic change can effectively revise the rules, change the game, extend the policy space of (in this case) the 'industrial lobby' within the authority and, ultimately, reshape the impact of public policy upon the community. In any transformation of the policy game to promote economic well-being a strengthening of the chief executive's functions are important as both cause and consequence.

## References

1.  *Local Government and the Industrial Strategy*, DoE Circular 71/77; *Development Control: Policy and Practice*, DoE Circular 22/80.
2.  For the classic statement of this perspective see G. T. Allison, *Essence of Decision* (Little, Brown & Co., 1971).
3.  For a penetrating study of the use of rational planning and programming techniques primarily for purposes of organisational boundary maintenance, see H. M. Sapolsky, *The Polaris System Development: Bureaucratic and Programmatic Success in Government* (Harvard University Press, 1972).
4.  L. Mohr, 'The Concept of Organizational Goals', *American Political Science Review*, 67, 1973, pp. 470–81.
5.  The authority generously granted unrestricted access to policy and case files and permission to attend relevant meetings during the period 1978–80. To preserve confidentiality certain details, including the name of the authority and those of firms and sites, have been altered in the account which follows.
6.  For the development of this part of London see generally Peter Hall, *The Industries of London since 1861* (Hutchinson, 1962); H. W. Richardson and D. Aldcroft, *Building in the British Economy Between the Wars* (Allen & Unwin, 1968); K. Young and P. L. Garside, *Metropolitan London: Politics and Urban Change, 1837–1981* (Edward Arnold, 1982).
7.  D. E. Keeble, 'Industrial Decentralisation and the Metropolis: the North-West London Case', *Transactions of the Institute of British Geographers*, 44, 1968, pp. 1–54.
8.  F. Blackaby (ed.), *De-industrialisation* (Heinemann, 1979).
9.  *Local Government and the Industrial Strategy*, para. 3.

# 7  New Relationships in the Inner City

**MURRAY STEWART and JACKY UNDERWOOD**

## Introduction

The characteristic of the area-based initiatives of the late 1960s and early 1970s to combat deprivation was that they were built upon faulty interpretations of the nature of deprivation. Numerous writers, for example Hambleton, Edwards and Batley,[1] have pointed out the key assumption upon which area policies in general, and inner city policies in particular was founded. This was that problems of deprivation derived from the physical conditions of particular areas and/or from the characteristics (usually defined as failings) of the particular people living in the area. The mid-1970s saw a gradual awareness of the inadequacy of this assumption, thanks largely to the work of the Community Development Projects,[2] but also in part as a consequence of the desk and action research of the *Inner Area Studies*[3] and of numerous reports from the major metropolitan authorities. These studies emphasised the need to see 'inner area' change as a part of a broader process of economic and social change in society as a whole, and to understand the problems of 'inner areas' in structural as opposed to 'pathological' individual-based terms. The 'structural' argument was in essence that the conditions experienced by 'deprived' families, or by groups concentrated in 'deprived' areas, were the consequence of public and private investment decisions and of the operation of labour and housing market structures which systematically produced concentrations of low-income households in older urban areas (amongst other places). The explanation of the inner city problems thus lay in

131

*economic structures* and in the factors which produced and perpetuated such structures. At the same time the beliefs which coloured the setting up of the CDPs and IASs were revived: that the attempts by government to meet the needs of deprived areas were hindered by inadequate *administrative* structures which hampered the delivery of services to those in need, discouraged co-ordination and co-operation between the agencies involved, inhibited the local political system in its articulation of redistribution issues, and precluded the redirection of resources to areas of greatest need.

These structural arguments were understood, interpreted, and acted upon in different ways by different bodies. Central government, reinforced by the series of metropolitian conferences of 1975 and 1976 and by the special case made out by the six big cities (Birmingham, Leeds, Newcastle, Sheffield, Liverpool, Manchester – the central districts of the Metropolitan Counties) perceived the need for a further initiative. In September 1976 the then Secretary of State for the Environment was given special responsibility for Urban Affairs and a Cabinet Committee was established. In April 1977 it was announced that there would be a major 'enhancement' of the Urban Programme, a system operating under the Home Office for the previous decade or so, under which local authorities put forward their own and voluntary bodies' schemes for grants for cases of special need in urban areas from an annual allocation of funds under the Local Government Grants (Social Need) Act 1969.[4] The aims of the Urban Programme were to be enlarged and responsibility transferred from the Home Office to the Department of the Environment (DoE) and the Welsh Office. In June 1977, the government set out its policies in the White Paper, *Policy for the Inner Cities.*[5]

The White Paper partially recognised the structural questions (although it still refers to those 'least able to cope' and with 'personal problems') and sought to address them as best as the government saw fit. Considerable emphasis was laid on *economic* problems and policies. The enhanced urban programme would be used to support economic and environmental projects as well as social ones, legislation would be passed to assist authorities to counter disinvestment and employment rundown in inner areas, the private sector would 'play its part'. On the *administrative* side the government announced its intention of entering into special arrangements, known as 'partnerships', with the county and district authorites and the health authorities of the most deprived cities with the object, first, of bringing together within one set of administrative arrangements the range of agencies responsible for action in the inner areas of those cities, and second, of redirecting main policies and programmes in favour of inner city areas.

This chapter focuses particularly upon the administrative structures and arrangements developed within the inner cities policy as they affect economic development. In this first section are some preliminary background remarks on the nature of the policy and the opportunities and limitations this sets upon new relationships; in the second section some of the more recent developments affecting public sector organisations, the non-statutory sector, and the private sector are set out; while in the third section some of the more general issues and implications are drawn out.

**The nature of the policy**

The development of inner cities policies and programmes has occurred in a period marked by a change of government. Despite the very differing ideological positions in relation to intervention, public spending, and support for deprived areas or groups occupied by the Labour and Tory governments of pre- and post-1979, inner cities policy has remained intact and even reinforced by Michael Heseltine's announcement in February 1981.[6] Nevertheless, as might be expected, the emphasis of policy has shifted (towards the economic and the private sector) and the methods of intervention have been extended.

Two perspectives on the scope for new approaches to policy development and implementation can be taken. The first, following Lewis and Flynn, suggests that central government may adopt any one of a variety of modes of implementing policy and that it will choose whatever one is appropriate at a particular time in the light of the history and current circumstances of the policy area in question.[7] Thus regulation, judicial control, procedural control, hiving off, consent, bargaining, execution and finance can be employed as modes of action from time to time.

Alternatively, as Cox argues, illustrating specifically the question of inner cities policy, administrative inertia severely limits the scope for policy shift and 'the hallmark of British policy-making . . . is an incremental adjustment to existing constraints in which the desire to deal positively with the problems [tends] to be lost, due to the need to appease the array of competing interests and responsibilities in the administrative process'.[8]

Inner cities' experience to date suggests some truth in both these perspectives. On the one hand, arrangements for alleviating the problems of inner areas appear in at least four forms:

1. As the creation of Urban Development Corporations, operating with special powers and funding as single purpose agencies for the renewal of London and Liverpool docklands (an 'agency' or hiving-off mode).
2. As Enterprise Zones, offering minor fiscal reliefs and relative freedom from bureaucratic government intervention for firms wishing to locate or relocate investment in selected derelict areas (the 'incentive' or finance mode).
3. As powers available in certain designated local authority areas under the Inner Urban Areas Act to make loans, establish Industrial Improvement Areas, assist with site preparation, etc. (an 'enabling', 'permissive' or consent mode).
4. As the establishment of joint machinery for central and local government partnership in the reappraisal of policies and the development of special programmes for selected inner areas (the 'collaborative' or 'bargaining' mode).

On the surface at least, therefore, there is a variety of approach to the problems of local economic regeneration. At the same time, while it is premature to comment on the progress of urban development corporations or enterprise zones, it is clear that the pessimistic 'administrative inertia' view of Cox is borne out by the recent experience in partnership and programme authorities and that there are major constraints to the development of new initiatives in the inner city. Collaboration and bargaining in a spirit of 'partnership' are not so simple as the White Paper suggested, given the differing stances of the various participants.

Initially the proposals for inner cities, as set out in the 1977 White Paper, were perceived to be fairly innovative – selective, locally based intervention; joint working between central and local government, other public agencies, the private sector and voluntary organisations; the re-examination of main policies and programmes; the identification of key issues and the concentration of resources upon them; an emphasis upon innovative, stimulating, novel projects. In the evolution of the policy, however, it is possible to see the shift from the aspirations of the White Paper to the reality of constrained and relatively unambitious implementation. The development of the policy has been documented elsewhere.[9] Four phases of policy have been evident:

1. The 'policy launch' in 1976 and 1977 incorporating the transfer of the 'urban' initiative to the Department of the Environment, the publication of the White Paper, the establishment of partnership and programme arrangements with selected local authorities, and the recasting of the Urban Programme.
2. 'Preparing for action'. While 1978–9 saw considerable implementation activity on the spending of the special 'construction package' funds found by government in 1977, the second stage of policy development running through the whole of 1978 and early 1979 was involved mainly with groundwork for future action. There were two strands here: introducing the Inner Urban Areas Act giving additional powers to local authorities; and preparing the first Inner Area Programmes for the period for three years from April 1979.
3. 'Changing direction' was an inevitable result of an incoming government and the need for ministers to review the policy. In September 1979, the Secretary of State announced the continuation of the initiative, albeit with simplified partnership procedures, with 1980–1 funding at the same level in real terms as 1979–80. He stressed the limits to public sector action, and urged local authorities to stimulate more private sector activity while also announcing Urban Development Corporations for the London and Liverpool Docklands.
4. 'Consolidation' is an appropriate term to describe the relaxed continuation of the initiative in 1981 following the government's recent review of the policy.[10] Inner cities policy is being maintained, the Urban Programme (including provision for UDCs) was allocated £224m. in 1981–2 (PESC 1980 Survey Prices), the partnership and programme authority arrangements will go on with no relegation or promotion of authorities, and private sector involvement will be emphasised.

Within the period of launch, preparation for action and change of direction, it is possible to observe in retrospect the seeds of inertia and disillusion particularly as joint working became the exception rather than the rule, as main programmes remained unbent, as administrative requirements came to dominate the identification and implementation of projects and as 'conformance' rather than performance became the norm.[11] The independent Liverpool three-man monitoring team concluded in 1980 'that "Partnership" is no more than the latest term for the involvement of Government in Inner City regeneration'. A similar view is that the introduction of programme procedures, akin to the Housing Strategies and Investment Programmes (HIP) and Transport Policies and Programmes (TPP) procedures, has reinforced the bidding/allocation relationship of local to central government and the mode of implementation of the policy has in consequence shifted from the collaborative to the negotiated with the resulting emergence of a more explicitly administrative and bureaucratic style than was either necessary or desirable.

It is therefore important to recognize the limitations of the inner cities initiative and the constraints upon the scope for change in relation to local economic development. At the same time it is possible to identify new relationships, modifications to practice and innovative developments in the public sector, voluntary sector and private sector; the subsequent parts of this chapter pick out some of these features.

### Recent developments in inner cities

*The public sector*

Reflecting the main theme of the White Paper, a central feature of individual local programmes has been 'the economy'. In organisational terms an 'economy', 'economic development', 'industry', or 'employment' key issue or topic working group has been virtually universal and 'economic' objectives, policies, and projects dominate the annual programme documents. In partnership areas the tendency is for a largish working group, normally without politicians, but including membership not solely from various departments of the district but also from the County Council, from the Manpower Services Commission, on occasions from the Departments of the Environment and/or Industry and/or Employment, from local industry (either Chamber of Commerce representatives or alternatively one or two key individuals) and from the local voluntary sector. Chairmanship depends on local circumstances and personalities, resting sometimes with the county, sometimes with a chief officer of the district. An important relationship is with pre-existing bodies operating in the economic field, most areas already possessing at least an industrial development officer and more likely an inter-departmental or inter-agency unit established to combat problems of economic decline and unemployment and/or an economic development subcommittee. Partnership work can be subsumed within such organisations (but strengthen them), operate in parallel in a complementary fashion, or seek to compete with existing activity. In general, given the significance and legitimacy attached to economic work, the relationship is a complementary one. In practice the major inter-organisational issues have been, on the one hand, the sharing of the Inner Urban Areas Act powers between county and district, particularly in relation to the establishment of industrial improvement areas, and on the other, the relative priority of partnership and programme areas given the county-wide phenomenon of economic change. In Greater Manchester, for example, the GMC has to take a view not solely on the position of the Manchester/Salford partnership area but also on the priority to be given to the programme areas of Bolton and Oldham in relation to other areas of need.

In programme areas the organisational arrangements are less extensive or complex,[12] although the same question of relating to existing arrangements exists. Structures for articulating economic development, however, are in general less well advanced in programme authorities and some have been stimulated into the creation of new structures. Wirral, for example, has introduced a new Economic Development Subcommittee which has responsibility for the preparation and implementation of the whole inner area programme.[13]

Finally, in commenting upon the organisational innovations that have occurred, two points are worth noting. First, in many partnership and programme areas 'economic' issues are dealt with by a number of groups. There are several examples of land or derelict land groups, of environmental groups which handle industrial refurbishment questions, of 'learning' groups which pick up questions of training and of 'social' groups which are concerned with low pay. Thus the economic problem pervades the whole programme. Second, the significance and status of 'economic' groups (however defined) has increased over the last two years as 'streamlining'[14] has whittled away the other activities of partnership. Thus organisational change has reinforced the central position of economic considerations in the inner city debate.

The processes of annual review, formulation (or reformulation) of policies and programmes, selection of projects and presentation of the bid to DoE varies from one area to another. Some authorities, for example, merely modify the previous year's statement while others carry out a reanalysis; some authorities divide up available funds by topic area, others by spending agency; some specify given proportions for voluntary funding, others allow voluntary and statutory bids to be competitive; a variety of approaches to implementation exist involving main departments (often with nominated project officers) and/or an inner cities unit which may well have a special implementation officer. In general, however, implementation work lies with those who normally carry out environmental work, land preparation, improvement, training or whatever, whereas planning more often rests with newer machinery set up for the purpose of developing an inner city strategy. This separation of planning and implementation remains one of the major organisational tensions within the inner city arrangements, a microcosm within local authorities of the more general tension between central and local government.

In relation to the content of policies and programmes, as opposed to organisation, the orientation ranges from the predominantly *developmental* where the concern is primarily for economic efficiency (through the retention/attraction of economic activity, through investment in buildings and plant, through infrastructural and environmental improvement) to the *social* where the emphasis is upon the distributional implications of economic change (through the provision of jobs for particular groups of people, through  policies for matching job and people, through programmes designed for employment ends rather than growth ends). The tendency in inner city documents is to assume consistency between these concerns rather than to recognise their interdependent but potentially conflicting nature[15] and in general there is little attempt in inner city planning to reconcile economic development with employment objectives. Thus while the major 'problem' is often – though not universally[16] – seen as unemployment and job loss, policies and programmes fail to make clear or to connect the stages of programme *input* (economic development towards which much funding is directed), programme *output* (the provision of land, infrastructure, premises, training, etc.) and programme *impact* (the extent to which outputs help to achieve the objectives – jobs for those most in need in the area). It is widely argued of course that any growth is worth having, whether it provides employment opportunities for those in need or not, and that in any case employment planning and the distributional goals of the programme are consequent upon growth rather than an element to be planned into growth. Nevertheless some authorities have been able to make connections, either because their analysis has suggested that development strategies are not the only ones (Oldham) or because their growth strategies offered scope for achieving employment objectives (Hammersmith), or simply because the need for monitoring and evaluation has begun to pose questions about impact. On the other hand, the implicit guidelines of central government have pushed authorities towards a simple developmental approach emphasising physical and environmental improvement and the provision of the basic preconditions for growth. In consequence, several authorities are being driven away from an approach which looks to the distributional aspects of the policy.

One indication of the direction of policy so far comes in the Department of Environment's *Partnerships at Work*.[17] This identifies eighteen schemes of economic regeneration involving expenditure of some £4.4m. per annum. While the list of schemes does not pretend to give a cross section of work being carried out with Urban Programme funds in partnership areas it is not atypical in its make-up. Site preparation projects range from the enormous five-year £300 000 per annum Derwenthaugh industrial improvement area site(s) in Gateshead, to a small half-hectare industrial infill site in Newcastle. Nursery factory units predominate, as they had begun to prior to the inner cities initiative, and in many authorities small industrial/workshop units take a large share of Programme funds since such schemes are generally expensive, often at the £500 000 plus level.

Refurbishment of older buildings (factories, sheds, mills, etc.) occurs in many programmes, often associated with industrial improvement area work (involving grants and loans), while the other main components of economic development are seen to be the encouragement of small businesses (small workshops and/or advice services) and skill training – the only economic activity with a voluntary sector input.

The emphasis in economic programmes is almost entirely upon capital projects rather than revenue expenditure and many of the projects are ones which would have appeared previously under derelict land, community land, or locally determined sector programmes. The same can be said of much of the environmental improvement work (for example, Liverpool's Environmental Improvement Area programme costing up to £2m. per annum for three- to five-year area uplift), although it is clear that tree planting – particularly beside the main radial routes along which potential investors are assumed to pass – has become a major (though inexpensive) new activity.

The economic programmes of partnership and programme authorities are, in short, entirely unsurprising. This is not to say that they are not sensible or useful; it is clear that nursery factory provision and refurbishment programmes, for example, produce units which are in considerable demand. What is evident, however, is that the inner cities initiative has not as yet produced particularly novel or innovative practices. Indeed it is arguable that the inner cities machinery and procedures have inhibited innovation and risk since there is evidence of experimentation in non-partnership and programme authorities elsewhere[18] as well as evidence of disincentives to risk in inner city areas. This view is given further weight by a brief consideration of the role of the voluntary and private sectors, both perceived as sources of new ideas and approaches in the White Paper.

*The non-statutory sector*

Traditionally voluntary organisations have not been heavily involved in economic development work, and the Wolfenden Report for example, largely ignored this area of activity in its 1978 review.[19] Up to the 1977 White Paper, Urban Programme rules precluded the use of funds for economic purposes, but the subsequent recasting of the Urban Programme to cover industrial and environmental as well as social schemes opened up opportunities for both statutory and non-statutory urban projects and the official review of the 'traditional' Urban Programme confirmed to central government the potential of voluntary effort, a potential which they have stressed in the guidelines given to partnership and programme authorities.[20]

Inner city programmes have thus opened up opportunities for the heterogeneous organisations conveniently labelled the non-statutory sector, although these opportunities have posed major problems for organisations not traditionally accustomed or suited to involvement in the economic field. Nevertheless, increasing involvement in the partnership and programme authority work has clearly had an impact. The combined effects of the consultation/participation involved in bidding for project funds, the occasional contributions to decision-making on voluntary sector bids, the advisory/encouraging activities of the NCVO and local CVSs (often with a special inner city person), the involvement of 'umbrella' organisations such as the Inner Cities Consultative Group in Lambeth, plus the guidelines welcoming voluntary schemes have led to a variety of initiatives predominantly in the work experience/training field and predominantly for young people, often from ethnic minorities.

The level of activity is low since only 14 per cent of Urban Programme money as a whole (including the traditional Urban Programme) is devoted to voluntary schemes and the proportion of this going to 'economic' projects is only a small one. Nevertheless initiatives come both from existing groups diversifying in the face of the advantageous position of 'economic' projects and from new groups established for the purpose of carrying out employment-related voluntary work. In both cases the inter-organisational relations being developed are fragile. This is partly because of the novelty of this area of voluntary activity, but partly also because relationships are being struck in a policy area with which local authorities are themselves unfamiliar; indeed local authorities are only just coming to terms with the way in which Job Creation, Community Enterprise and other Manpower Services Commission programmes (which themselves can and often do involve voluntary organisations) fit into the Urban Programme scheme of work.

*The private sector*

Despite the blandishments of both Labour and Tory governments
the private sector has been slow to become involved in the inner
cities – indeed their most obvious contribution over past decades
has been to the creation of inner area problems rather than to their
solution. It seems that this disinterest has been the product of a lack
of awareness of the existence of problems of the kind described in
the 1977 White Paper, a lack of interest in the problems even where
some awareness did exist, and a lack of practical involvement even
where some interest exists. As Hambleton points out, the
predominant view within the private sector has been that until inner
cities offer opportunities for profitable operation there is little that
the private sector can or should do.[21] Inner cities policy seeks to
alter this position and it is possible to identify three strands of
activity where new relationships may be being formed and
amendments to attitudes and practice occurring.

The first is in relation to the Urban Programme itself and the
preparation and evaluation of Inner Urban Programmes. The
Secretary of State has made it clear in two ways that private sector
involvement in partnership and programme authority work is
essential. First, there has been established the 'team of three'
independent review activity which, initially in Liverpool and
subsequently in Manchester/Salford and Newcastle/Gateshead,
has involved the private sector (and others) in monitoring
partnership activity. The first reports of the teams offer a mix of
laudatory and semi-critical comments on partnership in general and
on the potential contribution of the private sector in particular.[22]
Second, in February 1981 the Secretary of State announced that
effective consultation with local industry, normally the local
Chamber of Commerce, would be a prior condition of approving
an urban programme grant.[23] At the same time, he suggested that
the private sector should not become members of partnership
committees, preferring to see the latter as predominantly
governmental bodies whose increased size would be counter-
productive. Over and above these organisational arrangements the
private sector has been directly involved in inner city work
following Industrial Improvement Area declarations and
subsequent grant take-up. In some partnerships, declarations have
led to the formation of local industrial associations and to high

publicity for and take up of grants under the Inner Urban Areas Act. In Birmingham the creation of 'company consultants' with a brief to stimulate interest in partnership activity is seen as an effective measure, while the Liverpool monitoring team looked favourably on the Business Advisory Officer, whose functions are to open up communication with local industry over a range of issues, but particularly improvement area work. Thus the first strand of private sector inner city activity is the direct involvement with governmental programmes, albeit without formal involvement in partnership machinery.

A second strand is that where private sector expertise and resources are being sought outside the framework of the Urban Programme. In the most simple instance this takes the form of private sector initiatives over particular sites or developments in the inner city, either in conjunction with the public sector in a traditional form (see Chapter 3) or directly without public sector involvement. The evidence is that partnership is having some impact here in so far as appropriate sites are being identified by partnership machinery and more particularly, as partnership or programme authority schemes begin to have a demonstration effect. The success of the widespread public sector nursery factory initiatives, for example, has begun to convince private sector investors that small units in the inner city are not a high-risk investment, while in Birmingham some of the 1979–80 programme slippage occurred as a result of the private sector's eleventh hour interest, and subsequent investment, in a project which was initiated within the Urban Programme.

Private sector interest, however, outside the formal machinery has received most stimulus through the local enterprise agency movement still in its infancy but beginning to expand under the stimulus of the Enterprise Units established by the DoE in the Midlands and North West regions. The movement is not confined to inner cities but much of the stimulus comes from increased awareness of, and concern about the consequences of, inner area problems and many enterprise agency initiatives are directed to inner areas. There is no blueprint for an enterprise agency. Most to date take the form of a relationship between a group of local firms, usually associated with the local Chamber of Commerce, and other local interests, for example, the local authority or the local polytechnic, for the purpose of fostering the growth of new and existing firms in the area. Existing agencies –the London Enterprise Agency, Leeds Business Venture, and Birmingham Venture, for example –have tended to concentrate on the often under-resourced and inexpert small firms and to offer advice and/or assistance to them. Such advice can relate to management and finance, perhaps with a referral service to local banks, to innovation and patent advice, to marketing, to legal or administrative concerns, to premises, or on occasions to training. In broad terms, the enterprise agency has access, usually through a full-time director, to the resources of the larger local firms and is able to provide expertise either on an *ad hoc* or on a semi-permanent basis, for example through a temporary secondment. In some instances, as in the work of the Action Resource Centre, the advice may be given by a quasi-voluntary organisation financed by business (or perhaps through the Urban Programme) to run an independent source of assistance to firms, and in these instances the enterprise agency fulfils very similar functions to those falling on some partnership-sponsored bodies such as the Hackney Business Promotions centre. Other enterprise projects again, such as Park Royal and Trafford, lay a greater emphasis upon the improvement of the areas as a whole (both are established in massive old industrial parks) and focus predominantly on environmental and access problems – dereliction, landscaping, grant take-up and so on.

As a third strand of private sector involvement there is the growth of what has been termed 'community involvement' – the mobilisation of corporate social responsibility towards combating the economic and social problems faced by local communities. Like the enterprise agency movement this was given an impetus by ministers who followed up a Sunningdale Conference which exposed UK firms to American experience with the formation of the Pilkington Group. The latter was concerned with ways in which the involvement of major employers might be extended and focused attention on the way in which the policies of major national companies might be affecting local communities (for example, through purchasing, recruitment or estates practices in major firms). Major companies, it is argued, recognise that changing technology can create redundancies and local unemployment, and the community involvement 'movement' seeks to alert firms in their own interest to do something to mitigate the economic and social consequences of their own actions. The models – publicly-owned British Steel and privately-owned Pilkington – have different constituencies, the first national, the second confined to St Helens, but the aim is common: the creation of greater social responsibility.[24]

Together the enterprise agency and community involvement initiatives approach the problems of the decline of older communities as a pincer-like movement. The enterprise agency is locally based, rooted in the local Chamber of Commerce and the responsibility of local industrialists. It is matched by the corporate social responsibility of major firms established and committed at headquarter level and hopefully transmitted throughout the company organisation. If the impression is given of major new initiatives actually operating on the ground this is mistaken. Most effort so far has gone on discussion and ideas, even if there are now some half-a-dozen enterprise agencies at work. The stimulus to discussion is perhaps the most interesting feature that has emerged from the inner cities debate even if enterprise agency and corporate social responsibility initiatives are not confined to inner cities. A major lead to private sector involvement has been given by ministers of the DoE[25] but at the same time the Department itself is hesitant about its own involvement and role. Indeed, while on the one hand it is argued that better links between private and public sector are essential, on the other hand it is felt that some distancing between the two parties is essential. Thus the new 'Business in the Community' initiatives are being clearly distinguished as a private sector initiative reliant on private funds and premises (albeit with a senior DoE secondee to assist) and the point is made even more clearly in the Liverpool monitoring report. In relation to the Business Advisory Officer, it was pointed out that 'there was a strong need for an agency of this nature to be identified with the private sector as there existed an innate distrust of government involvement'. New relationships are therefore being forced around inner city issues but they are not necessarily relationships which break down traditional attitudes. As it becomes clearer precisely how the private sector might play its full part, so also does it become clearer that there exist widely differing motivations for inner city involvement and that although new forms of working may well stimulate compromise and collaboration in some areas, in others conflict may well remain.

## Issues and implications

It is evident that the 'new relationships' in the inner city over economic development are neither new nor independent of a much wider network of inter-organisational and inter-governmental relationships. The different parties to the inner city partnerships have, in practice, brought differing experience and aspirations to the new policy. The nature of central–local interaction in particular partnership and programme areas is in part a function of the history of that area – the history of previous relationships with the Department of the Environment over housing or planning policies and the history of previous involvement in inner city initiatives. Most, but not all, of the areas currently selected for attention have been involved with one or more inner city experiments of the past and the perceptions of current participants in inner cities policy are very much coloured by their previous experience of such experiments. In addition, there is the history of relations with other government departments – Education and Science, Health and Social Security, Industry, Home Office, etc. – a history which, as the CPRS have shown, may have been one of ambiguity and misunderstanding over the different messages flowing from central to local level (and vice versa).[26] Finally, there is the fact that the contemporary political climate varies from authority to authority. Local governments are autonomous political institutions and view inner cities policy as they view other policies, as a vehicle for achieving their own declared aims and objectives. Local political circumstances vary widely according both to the perceived problems and needs of the area and to such factors as political leadership or officer–member relations.

The consequence of this for economic development is that in many areas new powers, machinery and funds are directed towards activities with which authorities are familiar and indeed to which they are already committed. Thus the inner city programme of economic development reflects a tradition of local activity stemming from the early local Acts of the 1930s through the predominantly estate development era of the 1960s and early 1970s (largely associated with, or in response to, regional policies) to the wider range of initiatives attempted in the second half of the 1970s. This influence of existing behaviour upon new policy initiatives is not confined to inner cities policy; the same experience has been documented in relation to the Community Land Act.[27] It sheds an additional light on the inertia observed by Cox, however, and suggests that it is not solely the need to appease competing interests and responsibilities in the administrative process that induces inertia; it is also that participants have different objectives, and/or approaches to achieving those objectives, which are rooted in the past and that this experience of the past will in fact be brought to and used in a new policy area.

If the inner city relationships are influenced by history, they are also influenced by contemporary events and it is clear that the concept of 'partnership' over inner cities is almost an irrelevance at a time when it is felt (correctly or incorrectly) that one of the partners is doing its best to reduce the general status of the other to, at best, an agent and, at worst, a corpse. The ambiguity inherent at present in the central–local relation is clear, particularly for those metropolitan authorities threatened with penalties for overspending. How is it possible for 'partners' to develop a constructive, positive, joint relationship over extra spending for the special needs of the inner area while at the same time conducting a wider battle over the general question of expenditure targets?

The combination of these influences – the one historical, the other contemporary – has a particular significance for the content of inner city programmes. There is a tradition of developmental activity for economic purposes in local areas traditionally financed by locally determined sector capital spending, derelict land grant, community land allocations and the like. With the disappearance or drying up of these funds, the inner cities programme becomes the source of funding for such activity. With the emphasis in central government thinking on economic objectives and capital spending, the inner cities programme in practice has become akin to a local economic development key sector. It is scarcely surprising, therefore, to note the preponderance of traditional activity within the projects being carried out, and the dominance of predictable administrative concerns in the planning and implementation of the programme. As we argued above, the central–local relationship has become a more traditional one than was either necessary or desirable.

It is possible that political shifts at the local level – the move to Labour in metropolitan counties in May 1981 – will induce a different pattern of activity which will give more attention to the local control of investment and to the distributive consequences of economic development. What is clear, however, is that the stimulus to such shifts will not emerge through partnership and programme channels, since these are predominantly apolitical, despite the presence of significant local politicians in the process.

The early years of inner cities policy, therefore, have brought only marginal innovation and change. Despite the fairly extensive new contacts established within and between the different parties to the policy, inter-organisational learning has been limited and the application of learning has been even more limited. Individuals rather than organisations have been the focus for much of the work with the consequence, as individuals begin to shift jobs, that continuity and consistency in the policy become diluted.

The institutional stances after four years of the policy can easily be summed up. The behaviour of central government has increasingly demonstrated the difficulties of any kind of corporate approach and the economic departments originally involved – Industry and Employment – have by and large disappeared from the scene with the exception of some Department of Industry interest in the Northern and North West regions. DoE officials have battled on with the policy but have come to see it more as a traditional local authority programme to be planned, resourced, implemented and accounted for much like the HIP or the TPP. Attention has shifted to the Enterprise Zone and Development Corporation modes of intervention suggesting, in the terms of Lewis and Flynn, that traditional modes of policy implementation ('finance' and 'agent' modes) are easy to manage while 'collaboration' and 'partnership' are easier in theory than in practice. Inner cities policy has been a catalyst to link together county and district policies on economic development, but here again considerable progress had been made before partnership and programme arrangements were set up and what has occurred has been the adjustment of existing relationships to accommodate local government in relation to a wide range of functions and services.

The caricature of the inner cities programme as an economic key sector has already been drawn and it is quite noticeable how the economic elements in partnership (working arrangements, implicit policy guidelines, allocation of funds) have been strengthened at a time when other elements (for example, working parties on special needs groups) have been dismantled. This inexorable trend to the economic has important features. It transcends, for example, party political differences both at the local level and between national and local levels. In general the inner cities policy has been unaffected by political control. Although the Tory government has speeded up and emphasised the economic since late 1979, it would be quite wrong to say that the direction of the programme has shifted, and while there have been arguments about the balance of particular programmes this has been conducted as much in administrative as in political terms. Indeed it is quite clear that the tone and style of most partnerships is set more by the personal characteristics of the politicians involved than by their political perspectives.

In conclusion, the emergence of a predominantly 'economic' inner cities policy, foreshadowed in the 1977 White Paper and developed by successive governments up to 1981, and currently directed towards wealth creation and capital investment has been marked by three related major features. First, there has been the absence of any positive central–local interrelationship. The partnership between levels of government has been undermined by other elements, historical and contemporary, in central local relations, with the consequence that the main government policies and programmes at both centre and periphery have remained unexamined while existing, traditional, practices have in general been maintained. Second, the inner cities programme has been administered like any other programme and the aspirations towards innovation, experimentation and support for non-traditional activity has been submerged in a sea of traditional administrative practice, which has tended to legitimate and sanction many of the existing economic development activities already being planned or carried out. Finally, it seems that the inner cities policy may become overtly what it has always been implicitly – a partnership of interests in economic growth. The partnership of government is having only partial success; increasingly the involvement of the private sector – in the direction and to some extent the procedures of inner cities policy – represents a recognition of the dominant interests underlying the concern with the decline of inner areas. The partnership of government continues to pay lip service to a deprivation-oriented strategy; the partnership of interest pushes ahead with an economic development programme.

**References**

1.  R. Hambleton, 'Implementing Inner City Policy: Reflections from Experience', *Policy and Politics*, 9 (1), 1980, pp. 51–71. J. Edwards and R. Batley, *The Politics of Positive Discrimination* (Tavistock, 1978).
2.  For example, CDP Inter-Project Team, *The Costs of Industrial Change* (London: CDP, 1977).
3.  Department of the Environment, *Inner Area Studies: Summaries of Consultants' Final Reports* (HMSO, 1977).
4.  Announcement by the Secretary of State for the Environment, April 1977.
5.  *Policy for the Inner Cities*, Cmnd 6845 (HMSO, 1977).
6.  'Inner Cities Policy', *Hansard*, 998 (43), col. 603, 9 February 1981.
7.  J. Lewis and R. Flynn, 'The Implementation of Urban and Regional Planning Policies', *Policy and Politics*, 7 (2), 1979, pp. 123–42.
8.  A. W. Cox, 'Administrative Inertia and Inner City Policy', *Public Administration Bulletin*, 29, April 1979, pp. 2–17.
9.  R. Hambleton, M. Stewart and J. Underwood, *Inner Cities Policy: Management and Resources*, Working Paper 13 (Bristol: School for Advanced Urban Studies, 1980).
10. 'Inner Cities Policy'.
11. W. Williams, *Social Policy Research and Analysis* (Elsevier, 1971).
12. Hambleton, Stewart and Underwood, *Inner Cities Policy*.
13. Wirral District Council, Inner Area Programme 1980–3.
14. Secretary of State for the Environment, *Inner Cities Policy* (Department of the Environment, September 1979).
15. T. Davies, *Building Bridges: Linking Economic Regeneration to Inner City Employment Problems*, Working Paper 8 (Bristol: School for Advanced Urban Studies, 1980).
16. In Oldham, for example, in the early years of the programme low pay was perceived to be as significant an issue as unemployment.
17. Department of the Environment, *The Urban Programme: the Partnerships at Work* (DoE, 1981).
18. S. Barrett and M. Boddy, *Local Authority/Private Sector Industrial Development Partnerships*, Working Paper 18 (Bristol: School for Advanced Urban Studies, 1981).
19. Wolfenden Committee, *The Future of Voluntary Organizations* (Croom Helm, 1978).
20. Department of the Environment, *Review of the Traditional Urban Programme: Consultation Document* (DoE, 1980). See also the guidelines issued to partnership and programme authorities by DoE in July 1981.
21. R. Hambleton, *Inner Cities: Engaging the Private Sector*, Working Paper 10 (Bristol: School for Advanced Urban Studies, 1980).
22. The Independent Teams engaged in reviewing the partnerships comprised evaluators 'independent' of public agencies

(representatives of the private sector and academic world) and reported to the partnerships in Autumn of 1980 (Liverpool) and Autumn 1981 (Manchester/Salford and Newcastle/Gateshead).
23. 'Inner Cities Policy'.
24. *Handbook for Action: Report of a Working Group* (Business in the Community, 1981).
25. Secretary of State for the Environment, speech to the London Chamber of Commerce, June 1981.
26. Central Policy Review Staff, *Relations Between Central Government and Local Authorities* (HMSO, 1977).
27. S. Barrett, M. Boddy, M. Stewart, *The Implementation of the Community Land Scheme*, Occasional Paper 3 (Bristol: School for Advanced Urban Studies, 1978).

# III   EVALUATIONS

# 8   The Impact of Local Authorities on Manufacturing Firms: Recent Experience in London

DAVID J. NORTH and JAMIE GOUGH

## Introduction

The role of local authorities in alleviating the current crisis of manufacturing industry in Britain is currently the subject of considerable academic and political debate. As yet, however, there has been very little published analysis of the impact of local authority activities on manufacturing firms. In this chapter we present some research findings about the direct interaction between firm managements and local authorities in some London boroughs since 1976.[1] We shall be concerned with both traditional kinds of local authority intervention and with new policies such as those opened up by the Inner Urban Areas Act. Our aim is to assess the impact that the local authorities have had on firms in the period of study, the extent to which local authority interventions have met the expressed needs of firm managements, the perceptions of local authority policy by managements and the demands that they have to make on it.

The scope of our analysis here is restricted to the type of local authority activities which characteristically involve direct contact between the local authority and individual firms. We therefore discuss land-use planning and development control, key-worker housing, the supply of premises and sites, the provision of information on vacant sites and premises, and financial aid. Other fields of local government activity, which can have important effects on the context and structure of local industry, such as road investment, public transport and education, are not considered here. In London, these latter fields of activity involve the Greater London Council; the present paper is restricted to a discussion of the policies of borough (district) councils. The scope of our analysis here is also confined to the expenditure side of local authority activity and does not deal with the raising of revenue and its effects on firms.

The analysis of this paper is based on two types of empirical material. First, information on relevant local authority policies and their implementation, obtained from policy reports and interviews with local government officers; and second, information from interviews with the management of manufacturing firms or establishments on dealings that they have had with their local authority in the period 1976 to 1980. We discuss in turn these two aspects of our research material.

The boroughs in which our research was carried out – Hackney, Southwark and Wandsworth in inner London and for comparative purposes, Enfield and Merton in outer London – were chosen as ones having a high percentage of manufacturing in their employment. The policies of the councils towards industry was also a consideration. The inner boroughs were chosen on grounds of their interventionist policies towards industry in early 1979. Southwark was one of the first London boroughs in the field, first adopting policies explicitly aimed at countering employment decline in 1975. The emphasis was initially on strengthening manufacturing through a selective 'preferred industry' policy which was subsequently abandoned. In 1978 an Industrial and Commercial Development Fund was set up, financed from the rates and operating under discretionary section 137 of the 1972 Local Government Act powers. Wandsworth Council launched an industrial policy with the publication of a radical manifesto which proposed the coupling of increased provision of premises and finance to firms, with an increased control over the firms via planning agreements with the local authority; help for co-operatives was also envisaged. Section 137 finance was also used, but on a more modest scale than in Southwark. The change in control of the Council in 1978 from Labour to Conservative did not mean an abandonment of industrial intervention (though the conditions to be placed on recipient firms were dropped). It was not until 1977 that Hackney adopted policies of positive intervention into local industry. The powers and finance available to all three boroughs were greatly increased after the passing of the Inner Urban Areas Act: in early 1979 Wandsworth and Southwark were made 'designated districts', and the docklands part of Southwark and Hackney (in association with neighbouring Islington) were given 'partnership' status. It can be seen, then, that the policies and powers of the inner boroughs were in a state of rather rapid change over the period surveyed (1976–80). These changes should be borne in mind when we discuss the impact of the various policies.

The policies of the two outer boroughs, Enfield and Merton, remained essentially traditional, and were therefore more stable over the period surveyed. Enfield had had a *de facto* policy of favouring warehouse to manufacturing uses in order to ease the supply of labour to existing manufacturing firms, but this policy was dropped in 1976–7. In other respects both outer boroughs had by 1976 tempered the implementation of their traditional activities to cause a minimum of disruption to industry. Neither borough undertook any 'positive intervention' into industry, apart from the construction of some industrial units by Merton.

The selection of manufacturing establishments within the five boroughs was determined by the desire to analyse local industrial change in the context of national and international developments. The selection was therefore made from a limited number of sectors, taken for convenience as minimum list headings (MLHs) from the Standard Industrial Classification, so as to be susceptible to this type of analysis. The MLHs were chosen so as to be broadly representative of both the largest orders and the largest MLHs in the manufacturing employment spectrum of the five boroughs taken together. The resultant fourteen sectors are shown in Table 8.1.

The first round of monitoring was completed in October 1980, using a 1976 sampling frame of establishments. Of the 569 'valid' firms contacted, 25 per cent were found to have closed or moved;

**TABLE 8.1**   Number of firms interviewed, by sector, in the five
boroughs

| MLH | | Number of firms |
|-----|------|----|
| 213 | Biscuits | 1 |
| 231 | Brewing | 2 |
| 272 | Pharmaceuticals | 6 |
| 341 | Industrial plant and steelwork | 31 |
| 354 | Scientific instruments | 28 |
| 365 | Consumer electronics | 22 |
| 367 | Electronic capital goods | 13 |
| 395 | Cans and metal boxes | 2 |
| 443 | Women's and girls' tailored outerwear | 22 |
| 445 | Dresses, lingerie, infants' wear | 46 |
| 472 | Furniture and upholstery | 61 |
| 486 | Periodical printing | 4 |
| 489 | General printing | 58 |
| 494 | Toys, games, etc. | 23 |
| Total | | 319 |

of the remainder, 319 were interviewed – a 75 per cent response
rate. The 'firm-side' material contained in this paper is taken from
these interviews with owner/managers and senior executives. The
panel includes establishments from the whole size range found in
the boroughs. Of these 11 per cent had over 200 employees
(referred to in this paper as 'large' establishments), 20 per cent
between 50 and 200 employees ('medium-size' establishments) and
69 per cent 50 or less employees ('small' establishments). It should
be noted that establishments which started and those which 'died'
since 1976 are not included in this study.[2]

The substance of this chapter is divided into three parts. We first
discuss for each type of policy the activities of the boroughs and the
contacts of the firms in our panel with their borough councils. We
then examine the overall assessment of the contacts made by the
firm managers and their attitudes to the new industrial policies of
the boroughs. Finally, we highlight some of the implications of the
main findings of the paper.

**Contacts between firms and local authorities**

As part of the firm interview programme, owners and managers were asked to identify the types of contact that they had had with their local authorities since 1976. The various types of contact are listed in Table 8.2. They can take various forms, ranging from a telephone enquiry about the firm's eligibility for assistance or a written complaint about refuse collection services, to an application for planning permission or a financial grant involving several meetings with local goverment officers. Here we are interested in the contacts that any one firm has had over different matters rather than the number of contacts it may have had over any single issue. For example, if a firm made two separate applications for planning permission since 1976 this only counts as one contact in the following analysis.

Between 1976 and 1980 the majority of firms (about two-thirds) had some contact with their local authority, although in most cases this was on an infrequent basis, limited to one or two issues, and was conducted at arms' length. Only 15 per cent of the sample firms had dealings with their local authorities about three or more issues. Interestingly, a slightly higher proportion of outer than inner borough firms had cause to contact their local authority, which may seem surprising in view of the more interventionist policies of the inner boroughs. On the other hand, there are proportionately more large firms in the two outer boroughs and as will be shown below, the number of separate contacts is correlated with firm size. Furthermore, contacts about land-use matters, such as planning applications and car parking, tended to be more common in the outer boroughs. We would suggest, therefore, that the explanation for the difference had to do with the different types of firms in the inner and outer boroughs; it is certainly not the case that the outer authorities place greater emphasis on cultivating links with local firms.

The various matters over which contact between firms and the local authority can occur are potentially relevant to all firms, irrespective of their size. Moreover, many of the new economic policy initiatives in the inner areas are ostensibly directed towards the small firm sector. For these reasons, the finding that medium and large firms had significantly more contacts over different issues than small firms is somewhat unexpected (Table 8.3). 50 per cent of

**TABLE 8.2  Type and frequency of contact with borough 1976–80**

| Type of contact | Wandsworth | Southwark | Hackney | Merton | Enfield | Total inner boroughs | Total outer boroughs | Total |
|---|---|---|---|---|---|---|---|---|
| Financial aid (loans and grants) | 2 | 11 (14%) | 11 (12%) | 0 | 1 | 24 (11%) | 1 | 25 |
| Lease of local authority owned premises and sites | 9 (18%) | 11 (14%) | 11 (12%) | 3 | 3 | 31 (14%) | 6 | 37 (12%) |
| Information from local authority on vacant premises and sites | 7 (14%) | 11 (14%) | 11 (12%) | 4 | 3 | 29 (13%) | 7 | 36 (11%) |
| Applications for planning permission | 13 (26%) | 26 (33%) | 20 (21%) | 15 (37%) | 23 (41%) | 59 (27%) | 38 (39%) | 97 (30%) |
| Enforcement of non-conforming use provisions or of nuisance by-laws | 2 | 0 | 2 | 3 | 6 | 4 | 9 | 13 |
| Deferment of rates payment | 1 | 4 | 2 | 0 | 3 | 7 | 3 | 10 |
| Compulsory Purchase Order | 1 | 1 | 4 | 2 | 0 | 6 | 2 | 8 |
| Car Parking | 4 | 3 | 5 | 4 | 7 | 12 | 11 | 23 |
| Tender for contracts with local authority | 4 | 6 | 5 | 5 | 8 | 15 | 13 | 28 |
| Information or advice on aid available to industry | 1 | 1 | 1 | 0 | 1 | 3 | 1 | 4 |
| Housing assistance for key workers | 4 | 4 | 2 | 5 (12%) | 2 | 10 | 7 (7%) | 17 |
| Local authority contacted the firm (e.g. area survey) | 2 | 8 | 15 (16%) | 0 | 1 | 25 (11%) | 1 | 26 |
| Rubbish collection | 0 | 0 | 11 | 4 | 3 | 11 | 7 | 18 |
| Other type of contact, e.g. public transport, access | 9 (18%) | 9 (12%) | 13 (14%) | 7 (17%) | 11 (20%) | 31 (14%) | 18 (19%) | 49 (15%) |
| No contact | 18 (36%) | 27 (35%) | 34 (36%) | 12 (29%) | 17 (30%) | 79 (36%) | 29 (30%) | 108 (34%) |
| Total sample | 50 | 77 | 95 | 41 | 56 | 222 | 97 | 319 |

160

### TABLE 8.3   Frequency of contact by firm size

| Total number of types of contact with borough | Employment | | | | |
|---|---|---|---|---|---|
| | 1–10 | 11–50 | 51–200 | 201 + | Total |
| 0 | 42 (46%) | 48 (35%) | 15 (25%) | 5 (16%) | 110 (34%) |
| 1 | 35 (38%) | 54 (40%) | 15 (25%) | 6 (19%) | 110 (34%) |
| 2 | 8 (9%) | 15 (11%) | 17 (28%) | 11 (34%) | 51 (16%) |
| 3 | 4 | 12 (9%) | 6 (10%) | 6 (19%) | 28 (9%) |
| 4 | 1 | 3 | 2 | 3 (9%) | 9 (3%) |
| 5 and over | 1 | 4 | 5 (8%) | 1 | 11 (4%) |
| Total | 91 | 136 | 60 | 32 | 319 (100%) |

Number of firms (percentages of column totals)
Chi square significant at 0.001 significance level.

medium and 65 per cent of large firms had two or more contacts with their borough councils during the four years compared to only 21 per cent of the small firms. We would offer three explanations for this result. First, one matter on which medium and large firms are likely to have more frequent dealings with their local authorities is the need for planning permission for an extension or building alteration. This is because their demands for space are greater and the opportunities for 'in situ' expansion are generally better than for small firms, many of whom operate from short lease and subdivided premises. Nearly all the large firms in our panel made at least one planning application during the study period. Second, professional managers in large firms show more confidence and less reluctance in seeking assistance with particular problems than smaller firm entrepreneurs who may be too preoccupied with the day-to-day running of their businesses, unaware of the assistance that local authorities can offer, or opposed to involving government in their business matters. There is no evidence that they had fewer problems. Third, our evidence also suggests that local authorities tend to develop personal contacts at senior officer and councillor level with the managers of large firms because of their importance for employment and the local economy, thus raising further the propensity for large firms to request help from their local authority. Certainly there is a much wider communications gap between the owner/managers of small firms and local authority officers. Indeed, this is recognised by most of the local authority officers interviewed in this study and some of them are taking action in the form of business resource centres and publicity, to forge stronger links with the small business owner/managers.

We now turn to consider the experiences that firms have had of the various types of local authority activities, starting first with *land-use planning and development control policies.* By the late 1970s, all three of the inner boroughs had declared their intention to use their land-use development powers to facilitate industrial expansion. This would involve treating planning applications from manufacturing industry favourably and, for employment reasons, supporting an application for using premises for manufacturing in preference to one for warehousing. Much the same shift in the use of land-use powers has occurred in the two outer boroughs, despite the fact that the contraction of manufacturing employment has, until now, been less of a problem. Given these policy positions, we would expect the firms in our five boroughs to have had little trouble in obtaining planning permission from 1976 and few to have been the subject of compulsory purchase orders or other restrictions on their activities.

The results of the firm survey are consistent with the above policy intentions. Planning applications continued to be the most common form of contact between manufacturing firms and local government from 1976 to 1980 and far overshadowed in importance contacts in connection with local authorities' new economic policy measures. Nearly one-third of the sample panel made at least one application for planning permission in the period and there were notably more applications from firms in the outer than the inner boroughs. Further, a higher proportion of the applications from firms in the outer boroughs concerned major schemes like factory extensions and new factory units, which is probably attributable to the greater numbers of medium and large firms with the space for *in situ* expansion in the outer boroughs. It follows that it was more common for inner borough firms to be applying for conversions of warehousing or retail premises to light industrial uses or sometimes industrial premises to part office use (notably in the printing industry).

The success rate of planning applications was high (85 per cent being granted). Of the eleven firms which were refused planning permission, only five concerned major schemes which affected the development of the firm. Nearly all the refusals were because of conflicts with residential or conservation interests. We can conclude, therefore, that there is little support from this survey of managers for the argument that planning permission is proving an obstacle to firms' expansion and modernisation plans; on the contrary, the evidence here indicates that firms are able to obtain planning permission without difficulty.

Our evidence also confirms that compulsory purchase orders were not enforced against manufacturing firms. Only one firm (out of 319) was the subject of a CPO and this enabled a move to a council-owned site where it was able to build its own factory, which was beneficial to its subsequent development. However, a necessary caveat to this conclusion is that we are dealing with firms that have 'survived' at locations within their boroughs. We have no way of telling at this stage of the study how many of the numerous cases of relocation and closure (involving 25 per cent of the total sample of firms in existence in 1976) resulted from local authority action. However, according to the opinions of the local authority officers interviewed hardly any relocations or closures should have stemmed from compulsory purchase orders. Turning to the enforcement of restrictions on nonconforming industry, again we find that relatively few (thirteen) of the firms experienced any interference with their activities by local authorities, despite the large number which are clearly located in mixed land-use areas. Most of the restrictions related to smoke pollution and noise regulations in residential areas. Some firms had to restrict their hours of working as a result, but none considered the restrictions had imposed a serious constraint upon the firm's activities and development.

There is nothing, therefore, in the results of the firm survey here which would lead us to quarrel with the claims of the five boroughs to be implementing land-use policies which are supportive of the needs of manufacturing industry. Clearly the redevelopment schemes which swept away many factories and workshops during the 1960s had stopped by the mid-1970s, and since then enforced relocations and interference with the activities of nonconforming industries have been minimal. Overall, there is no evidence of local authority land-use planning acting as a constraint or hinderance to the operations of manufacturing firms.

Other areas of local authority land-use activity were only viewed as problematic by a minority of managers. Car parking was an important issue for some firms (5 per cent of sample); this was seen as especially serious by the managers of several large firms, who were putting pressure on their local authorities to find or provide a site close to their factories which could be used by employees travelling to work by car. However, the number contacting their local authority about this issue is small in relation to the number of managers identifying lack of car parking provision as a locational disadvantage. Complaints about access problems (5 per cent of sample) also often concerned parking, though this time they generally came from small firms operating in residential streets who wanted parking restrictions imposed to facilitate the access of large delivery vehicles. It is important, however, to place these various issues in proper perspective. Except for one case of a severe problem with goods access to the factory, none of them were seen as anything more than a nuisance to the firm and not a constraint on its growth or a spur to relocation.

*Housing* is one other traditional field of local authority responsibility which is important to industry via its effects on the labour supply. The possibility of local authorities reserving an allocation of council houses for the use of local firms, on either a temporary or permanent basis, who are recruiting workers from elsewhere has already been discussed at some length in Mason's contribution to this volume. Despite the fact that the shortage of suitable labour was probably the major single complaint of the firms surveyed, often blamed on the high cost of housing in London, very few firms in the panel actually applied to their local authority for housing assistance in order to attract skilled applicants from other areas. In each of the three inner boroughs, one employer had been given a claim on up to six council dwellings to use for workers moving to the area and this had been valuable to the firms. One major firm in Enfield had also been successful in obtaining key-worker housing, while another was lobbying for it at the time of interview. It is striking that it was only large firms that sought and obtained key-worker housing. The biggest demand came from the Merton firms with five of them applying since 1976 and only one case of success, Merton being generally opposed to such provision. This geographical distribution of demand is closely associated with the preponderant sectors in the boroughs. The demand for key-worker housing came entirely from firms in the engineering sectors (MLH 354, 365, 367) which had high demands for specialised skilled workers.

Having considered the effects of traditional local authority functions on manufacturing firms, we now move on to consider the new types of local authority intervention in the fields of industrial property and finance. A common feature of the industrial and employment policies of all five boroughs since 1976 has been to increase *the supply of industrial sites and premises.* Of the inner boroughs, Wandsworth and Southwark have been particularly successful in releasing land made vacant by the restructuring of public utilities (British Rail, the Gas Board, and the Port of London Authority) and previous industry for new industrial purposes. Besides assembling land for industry, the three inner boroughs (and Merton to a much lesser extent) have also become directly involved themselves in advance factory construction because of the private sector's traditional unwillingness to construct speculative premises in untried or declining areas. With the help of the last Labour government's 'construction package money', the inner boroughs have concentrated on building small and medium-size units (i.e. under 6500 square feet), including several flatted factory schemes. These developments were, of course, only a small increment to the total stock of industrial premises in the boroughs – about 1.5 per cent for the three boroughs taken together. Nevertheless, they constituted a very large fraction of the new building taking place: in Southwark, for example, local authority building was about 30 per cent of the industrial floorspace for which planning permission was granted in the three years 1977–8 to 1979–80. Local authorities are required to set 'market rents' for their units, except for leases of seven years or less (section 123 of the Local Government Act 1972). In fact one of the motives in setting high rents is to convince private developers that a market exists for modern premises at rents that give a commercial return on capital. Largely as a result of the termination of central government funding of local authority construction programmes in 1979, the policies in all three of the inner boroughs have switched from public sector to private sector developments. The council's role is now to act as the catalyst by negotiating lease or lease-and-lease-back arrangements with private developers on council land, an operation which is discussed in detail by Boddy.

How are these policies of land and site provision reflected in the contacts that local firms have with their local authority? For example, to what extent have firms in the sample panel approached their local authorities about leasing premises and sites since 1976? What has been the structure of demand for premises? Have the firms been helped to stay in the borough or to expand? The client group for these local authority services is represented in our panel by the 107 firms that have either moved within or into each borough since 1976, or which at the time of interview had some intention of relocating within each borough in the near future; these are the firms that have had reason to approach the local authority concerning land and premises. We have divided these firms into the sixty-seven 'definite relocators', those which had actually moved or which had a definite intention to do so, and the forty 'potential relocators', those which had a vague intention to move.

Looking first at the number of definite and potential relocators that enquired about local authority premises, we find that in the three inner boroughs, all of which embarked upon major council building programmes in the late 1970s, no less than 39 per cent of the definite relocators and 33 per cent of the potential relocators enquired about leasing local authority premises. Since the level is much lower in the two outer boroughs (where very little actual council building of industrial units took place), the evidence here does show an encouraging initial response (at least in the form of enquiries) to the factory building programmes of the inner boroughs.

However, compared to the numbers of enquiries, the number of firms that reached the stage of making a formal application for the lease of council premises or sites is actually very small. Taking the three inner boroughs together, only four out of the thirty-one enquiries reached this stage. The reasons for this high dropout rate indicate a mismatch between the type of factory premises demanded and that supplied. The majority of firms decided not to pursue a formal application after making enquiries about rents and conditions and visiting the sites. Among the small firms this was undoubtedly because they found the rents too high (often necessitating at least a doubling of the rents they were already paying, many of them paying historic rents at the end of long leases) for what was perceived as a factory shell requiring heavy expenditure on fitting out. Other very small firms considered the units too large for their immediate requirements. Out of the four firms which did move into council-rented premises, one was given a short lease on old premises and the other three obtained leases for new units, the financial costs for all three being reduced during a two year transitional period by the awarding of rent grants. That two of these firms were larger than most of those which enquired initially about local authority premises (one a Southwark furniture firm employing 100, the other a Hackney clothing firm employing 90) is a point worth noting. In both cases the local authorities stood to lose these key employers to other 'assisted' locations (Development Areas) unless they were able to provide a competitive package of premises and financial incentives.

The significance of local authority involvement in the industrial property market is reinforced by the fact that more managers had suggestions to make about local authority site and premises provision than about any other matter (17 per cent of firms). There is clearly a latent demand for industrial premises in all five boroughs, but the demand is complex and varies according to the size and profitability of firms. At one end of the size spectrum, some large firms would like their local councils to provide large, greenfield sites on which they can erect their own, low-rise factories. Typically these firms have high operating costs arising from having production split between a number of separate buildings, not necessarily adjacent to each other, which they have acquired for their expansion over the years. Relocation into new, purpose-built premises was usually a part of a broad strategy concerned with the reorganisation of production to increase competitiveness. The management of these firms generally had a preference for moving locally, not least to retain existing labour, but the difficulty of finding a large enough site already prepared for development in their existing or neighbouring boroughs was, according to the managers, the main reason for staying put. If large numbers of jobs are not to be put at risk in both inner and outer areas, then a solution has to be found to the space needs of this dwindling number of large expanding firms.

As already discussed, the local authority's own factory developments are directed at medium and small firms. Because the local authorities are only able to provide a fraction of the total stock of industrial premises themselves and also have to set rents at market levels, it is not surprising they can satisfy only the more buoyant firms and that a large portion of the demand for premises remains unfilled. A common suggestion from managers is that local authorities should be providng subsidised premises at rents firms can afford.[3] They take the view that there is little point in local authorities being involved in industrial building unless they can undercut the private developer. Of course, it is true that the inner boroughs are able to grant rent-free periods to help firms during the adjustment phase following a move, but managers are still concerned about being able to afford the increased rent in later years. We must stress that there is an important category of firm (usually small, performing a jobbing activity and operating on very low profit margins, typical of industries like furniture and clothing) which needs larger, long-lease premises when demand is strong, but simply cannot afford the kinds of new units available, whether built by local authorities or private developers. If local authorities are to meet this demand, the solution may be the conversion of large factories into smaller units if it can be clearly demonstrated that the costs of doing so are well below those of constructing new units. Hackney, for example, has been using the Inner Urban Areas Act in its two Industrial Improvement Areas to assist developers in the conversion of old industrial or warehouse premises into small units and workshops.

To conclude therefore, on the question of local authority industrial premises, our survey evidence indicates a high level of interest amongst the managers considering moving locally; over one-third enquired about the council's own lettings. But very few of these actually found council premises which met their requirements in terms of price and size; several of them clearly expected the local authorities to be setting lower rents than the private developers. From this we must conclude that the direct involvement of local authorities in the industrial building market in the late 1970s has begun to meet the needs of a particular group of buoyant firms but the needs of many more less successful firms remain unsupplied. Of course, it would be unrealistic to expect local authorities to be able to transform the industrial property market within a few years, given the limited resources at their disposal. Nor is it the intention of local authorities to replace private developers as the dominant industrial landlords. Rather, they are carrying out a 'pump-priming' role by providing small to medium-size units which it is recognised will satisfy only a limited number of demands. In this way they hope to give a lead to the private developers who, it is thought, will be in a better financial position to provide a greater range of types and sizes of units. Given the varied nature of the demand it is clearly important that one kind of policy for increasing industial space is not pursued to the exclusion of all others.

As well as the direct provision of sites and premises, some local authorities have attempted to improve the workings of the local market for industrial premises by improving the *supply of information about vacant premises* available to managers. Thus, to assist firms considering local relocation or moving into their areas, all three of the inner boroughs have in recent years produced registers of vacant sites and premises, which aim to include freehold and private leasehold as well as council leasehold ones. These lists are compiled using a variety of sources, such as the records of borough valuers and local estate agents, and are therefore aimed at being more comprehensive than a single estate agent's list.

Local authority information on premises was used by just under half of the firms considering local relocation, but was only rarely likely to lead directly to the final choice of premises. Managers see the local authority lists as one source of information amongst many, and do not give it any special weight. Managers had a mixed response to the value of information on vacant sites and premises given to them by local authorities. Some have found the lists of property very helpful and have found their new premises as a result. But four times as many said the lists were unhelpful, the main criticism being that they were out of date, and included premises that were no longer on the market. Another complaint was that the lists were restricted in their coverage, but it is difficult to know the extent to which this is a criticism of the lists themselves or a reflection on the stock of premises available. Managers' criticisms of the lists may actually help create an unfavourable image of the local authority in the minds of some of them.

The other major new development in local authority economic and employment policies in recent years has been *financial assistance to firms*. The three inner boroughs each have the necessary powers under the Inner Urban Areas Act to offer certain types of financial aid to firms, though there are some important differences in the ways in which this part of their industrial development policy operates.[4] Whereas in Hackney all the finance is made available under this Act, in Southwark and Wandsworth section 137 of the 1972 Local Government Act has also been used to set up a fund financed through the general rates. Wandsworth allocated £165 496 to an 'Employment Fund' in 1980–1, whereas Southwark managed to devote as much as £3 million to their 'Industrial and Commercial Development Fund' which was set up in 1978. This action enabled Southwark to start giving aid to firms before receiving the additional powers under the Inner Urban Areas Act. Since we are interested in contacts between firms and their authorities from 1976 to early 1980, we can therefore expect some difference in the degree of contact to stem from the varying lengths of time over which the three boroughs have been giving financial aid to firms. Hackney and Wandsworth only started applying the financial policies in 1979 and 1980 respectively, so these results will tend to underestimate the demand of local firms for local authority financial assistance in these boroughs.

Leaving aside the outer boroughs which have neither the powers nor the political volition for government intervention of this kind, we find that twenty-four firms (11 per cent) in the three inner boroughs enquired about various forms of financial assistance. Twenty-two of these were in Southwark and Hackney where the policies have been running longer and were better publicised than in Wandsworth. Most of the enquiries were either for rent grants to assist with proposed relocations or loans and grants for extending, improving, or equipping existing premises. However, not all of the enquiries were converted into a formal application for aid: three out of eleven enquiries in Hackney, and seven out of eleven in Southwark.

It is interesting that so few of the cases advanced beyond the enquiry stage to a formal application. Again (as with premises) the pattern is of a latent interest and demand for this kind of assistance, but a shortfall between this and the reality of assistance. Several factors account for this. In some cases, managers never went beyond the initial enquiry stage because they abandoned their relocation plans. Some enquiries concerned types of aid not covered by the Inner Urban Areas Act or the council's policy, such as aid for investment in plant or machinery. In other cases, managers decided not to pursue their application when they discovered the amount of information they would have to supply to the local authority about their operations or the length of time a decision would take. These managers were probably unrealistic in their perception of the conditions under which aid would be made available to them. In some cases managers maintain that they were actually discouraged from pursuing their applications by council officers since they did not meet profit or locational criteria. However, there is a conflict of evidence here between the managers and local officials who maintain that such judgements would not be made without formal applications being submitted. This suggests that at times communication between managers and council officials is imperfect and managers may draw wrong conclusions from advice given informally. It is clear that aid programmes do not reach all the potential client firms and that some managers become disillusioned about local authority policies, having had their expectations raised but not fulfilled.

Once again there is a size difference between the firms in our panel which did not progress beyond the enquiry stage and those that did make a formal application. Nine of the twelve firms which did not get beyond the enquiry stage employed fewer than fifty people; in contrast, nine of the ten firms which actually made an application employed more than fifty as did all firms in our survey whose application was successful. Possibly smaller firms do not follow up initial enquiries because they lack management time and experience to sustain an enquiry, expect rapid results and are prone to change their plans. On the other hand, since it was the medium and large firms in our panel which were successful in obtaining financial aid, then this may indicate that local authority officers put more effort into enquiries made by larger firms, especially if there is a high risk that the firm will move or locate new investment elsewhere and thereby remove a significant number of actual or potential jobs. Taking the inner boroughs together, therefore, our evidence is unequivocal in showing that larger firms are more likely to follow an enquiry through to a successful application than small firms.

Various central government references in the early stages of the inner cities programme led us to the supposition that new local authority initiatives including financial aid would be directed primarily towards small firms.[5] But apart from the interest relief grants which can only be paid to firms employing fewer than fifty people, the Inner Urban Areas Act makes little mention of the size or type of firm; for example, 'the new powers are intended to allow authorities to encourage firms to develop and expand in inner area locations when they might otherwise have gone outside the area, or not undertaken the development at all'.[6]

In principle, therfore, all sizes of firm are equally eligible for most forms of aid provided by the new powers. There is nothing in our survey evidence to show that local authorities are discriminating against larger firms in favour of small ones. If anything, because of the confidence of professional managers in dealing with local authorities and the importance of these key firms to the local economy, the reality suggests that there is some discrimination in favour of the larger firms. At the very least, therefore, our evidence seems to indicate that the practice comes closer to the Act's indiscriminate approach rather than the small firm orientated policies advocated by many participants in the inner cities debate.[7]

Finally, it is worth looking closer at the eight firms which were successful in obtaining grants or loans from their borough councils. This will enable us to shed some light on crucial questions relating to the impact of the aid on firms and their employment levels. For example, was the aid a necessary condition for making the investment decisions or would the firms have gone ahead anyway? Did the aid lead to any net increase in employment within the firm or did it purely prevent jobs moving out of the borough? The latter is an important distinction when assessing the effects of spatial policies (whether regional or local) on employment. Ideally, we need to separate the absolute change (i.e. a net increase or decrease of employment in the firm irrespective of location) from the locational change (i.e. a shift of jobs within the firm between the borough and other locations).[8] Using the information supplied by managers in the interviews on the firm's overall strategy, production and employment history, and financial position, we have been able to make some assessment of the role the financial aid plays in the investment decision of the firm and the impact of the grants and loans upon employment in the firm.

The first point to be made is that the level of financial aid offered by the boroughs cannot compensate for basic weakness in the position of a firm or establishment. Three of the eight firms did not in fact take up the aid offered because their investment plans were scrapped, due to problems of low productivity or declining markets resulting in falling profitability (one firm subsequently going out of business). The second point is that our evidence strongly suggests that in two of the five cases where aid was taken up, the relevant investment decision would have been made without it. In other words, as has been claimed of many cases of regional financial incentives, the aid represents a marginal bonus rather than a vital element in the investment decision.[9]

In assessing the employment effects of the aid, a distinction needs to be made between employment change that accompanied the relevant investment decision and the employment change actually attributable to the aid itself. This distinction is usually absent in the figures given by local authorities for the effectiveness of their aid policies, and it requires detailed information from firms such as we obtained in our interviews. Even so, our assessments involve a degree of judgement.

The employment effect of the relevant investment decision was either positive or, at worst, neutral within each of the five firms that received aid. Given the premises-related nature of the aid available, it is not surprising to find that the aid in all cases involved a move to new premises, while sometimes retaining the old. However, different kinds of employment effect arose: for example, two cases involved large increases in capacity of essentially the existing type, providing proportionally large increases of employment, while in another case, the investment was an intensive one, providing little new employment but strengthening the firm's competitive position.

The employment effect actually attributable to the aid given, however, was quite different. The 'absolute effect' on employment due to the aid was small: as stated, the firms which expanded employment immediately on making the investment made it clear that they would have made that investment anyway, either by a move outside the borough, or by a move to other premises in the borough, or by using other sources of funds. However, there was a distinct 'locational effect' on employment within the borough in two cases, where the aid prevented the movement of the expanding firms to Development Areas. Thus while the effect of the investment decisions was certainly to produce an absolute increase in employment in the firms, the effect of the aid given was at most a locational one and then confined to two firms only.

The key issue which our evidence raises is that the various types of investment context in which financial aid is granted relate very differently to general employment and industrial policy and would be viewed differently from the point of view of local, regional and national employment policies. At present, these policy implications have not been elaborated (at any rate publicly) by either the boroughs or central government. There would thus seem to be the need at both levels of government for more clearly defined objectives for the local financial aid programmes.

### Managers' assessment of local authority policy

Having analysed in some detail the various industrial development and employment policies of the five boroughs, together with managers' own accounts of their contacts with their local authority, we now try to summarise managers' overall assessment of their local authority based on their experiences since 1976. Obviously, it is difficult if not impossible for respondents to restrict their opinion to a particular period of time. Opinions evolve over a long period and in a few cases unfavourable contact with the local authority prior to 1976 had clearly affected a manager's judgement. However, apart from this limitation, the answers provide a useful summary of managerial response to local authority policies relating directly or indirectly to manufacturing industry.

Not surprisingly in view of the very occasional and often arms' length nature of the contact which took place since 1976, three-quarters of the respondents felt unable to arrive at a definite opinion. They tend to regard the local authority as a fairly neutral agency, carrying out its traditional environment functions in a 'normal' way, and having little direct bearing on their activities.

We need to look closer, therefore, at the quarter of managers who had formed a definite opinion. These were usually firms which had had dealings with their local authority during the last three years and based their views on the result of these contacts. Taking the five boroughs together they were split fairly evenly between those forming helpful and unhelpful judgements, although there are some marked differences between the boroughs. Southwark emerges as the authority thought to be most helpful and the least unhelpful by the resident firms, followed by Wandsworth. This is consistent with the higher proportion of panel firms in Southwark following enquiries about premises and financial aid through to a successful conclusion, than was the case in other boroughs. Most of those giving an unhelpful judgement in Southwark had been refused planning permission. In Wandsworth it is the largest firms which regard the local authority as helpful, primarily because they had developed a good relationship at a high level within the Council.

Hackney, on the other hand, has not achieved the same image amongst the managers who had formed a definite view, with over four times as many considering the local authority unhelpful as helpful. There is no single reason why managers give this judgement. Some attribute it to their disappointment after contacting the local authority about premises and financial aid. As discussed previously, many of them never reached the stage of making a formal application because they had failed to appreciate initially the procedures involved. But it should be emphasised that the main grounds for disapproval with Hackney Council were not related directly to the new industrial policy initiatives. Instead, they concerned the traditional local authority functions. For a few the assessment was connected with having a planning application refused, while others were generally critical of the poor quality of public services and the high rates. It is also evident that seven out of the nineteen managers regarding the local authority as unhelpful were in the furniture industry and this includes all the largest furniture firms. The inability of the local authority to help with their labour shortages may contribute to their negative attitude. The Hackney Business Promotions centre, set up in 1978 and financed by the Urban Programme, is intended to give expert advice and assistance, especially to small firms, but it will take a long time to reverse the anti-local authority view which many small firm managers have in this area. In the two outer boroughs, most of the strong opinions relate to success or failure with planning applications. Even some of the large firms in Enfield have had few direct dealings with the local authority – in the words of one executive, 'the local authority is transparent'.

Finally, since the size of the firm has so far in this paper been shown to be an important determinant of not only the amount of contact with the local authority, but also the probability of obtaining a successful result, it is worth looking more closely at the relationship between managers' attitudes to their local authority and the size of the firm. The analysis reveals that large-firm managers are more likely to have a definite view about the local authority than their equivalents in small firms, possibly because they have had more contacts. But there is also a difference in the direction of the attitudes. Of those having definite opinions, more medium- and large-firm managers (i.e. those employing over fifty) regard the local authority as helpful, and conversely, more small-firm managers as unhelpful than we would expect if firm size was not a factor (chi square significant at the 0.01 level). 22 per cent of medium/large-firm managers regarded the local authority as helpful compared to 8 per cent of small-firm managers. It would seem to follow, therefore, that it is largely because they have both more contacts and more favourable ones with their local authorities that the managers of medium and large firms are more inclined to regard their local authority as helpful than their counterparts in small firms.

**Managers' attitude to the role of the local authority in the local economy**

The above discussion was essentially based on managers' past experiences. We now want to consider more generally managerial attitudes to local government involvement in the local economy. Do the majority support the new types of initiatives taken by some local authorities in recent years to try to promote industrial regeneration and provide for the needs of firms, or do they oppose such policies? Arguably, a knowledge of managerial attitudes will give us some indication of the future demand conditions for local authority business services and aid. For example, if the majority of managers are ideologically opposed to local government intervention in the local economy then this will surely inhbit the effectiveness of the new economic policy initiatives by restricting the client group to firms who may not be in the greatest need of help.

We have made an attempt to categorise the opinions of the respondents in order to shed some light on the above questions. The views of most managers were exposed in answer to the question about what the local authority should be doing to help local industry, although answers to other questions in the course of the interview were also useful. Five categories of opinion have been devised:

1. Those who are strongly opposed to local government becoming

involved in local industry in any way apart from conventional land-use and infrastructure responsibilities.

2. Those who, while not being ideologically opposed to local authority involvement, were clearly sceptical about its usefulness.

3. Those who essentially supported recent industry-oriented policies of local authorities and take a pragmatic view of the need for them to intervene in helping to solve local economic and employment problems.

4. Those who think that local authorities have not gone far enough and are in favour of stronger policies than have been adopted hitherto.

5. Those who were impossible to assign to the above categories either because we didn't have enough information to make a confident judgement or because the managers clearly had no thoughts on the subject.

This exercise has obvious limitations, not least because in large firms these are the views of the managers who happen to have been interviewed rather than those of the firms. Further, some managers obviously have contradictory views, such as that of the owner/manager who was full of praise for the local authority in providing him with one of their units but was totally opposed to local government intervention of any kind in the market economy! Moreover, it is surprising how many managers do not have a clear conception of the local authority and its functions; some, for example, do not distinguish local authorities from Job Centres.

The results indicate a large degree of support for recent local government initiatives, with about half of the managers either taking a pragmatic view or favouring stronger intervention. Most of these managers either have made little use of local authority services as yet and therefore haven't experienced the realities of applying for premises or finance, or they have had successful contacts in the last few years. Many of the pragmatists took the view that it was senseless not to take advantage of any assistance that was available, no matter what its source. Only a quarter of the managers appeared to be either totally opposed to the new policies or strongly sceptical about their effectiveness. The few opponents were generally those who had an ideological commitment to the free working of the market system, thinking that government help invited industrial inefficiency, or thought the policies were doomed in practice because of the inefficiencies of local 'bureaucracies' and their inexperience of dealing with business matters. Entrepreneurs from a craft (as opposed to technical or managerial) background who valued their independence were strongly represented in this group. The sceptics category, on the other hand, included most of those firms which had been disappointed by their experience of contacting the local authority. These tended to be the managers who were discouraged by the procedures for obtaining financial aid or had found that council-owned premises did not meet their requirements. This group also included those managers who think that because the major problems facing industry are national ones (for example, import levels in the clothing industry, the collapse of markets or the rate of inflation), local authority action is irrelevant. This view may be becoming more widespread as many firms fight for their survival during the present recession.

From the local authority viewpoint, therefore, our evidence indicates that only a minority of managers are totally opposed to the more active involvement of local government in the economy of their areas. While enthusiasm for even stronger intervention is equally limited, the present level of government involvement typical of the inner boroughs in this study is endorsed by a substantial section of the local business community. It follows that managerial attitudes in themselves should not obstruct the implementation of local authority policies. However, there may be one significant exception. It was noted above that one group of managers, the craft entrepreneurs, were inclined to show greater opposition to local authority intervention than other types of managers; they are also associated with the smallest firms. It is this group which will be the hardest to reach by the present policies. In the short term, there is probably nothing that can be done by the local authority to break down the hardened attitude of many of these working proprietors and it is a far more efficient use of limited resources to concetrate on those who are willing to accept local authority help, even at the risk of some bias towards owners and managers who are not so directly involved in the production side of their business. If there is a favourable 'demonstration effect' from local firms that are in receipt of local authority services and aid, then the opposition of others may decline over time.

**Contacts between firms and local authorities during the 1980–1 recession**

The second round of monitoring carried out at the end of 1981 enables us to update the information on the contacts between a reduced panel of 248 firms (a fifth of the original panel having closed down) and their local authorities. It might be thought that the level of contacts would rise as managerial awareness and acceptance of local authority economic policies increases. However, our evidence shows that the effects of the economic recession have been much stronger than these behavioural factors. Although the average propensity for small firms (under 50 employees) to contact their local authorities was similar between the two monitoring periods, that of larger firms (over 200 employees) was much lower in the second period (falling from an average of 0.44 per annum in 1976–9 to 0.25 per annum in 1980–1). The main reason was the much lower rate of extensive investment in the larger firms during the recession years, reducing the need to apply for planning permissions to extend or convert factory space. Demand for local authority economic services was also lower. Fewer firms implemented relocation plans during the recession years, leading to fewer enquiries about leasing local authority premises. The previous pattern of most firms deciding against applying for local authority units and sites either on grounds of cost or inappropriate size and layout still held among the reduced number of firms which did consider relocation. Similarly, the rate of enquiries about financial aid was also down in the second period, and only six of the nine enquiries resulted in a formal application. It is striking that four of these came from firms which had put in successful applications in the previous period and were therefore encouraged to try again. Allowing for these repeated clients, there were therefore even fewer new clients for local authority financial aid after 1979. We therefore conclude that since most local authority services are directed at the needs of expansionist firms, any significant increase in the level of contacts is likely to be dependent on economic recovery.

**Conclusions**

Finally, we summarise the main results of our analysis of the contacts between London borough councils and manufacturing firms and consider briefly their implications, some of which will be taken further in the final chapter.

The first point arising from our evidence is that the traditional land-use powers and policies of local authorities in the late 1970s have clearly been used in the interests of manufacturing firms. There were very few cases where refusal of planning permission interfered with a major project of a firm, nonconforming use restrictions and nuisance bye-laws have been enforced very little, and compulsory purchase orders have affected very few firms. This suggests that further relaxation of planning controls on industry, such as has been proposed for the Enterprise Zones, will make negligible difference to firms as this is no longer considered by the majority of them to be a constraint upon their development.

The second point is that there does not appear to be the kind of suspicion or hostility from firms towards the 'new' types of intervention by local government in the provision of premises and finance that is sometimes expected, with the partial exception of craft entrepreneurs. Many firms would be prepared to use these types of aid if provided and few would rule themselves out for ideological reasons. The provision of these services by local authorities appears to stimulate the demand for them. There is a strong demand from manufacturers for greater local authority involvement in the provision of land and premises, whether through council building programmes or partnerships with private developers, but it is important to stress that the demand is highly differentiated and it is only the more successful firms which have been able to afford the full market rents which are set. Again, the level of demand for financial aid as measured by the number of enquiries and the support in principle is strong and not inhibited by consideration of their possible fiscal implications. We can conclude, therefore, that there is general support amongst managers for the mild interventionist policies now being taken by most inner city authorities. However, very few managers would welcome stronger intervention, such as local government involvement in their policy-making through planning agreements or in their equity financing through a municipal shareholding in the firm. Local authority involvement is encouraged in the form of assistance, especially if it is on better terms than offered by private sector institutions, but not surprisingly, is unacceptable if it involves any loss of management independence.

It is sometimes maintained that local authority activity impinges more strongly on small firms than large ones. The limited resources available to the local authorities have also led to the supposition that new local authority initiatives would be directed primarily towards small firms. The third point is that neither of these expectations is borne out by our survey: rather the opposite. Large firms tend to have dealings with the local authority in more types of area than smaller firms; they make more planning applications; they tend to be more successful in carrying through applications for financial aid; they are more likely to seek and obtain key-worker housing; and they are more likely than small firms to find the local authority generally helpful. This difference between large and small firms is attributable partly to the greater management skills and time within larger firms, and partly to the greater interest of the local authorities in these firms and a greater receptiveness to their demands. The latter is attributable to real constraints acting on the local authorities. While the financial or resource outlays necessary to aid large firms are clearly greater per firm than for small ones, the local authority will tend to concentrate on the large firms partly because of their greater role and weight in the local economy, and partly because of the lack of officer time available for dealing with the multiplicity of small firms. It is hard to see how these very substantial pressures could be circumvented.

It follows from the above point that to some extent the success of local authority economic initiatives will depend upon an improvement in the relationships between the owners and managers of small firms and local authority officers. We have shown, both for premises and financial aid, that a large proportion of enquiries do not develop into formal applications and that in many cases this is due to misunderstandings between the authorities and managers. The latter is unlikely to be merely 'teething trouble' of the Inner Urban Areas Act powers. The considerable complexity of these powers, and the large degree of discretion possessed by the local authorities in their implementation, mean that there is likely to remain considerable ignorance and confusion among managers, particularly of small firms, of their local authority's policy in this area.

Under these circumstances, there is certainly scope for improvement in the presentation of local authorities' policies to the client group of local firms. There is some evidence that policies will fail to get across, or worse still firms will draw negative conclusions about the ability of the local authority to help them, because of failures at this point in the aid-giving process.

The final point concerns the need for greater clarification by both central and local government about the objectives of the new economic initiatives and measures of their efficiency. Our analysis of an admittedly small sample of firms receiving financial aid has pointed to some of the important questions which must be faced in both the implementation and evaluation of policy. For example, in the administration of discretionary aid there are difficulties for local authorities in assessing whether or not the aid is necessary in a particular case. If it is thought that local authority resources should be used only in cases where it is vital to the investment decision, then local authorities need to match the expertise of the managers in medium and large firms who are skilled at making convincing applications for financial assistance. In terms of assessing the effects of the aid, our evidence indicates that, while in most cases the aid was part of an investment decision that created extra jobs within the firm, the effect of the aid was on the location rather than the absolute level of employment. It is clear that many firms, especially the medium and large ones, will play inner city authorities off against each other as well as against the financial help obtainable in Development Areas. Certainly, the relative importance of the absolute and locational effects of these policies needs more consideration in government policy at the national and local levels, as well as in research, than it has been given hitherto.

## References

1.    This paper arises from a research project, financed by the Department of Environment, into the determinants of industrial change in London. The aim of the project is to analyse industrial decline in the inner boroughs of London over the period 1976-81, deduce its underlying causes and evaluate the impact of local authority initiatives aimed at industrial regeneration. A comparison is made

with trends and policies in outer boroughs. In so far as this paper is only concerned with part of the research it looks at local authority policies in isolation from the full explanatory context of the processes of change in manufacturing industry.

2. Contact with the managers of new firms and firms that 'died' since 1976 and the second round of interviews to monitor the impact of the recession are to be carried out later in 1981.

3. Rents in early 1981 varied over the five boroughs, being lowest in Hackney and Southwark (£2.50–£3.00), around £3.50 in Wandsworth, and highest in Merton (£3.75–£4.00). In contrast, most firms in the panel which were in rented accommodation were paying rents in the region of £1.50–£2.50 per sq.ft.

4. Under various sections of the Inner Urban Areas Act (July 1978) the three authorities are empowered to give loans of up to 90 per cent of the cost of land acquisition and development, loans or grants towards the cost of establishing co-operative or common ownership enterprises and, in the case of industrial improvement areas, loans and grants for improvements to the environment or amenities as well as towards the costs of converting, improving or modifying commercial and industrial buildings. These powers apply to both partnerships and designated districts. Three additional financial powers are available in the patnership authorities (Hackney and the docklands part of Southwark); these powers are, first, the making of grants to assist with rents paid by firms taking out new leases or having their rent reviewed on industrial and commercial premises; second, the making of interest free loans for up to two years for site preparation; and third, making interest relief grants to small firms (employing under fifty staff) for loans on land and buildings. The Department of Environment contributes 75 per cent of the cost of grants and loans made under the Inner Urban Areas Act powers. Each application for financial assistance from a firm has to be approved first by the local authority and then the Department of Environment.

5. For example, Department of the Environment, *Policy for the Inner Cities*, Cmnd 6845 (HMSO, 1977); and Department of the Environment, Circular 71/77.

6. Department of the Environment, *Inner Urban Areas Act 1978*, Circular 68/78, para. 14.

7. For example, N. Falk, *Think Small: Enterprise and Economy* (London: Fabian Society, 1978); and N. Falk, 'Small Firms and the Inner City', in A. Gibb and T. Webb (eds), *Policy Issues in Small Business Research* (Saxon House, 1980.)

8. D. B. Massey and R. A. Meegan, 'Industrial Restructuring versus the Cities', *Urban Studies*, 15, 1978.

9. House of Commons Expenditure Committee, *Regional Development Incentives*, Second Report, Session 1973–4 (HMSO, 1973).

# 9 Local Employment Initiatives in North East England: Evaluation and Assessment Problems

## D. J. STOREY

### Introduction

The North East of England is the classic English depressed area. Almost every schoolchild has heard of the Jarrow Hunger Marches in the 1930s and more recently the whole country was made aware of the implications for an isolated community when the Consett Steel Works closed. Along with Merseyside, the North East has been called the graveyard of British capitalism, and so it is, perhaps, not surprising that the public sector should have become more involved in the creation and maintenance of employment than probably any other area of England.

Public involvement in the creation of jobs has a long history. One of the most important actions of the Commissioners for the Special Areas in the 1930s was to obtain, for the first time, public funds to create Industrial Estates on which there was a variety of different-sized factory premises.[1] It is no coincidence that one of the first (and currently the headquarters of English Industrial Estates) was Team Valley in Gateshead. Since the Second World War central government, as part of its regional policy, has offered a variety of incentives to firms to locate in the Northern region. Over the years the nature of these incentives has varied, as has the eligibility of areas, but for most of the period since 1945 firms in the main urban areas of North East England have been eligible for the highest available rates of assistance.

184

Despite the efforts of central government the current economic problems of the North East remain, not dissimilar to those when the men of Jarrow took to the streets. There is still a dependence upon shipbuilding, heavy engineering and metal manufacturing. In other ways the problems have changed: the chemical industry, which came to Teeside in the 1930s and 1940s and provided the base for prosperity in the south of the region for a generation, shed more jobs than the steel industry between 1965 and 1976. Other industries which came to the North East, attracted by government grants and relatively buoyant market conditions, found by the end of the 1970s that production had to be reduced, and they retreated southwards or overseas. Even the North East coal mines, which in the 1930s offered employment to one-tenth of the male workforce, were not able to take advantage of the increased demand for energy. The area had no new resources of coal, and the pits that remained were often difficult to work. Finally the area showed no ability to pull itself up by its own bootstraps. New firm formation was, in the opinion of the Northern Region Strategy Team, the lowest of all the major English Regions.[2] Gone were the days when the North East produced great innovators or entrepreneurs such as Stephenson or Pease or Parsons. Instead, according to the Strategy Team, the region was characterised by a preference for collective rather than individual action; it is politically and culturally collectivist.

With such a tradition it is not surprising that publicly funded, locally based initiatives designed to create the conditions for prosperity were developed. The County Councils of Durham and Northumberland have, for many years, had powers to assist industry while many of the powers of the Tyne & Wear Act 1976 (such as the creation of Industrial Improvement Areas) were later embodied in the Inner Urban Areas Act 1978. Many local authorities in the region have developed considerable experience in using their own funds to clear derelict land, and build and lease their own factories. Consequently local authorities, while following broadly similar policies and contributing to regional organisations, such as the North of England Development Council, had by the end of the 1970s begun to compete with one another in the attraction of large new establishments. The reduced number of such plants meant there was intense rivalry between authorities to attract those firms which could create large numbers of jobs in 'their' locality.

To achieve these objectives all county councils, and many district councils, have substantial promotional budgets designed to communicate to potential industrialists the benefits of locating in their area.

Local authorities are not the only bodies involved in creating jobs. The North of England Development Council, founded in 1962, has a responsibility to 'sell' the region, both to overseas firms and to firms currently located elsewhere in the country but who are considering a site in the North East. More recently established is BSC (Industry), a wholly owned subsidiary of the British Steel Corporation, whose function is to encourage the creation of new jobs in areas affected by steel closures. In the North East it is primarily concerned with Consett and Hartlepool. Factories in rural parts of the region are constructed not only by the English Industrial Estates (EIE) and by the local authorities, but also by the Council for Small Industries in Rural Areas (COSIRA) which is able to offer a comprehensive package of incentives and advice to eligible small firms. The region also has new towns at Washington, and Peterlee/Aycliffe, which also have responsibilities for the creation of employment and wealth. Finally, there are a myriad of local agencies, some associated with local colleges, polytechnics and universities, who offer advice and information primarily to small and new businesses. In fact the present author showed that a new firm founder in Cleveland could approach up to twenty-five different agencies within a 40-mile radius of Middlesbrough.[3]

The number of public agencies undertaking apparently similar functions suggests that there may be some duplication of functions and raises some fundamental questions about local economic development. Could factories currently being constructed by local authorities be better managed by EIE? Why can such factories not be constructed and managed by the private sector? Is competitive advertising between local authorities wasteful? Are there too many bodies offering advice to small firms? Is there a need for a Northern Development Agency to take over the functions of the regional Department of Industry, Small Firms Counselling Service and North of England Development Council? These are important and relevant questions which cannot be answered until the objectives of the various agencies are clarified, and until an assessment is made of the effectiveness of their operations.

This chapter begins such a task by examining local economic development in North East England, and assembling the results of other studies which have conducted partial assessments of these issues. It assesses the effectiveness of creating jobs through attracting industry to the area as compared with policies to assist small firms, and highlights the need for specific criteria in measuring agency performance, together with an appropriate form of monitoring.

The methodology of approach, and the questions which the paper raises, are of interest not just to students of the economy of Northern England, but to all those interested in local economic development. The issue of competitive advertising between local authorities, the plethora of agencies offering outwardly similar services and whether services, currently provided by local authorities, would be better provided by the private sector are questions of national importance.

It is not our intention to describe in detail each initiative or to offer a detailed *raison d'être* for local authority involvement in the local economy. Those interested in such topics can consult a number of studies.[4] Instead this chapter examines the main initiatives taken by local authorities in Northern England and reviews those evaluations which have been made of the effectiveness of such expenditure.

## Expenditure on local authority employment initiatives in Northern England

Table 9.1 shows data on the various categories of local authority expenditure on economic development in the Northern region (i.e. including Cumbria), while Table 9.2 provides similar data for the expenditure by the new towns. Table 9.1 shows that expenditure on economic development in constant prices in 1979–80 was approximately three times that in 1974–5, although no such increases are apparent from Table 9.2 for the expenditure by new towns. Expenditure devoted to the various activities has varied considerably. For example, expenditure by Northern local authorities on loans in 1974–5 was more than three times their industrial promotion budgets, whereas by 1979–80 the two were almost identical. Expenditure on factory construction has also

### TABLE 9.1    Local authority expenditure[1] on economic development: Northern region 1974–5 to 1980–1

| | Gross expenditure (£m., 1978 prices) | Percentage shares | | | | |
|---|---|---|---|---|---|---|
| | | Industrial promotion* | Land acquisition† | Servicing land‡ | Factory construction | Loans**[3] |
| 1974–5 | 3.49 | 5.3 | | 58.0 | 20.5 | 16.2 |
| 1975–6 | 4.93 | 3.7 | | 67.2 | 16.2 | 12.9 |
| 1976–7 | 4.31 | 3.8 | | 65.0 | 17.9 | 13.3 |
| 1977–8 | 5.43 | 4.5 | | 54.7 | 9.8 | 31.0 |
| 1978–9 | 7.28 | 6.4 | | 56.3 | 30.5 | 6.8 |
| 1979–80 | 10.33 | 7.1 | 20.5 | 28.9 | 35.0 | 8.5 |
| 1980–1[2] | 9.94 | 7.6 | 7.2 | 29.1 | 37.2 | 18.9 |

1.  Data incomplete: Cleveland (1974–9) – expenditure of £0.5m. on loans by the district councils has been excluded for lack of an annual breakdown; Cumbria (1974–9) no data supplied by Allerdale or Eden districts and (1979–81) no data supplied by Eden district; Durham (1974–9) no data supplied by Darlington, Derwentside, Durham or Wear Valley districts and (1979–81) no data supplied by Chester-le-Street or Easington districts; Northumberland (1974–9) no data supplied by Berwick or Castle Morpeth districts and (1979–81) no data supplied by Berwick district; Tyne and Wear (1974–9) no data supplied by Gateshead or Sunderland districts.

2.  Figures for 1980–1 are based on budget provisions in contrast to the outturn expenditures for previous years.

3.  Expenditure on grants is not included since it represents less than £1m.

*   Excludes staff costs but includes contribution by local authorities to the North of England Development Council.

†   This figure represents gross expenditure (i.e. excluding disposals) by the local authorities.

‡   This figure represents gross expenditure (i.e. excluding income from the EEC or central government) on access work plus provision of on-site services.

**  Gross new loans paid in the year in question. Receipts and interest repayment from loans is not included.

fluctuated considerably from £530 000 in 1977–8 to £3 600 000 in 1979–80.

Table 9.3 subdivides aggregate expenditure in both 1979–80 and 1980–1 by counties. It shows that expenditure per head of population on economic development varies considerably both between the counties, and on a year-to-year basis. For example, in Cumbria in 1979–80 expenditure per head was only £1.36, whereas in Tyne and Wear expenditure was £5.94. From this low figure Cumbria in 1980–1 was planning to increase its expenditure to £3.58 per head. Durham was also anticipating a major increase in expenditure from £3.39 per head to £5.70, whereas both Cleveland and Tyne and Wear were expecting to just maintain spending and Northumberland was proposing to reduce expenditure.

There are also considerable variations in the priorities for

**TABLE 9.2   New town expenditure\* on economic development: northern region 1974–5 to 1980–1**

| | Gross expenditure (£m., 1978 prices) | Percentage shares | | | |
| --- | --- | --- | --- | --- | --- |
| – | | Industrial promotion | Industrial estates | Factory construction | Loans |
| 1974–5 | 8.47 | 0.9 | 16.4 | 82.7 | — |
| 1975–6 | 9.86 | 1.2 | 16.0 | 82.8 | — |
| 1976–7 | 5.46 | 2.1 | 23.0 | 74.9 | — |
| 1977–8 | 5.59 | 2.7 | 20.5 | 76.8 | — |
| 1978–9 | 8.52 | 1.8 | 18.0 | 80.2 | — |
| 1979–80 | 8.02 | 1.8 | 25.5 | 72.7 | — |
| 1980–1† | 6.39 | 3.1 | 21.6 | 75.3 | — |

\* Total expenditure by Aycliffe, Peterlee and Washington New Town Corporations, except for 1979–80 and 1980–1 for which data for Washington are not available.

† Figures for 1980–1 are based on budget provisions in contrast to outturn expenditure for previous years.

expenditure. In most counties industrial promotion expenditure takes rather less than one-tenth of the total economic development budget, but in many ways this is a false figure since it excludes staff costs. The acquisition of land is a particularly volatile element in annual expenditure on development, illustrated by the fact that County Durham devoted 41 per cent of its total budget to this activity in 1979–80, yet anticipated no expenditure in 1980–1. Expenditure on factory building and the servicing of land varies considerably between authorities. For example, only 14 per cent of Cumbria's expenditure in 1979–80 was on factory building compared with 56 per cent of that of Northumberland. There are also major differences in the expenditure incurred on loans, which are expected to be of negligible importance in Northumberland in 1980–1, whereas they account for 46 per cent of the total economic development budget of Cumbria in the same year. Alternatively expressed, the population of Northumberland will pay 12p per head, whereas those in Cumbria will pay £1.65.

Expenditure by local authorities on economic development is, however, relatively small compared to that of central government. For example, in Tyne and Wear between April 1977 and December 1979 expenditure by the local authorities on loans for land, buildings, plant and machinery totalled £3.9m. During that same period firms in the county received £23m. of Regional Development Grants and £9m. of Regional Selective Assistance.

**TABLE 9.3   Expenditure by local authorities on economic development by county, 1979–80 and 1980–1**

| | Cumbria | | Cleveland | | Durham | | Northumberland | | Tyne and Wear | |
|---|---|---|---|---|---|---|---|---|---|---|
| | 1979–80 % | 1980–1 % | 1979–80 % | 1980–1 % | 1979–80 % | 1980–1 % | 1979–80 % | 1980–1 % | 1979–80 % | 1980–1 % |
| Promotion | 14 | 4 | 8 | 11 | 2 | 5 | 7 | 9 | 7 | 8 |
| Acquisition of Land | 0 | 2 | 28 | 12 | 41 | 0 | 4 | 16 | 18 | 9 |
| Servicing of Land | 56 | 31 | 40 | 48 | 29 | 16 | 24 | 26 | 25 | 29 |
| Factories | 14 | 17 | 19 | 23 | 23 | 62 | 56 | 45 | 40 | 35 |
| Loans | 16 | 46 | 5 | 6 | 5 | 17 | 9 | 4 | 10 | 19 |
| TOTAL | 100 | 100 | 100 | 100 | 100 | 100 | 100 | 100 | 100 | 100 |
| EXPENDITURE PER HEAD (1980 prices) | £1.36 | £3.58 | £3.18 | £3.14 | £3.39 | £5.70 | £3.99 | £3.32 | £5.94 | £5.94 |

Note: Expenditure per head figures exclude population from those districts where returns were not made.

The discrepancy was even more marked in Cleveland where Regional Development Grant payments over the two-year period 1975–6 to 1977–8 totalled £269.5m., whereas total local authority expenditure was under £3m.


## Evaluation: some general comments

Local authorities have, as we have seen, a number of policies available to them to stimulate economic activity in their area. To assess the success of individual policies, and to derive priorities for expenditure, several different perspectives may be relevant.

The most obvious is that of the local authority itself, acting on behalf of the ratepayers of the area. It might be assumed that the intention of the authority is to either create new jobs in its locality, or to retain those jobs which might have been lost, either through transfer elsewhere, or through the closure of establishments. However, even this simple statement raises problems. Many local authorities, for example, may be more interested in reducing unemployment through the creation of jobs than, for example, by encouraging migration. In addition, there is no consistent relationship between the number of jobs created in a locality and changes in the local rates of employment. This will depend upon factors such as the number of male and female jobs to be created, whether they are full- or part-time jobs, whether they are created by large or small firms, whether they are skilled or unskilled and the travel-to-work patterns. If a high proportion of the jobs are part-time and for women, they are more likely to be filled by women who had not been registered as unemployed, and so the impact upon the published rates of unemployment will be negligible.

The impact which the jobs created for males have on local rates of unemployment will depend upon travel-to-work patterns, effect on out-migration patterns and upon the number of jobs to be filled by key workers. Let us assume, as in Figure 9.1, that hypothetically a new factory is to be located in area $X$ and it will create 1000 new jobs, 700 of which are for males, 100 are for full-time females and 200 for part-time females. From the diagram, for the variety of reasons shown, the number of individuals removed from the local register of unemployed is hypothesised to be only 325 despite the creation of 1000 jobs locally, and is chosen because it corresponds

**FIGURE 9.1    Job creation and unemployment: an illustration**

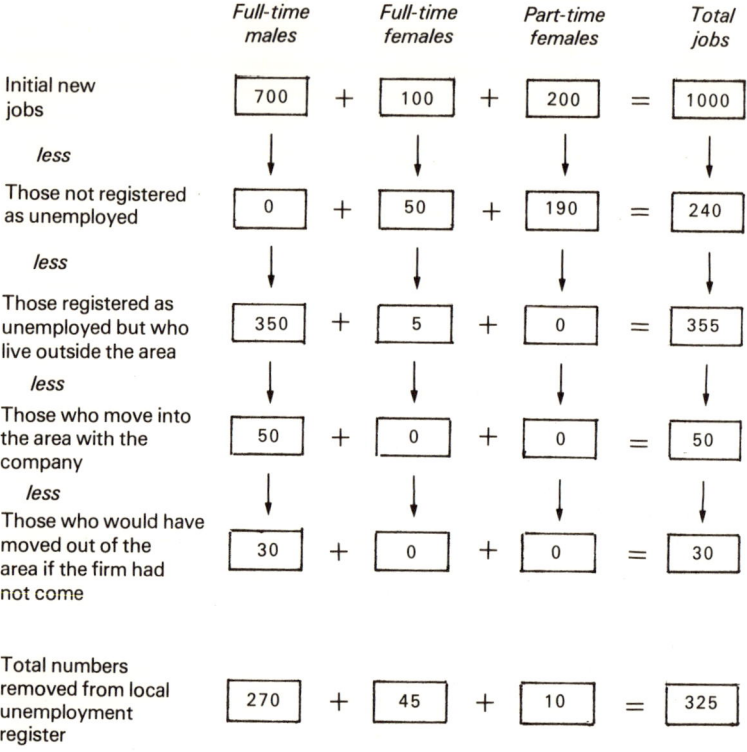

| | Full-time males | | Full-time females | | Part-time females | | Total jobs |
|---|---|---|---|---|---|---|---|
| Initial new jobs | 700 | + | 100 | + | 200 | = | 1000 |
| *less* | ↓ | | ↓ | | ↓ | | ↓ |
| Those not registered as unemployed | 0 | + | 50 | + | 190 | = | 240 |
| *less* | ↓ | | ↓ | | ↓ | | ↓ |
| Those registered as unemployed but who live outside the area | 350 | + | 5 | + | 0 | = | 355 |
| *less* | ↓ | | ↓ | | ↓ | | ↓ |
| Those who move into the area with the company | 50 | + | 0 | + | 0 | = | 50 |
| *less* | ↓ | | ↓ | | ↓ | | ↓ |
| Those who would have moved out of the area if the firm had not come | 30 | + | 0 | + | 0 | = | 30 |
| Total numbers removed from local unemployment register | 270 | + | 45 | + | 10 | = | 325 |

with estimates which have been made of the effectiveness of regional policy in Britain in the 1970s.[5]

The implications for policies of this asymmetry at local level of employment and unemployment are considerable. For example, a local authority whose ratepayers were able to travel easily into another, might be tempted to minimise its own expenditure on industrial development knowing that its fortunes are determined by its neighbours' expenditure, and that its residents cannot be excluded from the benefits of its neighbours' job-creating activities. This may be relevant in the case of outer metropolitan districts who would choose to exclude industry from their locality for aesthetic and environmental reasons, yet who wish to ensure their residents retain suitable job opportunities. Problems arise, of course, since it is often the authorities in the inner areas which have the highest local rates of unemployment, yet also have a labour force least able to compete for the jobs which are created.[6]

The local authority may also be concerned that the types of jobs which it creates should be capable of being filled, directly or indirectly, by those currently unemployed of which a dominant proportion are unskilled. A study of 301 firms new to Cleveland between 1971 and 1978 showed the largest five employers provided 23 per cent of all the skilled jobs in the sample, 35 per cent of the semi-skilled, but 69 per cent of the unskilled jobs.[7] This suggests that if new firms are to make an impact upon unemployment of unskilled workers, the area has to attract large employers rather than pursue currently fashionable policies of stimulating indigenous growth of small firms, since this type of firm does not employ the type of labour which is available.

Let us, however, assume that a decision is reached that the local authority is unconcerned about the impact upon local rates of unemployment. Instead, its avowed intention is purely to create new jobs of whatever type in its locality. To identify the real effect of economic initiatives by the local authority the analyst must be able to postulate the effect on new job creation, without the initiative – i.e. the 'policy-off' effect. The 1000-job factory described above might well have come to area *X*, irrespective of the actions of the local authority, central government or any other agency in providing loans/grants, sites/premises, etc. An estimate, therefore, has to be made of the number of jobs which would have been created if no incentives had existed.

This problem is identical to that encountered in assessing regional policy. Here, a period when policy was virtually non-existent is chosen as the policy-off period, and the expected numbers of jobs created had such conditions continued, holding industrial structure and demand pressure constant, is compared with the actual number of jobs created when policies are operative. Since different weapons are used with different intensities during the 'policy-on' period it is also possible to identify the relative effectiveness of each weapon.

The sophisticated testing which is possible for examining the effect of regional policy is not available to those interested in local authority initiatives, although the principles underlying such an evaluation remain the same. Public expenditure on local initiatives is, in Northern England as we have seen, about 2 per cent of expenditure on Regional Assistance, so it is correspondingly more difficult to isolate its effect. Second, local authority policy has been in operation for a much shorter period so any effects will be very recent.

In addition, local authority expenditure policies cannot be examined solely from the viewpoint of the authority itself, since there are regional and national implications of authorities becoming involved in these activities. For example, local authority activity in creating industrial improvement areas, or giving grants to new firms, may mean that authority *A* increases the number of jobs created in its area but these jobs may not be a net creation to the national economy, being merely diverted from an authority offering no such grant. Central government has therefore to evaluate the extent to which initiatives create net new jobs and the extent to which they merely divert jobs. Central government also has to determine the extent to which public investment in, for example, the provision of sites and premises, makes a private market unworkable. The extent to which shortage of starter premises, for example, has acted as a constraint on the birth rate of new firms in Britain is currently a lively issue of debate. It is suggested that because the management costs of small premises are higher than for medium and large-sized premises, the private sector has, with certain noted exceptions, avoided this type of investment.[8] The public sector, and particularly local authorities, have felt this to be an area in which they have an advantage. It may be, however, that the demand for such premises is now so great that the private sector would have been prepared to construct and manage such premises had not public involvement at least partially satisfied that demand at a price below that which was 'economic' for the private sector.

It is a matter of concern to a government trying to reduce public expenditure, if local authorities are incurring expenditure which would be willingly undertaken by the private sector. This may be regarded as a classic case where private capital is being 'crowded out' by the public sector. Furthermore, it may be thought desirable for services to be provided by the private sector which has greater incentives for internal efficiency, ultimately through competition and the risk of going out of business. The local authority, on the other hand, has no such incentives. Indeed there is a considerable body of thought suggesting that public bureaucracies may exploit their position, not for the benefit of their ratepayers, but for the benefit of the staff employed in such bureaux.[9]

The difficulties of conducting a detailed financial appraisal of policies is often cited as a symptom of such activity. For example, it can be difficult to determine the extent to which local authority factory building is subsidised. Records of management expenses are rarely kept, and there seems little pressure from within the authority for such records. It is, therefore, unclear whether there would be opportunities for profitable investment by the private sector if public sector involvement were reduced.

The above evaluation problems both at a local and national level assume local authority incentives are designed solely to create employment, but in fact the authority may have other objectives. For example, it may build new premises in a specific location in order to relocate firms currently in areas close to residential dwellings. The authority may be concerned with redevelopment, or with general environmental improvement, so its function may be to improve the spatial distribution of existing jobs, rather than the creation of new jobs.

## The initiatives

In this section a review is undertaken of the relatively few studies of local economic initiatives in the North of England. No single study covers all initiatives, including those undertaken by regional and *ad hoc* public agencies, although all economic initiatives taken within the metropolitan county of Tyne and Wear by the local authorities have been analysed. For ease of exposition, therefore, each of the initiatives listed in Table 9.1, i.e. industrial promotion, land acquisition and servicing, factory construction and loans/grants will be discussed separately.

### Industrial promotion

Industrial promotion in a local authority may take several forms. A number of authorities have a budget to cover the costs of placing advertisements in national newspapers and trade journals designed to encourage industrialists to locate in their area. A variety of approaches are used. Some stress the good features of the area, such as communications, labour relations, availability of skills, etc. Others list the firms that have recently come to the area, often with either quotations from senior personnel on their experience, or an indication of the growth of the company, etc.

A second aspect of industrial promotion is the 'mail-shot'. Here the local agency identifies a sample of firms whom it feels may be receptive to information about sites in the agency's area. Such firms may be selected because their industry shows growth potential, or because the firm is likely to find attractive the skills of unemployed labour in the area. These firms would receive information about the area with an indication that a council officer would be prepared to discuss relocation. Some authorities also isolate specific towns which have low rates of unemployment, and where firms are known to have difficulty recruiting labour. The authorities circularise firms inviting them to a lunch at which relocation can be discussed.

Most promotional effort is directed towards established firms, encouraging them to expand in the agency's area and, in times when such expansion might have been constrained by shortage-of-labour pressures in the prosperous areas, it was more likely to be in both the regional and national interest for it to take place in an assisted area. It is less clear whether relocation policies (and hence advertising/industrial promotion expenditure) are in the national interest, although they clearly remain in the regional interest, when development in many of the 'prosperous' areas is not constrained by shortages of labour and/or premises. The decline in economic activity in Britain since the mid-1970s has resulted in fewer firms considering expansion, but it has also coincided with an intensification of local authority activity as was seen in Table 9.1. Hence there are now more authorities with increased budgets chasing fewer firms.

There are two separate problems associated with industrial promotion. The first concerns the internal efficiency of the effort, i.e. how can the authority/agency be satisfied that it is having the maximum impact; and the second is whether it is an efficient use of resources, on a national basis, to have a large number of agencies attempting to encourage the relocation of plants.

The best-known (and certainly the most contentious) study of the performance of industrial promotion agencies in Northern England was conducted by Coopers and Lybrand.[10] Their approach was to discuss the aims and objectives of the agency with its executives and then to conduct investigations into recent enquiries from prospective investors. Finally, the views of other relevant parties on the performance of the agency were obtained. Since the investigations were of agencies at the regional level, local authorities were the prime source of subjective opinions on agency performance. Coopers and Lybrand were satisfied with the performance of the Department of Industry, the new towns of Peterlee/Aycliffe and of Washington, but were critical of the North of England Development Council. The latter, they felt, produced an insufficient number of enquiries for the expenditure incurred, and these enquiries subsequently resulted in an insufficient number of new establishments in the region. These conclusions were subsequently publicly challenged by NEDC and the debate which took place illustrates the difficulties of conducting satisfactory evaluations on this topic.

Coopers and Lybrand recognised that the prime function of a regional agency such as NEDC is to create interest in the region among potential industrialists. The consultants also recognised that the ultimate responsibility for 'converting' that interest into actual locations depends upon the performance of both the local authorities, the organs of central government and, in the case of major overseas locations, even the European Commission. The 'conversion' of enquiries must therefore be a team effort, with poor performance by one part of that team risking the loss of a relocation.

The consultants also recognised that, although NEDC might create interest amongst potential industrialists, this need not be manifest by enquiries directed through NEDC. The NEDC argued that its major function was to change the image of the North held by Southern England and overseas industrialists. Hence, although NEDC may have been instrumental in influencing opinion, the industrialists might legitimately make a relocation enquiry through another agency such as the Department of Industry, or even directly to a local authority.

Although Coopers and Lybrand recognised these points, they were ignored in the quantitative evaluation. Here the consultants estimated three coefficients in their assessment of NEDC:

1. The ratio between industrial enquiries and visits to the region was 3:1.
2. The ratio between visits to the region and decisions to invest was 20:1.
3. Each project which comes to the region will create, on average, fifty jobs.

Using these assumptions, and knowing first, that in one year 114 enquiries were generated and second, the total expenditure by the NEDC, the consultants were able to derive a cost per job figure of around £4600. This they felt to be high.

Even if the basic approach was valid, a number of criticisms may be made of its use. The first is that definitions of what constitutes an enquiry differ from one agency to another. This is irrelevant if the criterion for success is number of jobs created, but if the criterion is generation of enquiries then it becomes of paramount importance. If the criterion is that of the creation of new jobs there are problems first, with the nature of enquiries converted and second, over the build-up of employment.

In the case of a number of agencies the conversion of one major enquiry in one year, and not in another, which in itself may be a matter of luck or issues outside the control of the agency, or of expenditure and effort incurred several years previously, will significantly alter the implied efficiency of the agency, because the total number of conversions in each year is so small. In no way, therefore, can the coefficients used by Coopers and Lybrand be regarded as being invariant from year to year. In principle what is needed is an examination of agency performance over a number of years, but this in turn raises the difficulty that economic conditions change since it will be easier to recruit firms during prosperous times. Only if a group of agencies were evaluated, on identically the same bases over the same time period, could such problems be overcome. Since the reputation with industrialists of areas also changes for reasons outside the agency's control, due to bad publicity about strikes, closures, crime, etc., even this approach would need careful interpretation.

The number of jobs created by a new establishment are also difficult to determine in advance. It has been estimated during the 1970s that new plants establishing in assisted areas took up to seven years to reach their peak employment,[11] so that evaluation risks underestimating total impact. On the other hand, it is characteristic of industrialists (at least when discussing the matter with public agencies!) to overestimate the number of jobs which they intend to create. Also it is likely that a proportion of those new establishments attracted into the area will close fairly shortly after their arrival.

The present author took these criticisms into account in an examination of the industrial enquiries received by Cleveland County Council[12] and thus offered no estimates of the expenditure per job created, by the authority. Instead, all industrial enquiries received by Cleveland County Council in 1973 and 1976 were followed up and it was found that about 10 per cent of all firms, including those enquiring through other organisations such as the Department of Industry, NEDC, etc., had by 1979 located in the county or were about to locate. It was also found that the vast majority of firms making enquiries had by 1979 not moved anywhere, either because of the abandonment of expansion plans or because they were no longer in business. In fact, approximately half of the firms who made enquiries and subsequently moved, eventually located in Cleveland. This raises the problem of the appropriate index by which to judge the effectiveness of agencies. To examine only the total number of jobs created (whether or not this then becomes the denominator to determine a cost per job figure) means that the figures will vary according to the number of firms considering moving, which in turn will vary with the current and expected level of economic activity in the national economy. It is then relative efficiency that is important, since the agency cannot affect the overall economic climate; it can merely attempt to increase its market share at the expense of other agencies, and other areas.

Evaluation of the internal efficiency of agencies in industrial promotion should therefore be undertaken according to two indices over time. The first is the simple counting of the numbers of enquiries received, where the definition of an enquiry remains unchanged. This takes account of the role of the agency which sees itself as a promotional body, but which has relatively little control over the conversion of these enquiries. Nevertheless, the ultimate purpose even of a promotional agency is to create jobs locally. It should be measured (and compared) on the basis of its ability, together with other agencies in the team, to convert these enquiries into jobs. The formula for such an evaluation is shown in Equation (1).

---

**Equation (1)**

$$H = \frac{\sum\limits_{i}^{K} E_i J_i}{\sum\limits_{i}^{K} E_i J_i + \sum\limits_{j}^{L} E_j J_j}$$

$H$   = performance index
$E_i$  = $i$th enquiry which located in area
$J_i$  = Number of jobs associated with enquiry $i$
$K$   = Number of enquiries locating in area
$E_j$  = $j$th enquiry which located outside the area
$J_j$  = Number of jobs associated with enquiry $j$
$L$   = Number of enquiries subsequently located outside area

---

Even this index has one major fault. Firms who would have chosen to locate in area $X$ and nowhere else, but because of the agency abandoned their plans, would not be identified in such a measure. Apart from such cases the index offers probably the most satisfactory measure of the internal efficiency of agencies.

Whether agencies, in current economic conditions, operate in the national interest remains unclear. It seems likely that those agencies concerned with obtaining the location in Britain of overseas firms may be judged purely in terms of their internal efficiency unless there is evidence that several British agencies are competing with each other for the same firm, which has decided to locate in Britain. In most cases, however, the agency will be competing with overseas countries for such firms.

For firms moving from one part of Britain to another the matter is more difficult, but in essence the analyst must determine the level and nature of movement which would have been undertaken without the current level of agency involvement, i.e. the policy off. This then has to be compared with the nature and level of current movement for the expenditure incurred.

*Loans and Grants*

Several local authorities in Northern England give loans and grants but the practice is most extensive in the metropolitan county of Tyne and Wear. The Tyne & Wear Act 1976 gave formal powers to that authority to provide loans for:

1. the purchase, leasing, preparation or improvement of a site for industrial purposes;
2. the provision, extension or improvement of industrial buildings or of facilities and services on which an industrial use depends;
3. the purchase of plant, machinery or equipment for use in industrial buildings.

Powers for the provision, both of loans and grants, were available under Acts of the pre-1974 counties of Durham and Northumberland, but the extent to which these powers have been used varied over time and between the two authorites. Tyne and Wear County Council have undertaken an evaluation of the success of these initiatives as part of the Structure Plan appraisal. They examined firms that received loans from the authorities and identified the net change in employment between receipt of the loan and the evaluation. This was then compared with the average firm in that industry during the same period. This may be expressed as in Equation (2).

---

### Equation (2)

$$J = \sum_i \sum_j E_j^i - E^i$$

where $J$ = Total number of net new jobs created
$E_j^i$ = Change in employment of the $j$th firm in industry $i$
$E^i$ = Change in employment of average firm in industry $i$

---

This procedure is unsatisfactory for several reasons. The first and most important is that no attempt is made to determine whether the firm might have obtained the loan from elsewhere, if the local authority had been unwilling/unable to provide finance. The true alternative or 'policy off' is not incorporated. Second, to take account only of the industry of the firm is not a satisfactory method for holding all other variables constant. For example, firms borrowing from the local authority for the purchase of plant and machinery are more likely to be expanding than contracting, and so comparisons with the 'average' of all firms in a given industry will tend to overstate the impact of the loan. Third, the relatively few firms receiving loans and grants means that the results are extremely sensitive to the performance of a few firms.

An alternative to this procedure is to ask the firms who received assistance whether they thought it significantly contributed to their growth, paralleling this by a statistical study examining employment change in those firms which received aid. This approach was adopted in a study by the Inner City Employment Project team of the Town and Country Planning Department, Newcastle University, of grants/loans distributed by Tyne and Wear County Council to firms in their inner city areas. It found that the 147 firms which received aid had increased their employment by 81 per cent or 967 jobs since the assistance was provided. The biggest increase took place in firms in local authority advance factories, which had also received financial assistance. These impressive figures contrast with the replies of industrialists to questions regarding the importance of aid, in which the majority felt it was relatively unimportant to the development of their firm. Of the 967 jobs created, only 182 were jobs which in the opinion of the owner/manager of the firm would not have been created without aid from the local authority.

This discrepancy between the replies of industrialists on the role of the loans and their apparent 'statistical' effect is easily explained. The statistical procedures by which the effect of the loan is determined are inadequate for the same reasons as the County Council appraisal, yet it is also clearly inappropriate to rely solely upon the responses of the industrialist who may perceive it to be in his own interests not to answer the question truthfully. For example, an industrialist may choose to view the growth of the firm as being attributable to his/her own initiative and enterprise, rather than being dependent upon local authority 'hand-outs'.

To resolve these difficulties, at least in part, Willis and Whisker have provided a more complete taxonomy for assessing the effectiveness of local authority aid.[13] They note that most local authority assistance has been directed towards subsidising capital expenditure rather than reducing the costs of employing labour, even though an increased use of labour is the object of policy. Subsidising capital will result in the cost of capital to the firm falling, relative to the price of labour, and induce the firm to use more capital and less labour (the substitution effect). If, however, this increases the efficiency of the firm, relative to that of its competitors, it may be able to reduce prices and increase output. The production of this extra output will require more inputs of both capital and labour (the output effect). If, and only if, the output effect outweighs the substitution effect will more labour be employed.

Willis and Whisker therefore propose to construct for each firm the parameters of a production function and then examine, in aggregate, the effect of a subsidy on capital expenditure. While this approach has some underlying rigour the practical difficulties are considerable. There is first the problem of choosing an appropriate production function. Willis and Whisker propose to use a constant elasticity of substitution (CES) function but other forms may be equally valid. All production functions, however, encounter difficulties with measuring the stock of capital at a point in time since machines, buildings, etc., will be of a variety of vintages and have values to the firm which are not accurately reflected either in resale or in scrap value. Finally there is, as always, the problem of data. A number of firms will not be able to provide usable data either because of differences in accounting practice or, in the case of multi-plant firms, because data are not available in a sufficiently disaggregated form. These factors, together with difficulties of handling the problems of technical change, make the merits of this approach to evaluation difficult to assess.

If, however, the above difficulties could be overcome it would be possible to estimate, both for each firm, and for all firms in total, the effect of a reduction in the price of capital and also determine whether the output effect exceeded the substitution effect in aggregate. At the individual firm level it would be possible to identify the types of firms where the output effect exceeded the substitution effect, so that aid could be directed more effectively.

*Factory construction*

Several studies of the problems facing employers in inner city areas have pointed to the poor quality of premises which they occupy.[14] In some cases this is due to poor layout, or to physical conditions, but primarily to the absence of any room for expansion. Even in less congested areas the absence of small premises, which can be used by those starting in business for the first time, has been cited as a major contraint on the British economy's ability to regenerate itself through a high rate of new firm formation.[15]

In the years immediately following local government reorganisation, several local authorities in the North embarked upon factory building programmes, without a clear understanding of the 'market gap' they were endeavouring to fill. Several developments, however, made them reduce the variety of unit sizes under construction. The first was the pressures from central government for controlling public spending, which affected all authorities. The second was the increased interest in the small firm taken by governments of both parties. The small firm, in the middle 1970s, had shaken off the stigma of being associated with technological backwardness and weak management. It was seen that despite the assistance given to large corporations, it was the small firms, in manufacturing, which were producing an increased proportion of total output and employment. The decline in the contribution to total output and total employment made by small manufacturing firms, which had continued for thirty years,[16] had been reversed and it was hoped that the small-firms sector could increase employment. It became clear that despite the increased importance of small firms, and the greater interest by individuals in starting their own businesses (partly itself due to the historically high levels of unemployment) there appeared to be a shortage of appropriate premises. The emergence of the inner city as a clearly identified problem area,[17] and the recognition that here small-firms policies were particularly relevant, meant that large metropolitan authorities came under pressure to fill what was generally perceived as a market gap. Authorities faced with a budget constraint shifted resources away from providing a variety of sized units towards concentrating almost exclusively on small units.[18]

The emphasis upon provision of small units in Tyne and Wear is shown in Table 9.4 which illustrates the difference between the size

**TABLE 9.4   Provision of advance factories by local authorities and the English Industrial Estates Corporation in Tyne and Wear 1976–9**

| | | Size of unit ('000 sq. ft) | | | | |
|---|---|---|---|---|---|---|
| *EIEC* | | *0–5* | *5–10* | *10–20* | *20+* | *Total* |
| Floor space ('000 sq. ft) | | 245 | 148 | 480 | 175 | 1,048 |
| Units (No) | | 92 | 18 | 30 | 7 | 147 |
| *Local authorities* | *0–3* | *3–5* | *5–10* | *10–20* | *20+* | *Total* |
| Floor space ('000 sq. ft) | 301 | 69 | 65 | 0 | 0 | 435 |
| Units (No) | 162 | 17 | 8 | 0 | 0 | 187 |

of units provided by the English Industrial Estates Corporation (as it was known prior to the 1980 Industry Act) and the local authority. The former has over 62 per cent of its total floor space in units of over 10 000 sq. ft. whereas no local authority has units of this size.

To evaluate the effectiveness of local authority involvement the issue is again one of deciding what would have happened in the absence of authorities providing these premises, and also to decide whether their involvement has, from an internal viewpoint, been efficient. Tyne and Wear showed that thirty-five nursery factory units had been built and let by the end of 1976 at a cost of £1.23m., with 139 new jobs created at an average cost of £8902 per job, but this cannot be regarded as the cost to local authorities of creating new jobs.[19] No attempt is made to determine whether the firms would have found alternative premises, and no attempt is made to determine whether the private sector would have found it worthwhile to construct such premises itself. The observation that the private sector had not, until that time, undertaken such projects, is frequently the justification for local authority action but, unless the private sector is ignorant of these opportunities, a more likely explanation is that despite the so-called 'shortages of starter premises' their price has not risen sufficiently to make them a good investment for the private sector. This, in turn, questions whether there is, in fact, a 'shortage'.

Tyne and Wear also assessed their expenditure on the acquisition and preparation of industrial land. They considered a total of 108 firms on ten industrial estates in a variety of locations and compared the increase in the number of jobs in each firm, from the time it had located on the industrial estate, with the performance of firms in that industry over the same period. The results derived for five industrial estates where cost data were available are shown in Table 9.5. It shows that it is possible for the number of additional jobs created to be negative, as in Gateshead. The total effect of the calculation was that for all the industrial estates taken together the cost per job created was £1065, although for areas outside the inner areas expenditure was only £415. These costs per job created were then compared to those of regional development policies, which were estimated at £21 000 by NRST.[20]

**TABLE 9.5   Job creation on industrial estates in Tyne and Wear**

| Estate | County division | Additional Jobs created | Cost (£) | | Cost per job (£) | |
|---|---|---|---|---|---|---|
| | | | Outturn | Nov. 1976 | Outturn | Nov 1976 |
| East | | | | | | |
| Gateshead | Inner | −51 | 202 989 | 567 804 | −3980 | −11 133 |
| Gosforth | Intermediate | +325 | 22 472 | 53 163 | +69 | +163 |
| Killingworth | | | | | | |
| (Stephenson) | Outer | +463 | 75 925 | 187 096 | +164 | +404 |
| Brunswick | Outer | +18 | 53 688 | 113 780 | +2983 | +6322 |
| Hetton-Lyons | Outer | +152 | 16 139 | 43 836 | +106 | +289 |

Note: To arrive at costs at November 1976 prices detailed information was obtained on expenditure year by year for each estate. For Hetton-Lyons, yearly expenditure was not available, so total expenditure is averaged out over the period 1960–72 (years during which firms have been known to have been moving on to the estate) and converted to 1976 prices.

The limitations of this analysis should be clear from our earlier comments. First, firms locating on industrial estates are not representative of the population of firms as a whole. They tend to be younger, more dynamic and more likely to increase in employment. Second, the derivation of a negative figure for Gateshead illustrates that the data cannot be true opportunity costs. Indeed this author finds it difficult to interpret such a measure. (Does it mean that expenditure was £11 133 for each job lost?) Third, the figures cannot be used to compare with those on Regional Development Grants (although this comparison was made) since a number of firms will have located on local authority trading estates and received Regional Assistance and because the data for regional grants is, in principle, closer to a concept of opportunity cost. Finally, and most importantly, the figures in no way estimate what would have happened to that firm in the absence of the initiative.

Analysis by ICEP attempts to overcome some of these problems by examining thirty firms in the inner area of Tyne and Wear that moved into an advance factory, but which received no financial aid from the Council. These firms increased their employment by approximately 105 per cent. Of sixty-eight firms that obtained both an advance factory and financial assistance the increase in employment was 211 per cent or 417 new jobs. The problem with such results, as we noted earlier, is that when firms were asked whether receipt of the local authority assistance had been a major factor in influencing their decision to expand, the majority said it was either unimportant, or of only minor importance. One is left with the choice of either believing the industrialist or of assessing the growth figures, neither of which are satisfactory, yet which are open to wholly different interpretations.

**Conclusion**

Although local initiatives designed to create private sector jobs are on a much smaller scale than those of central government, they represent one of the few areas of local authority budgets which is currently being increased. It is therefore of great importance that elected members should be satisfied that there are procedures for determining whether expenditure is being incurred to good effect. The evidence from this survey of Northern England is not promising. It suggests that only a few local authorities, or other public agencies involved in job creation, conduct detailed appraisals of the effectiveness of their operations. Without such appraisals, however, it is not possible to determine whether additional resources should be directed towards advertising in the hope of attracting new large establishments to the area, towards assisting small indigenous firms through loans or grants, or whether policies to improve land or construct factories are likely to be more effective. It is also not possible to evaluate whether the total budgets should be increased or decreased. This is due partly to difficulties of deciding whether it is the creation of new jobs or the reduction in the levels of unemployment which are relevant, and this may explain the wide variations in the proportions of total expenditure devoted to individual initiatives by each county.

Those studies of the effectiveness of local initiatives which have been undertaken suffer from several difficulties. Some were shown to be statistically inadequate because they were based on an insufficient number of cases. The major problem, however, is that few studies have satisfactorily grappled with assessing what would have happened in the absence of an initiative by the authority. Would, for example, the much commented upon shortage of premises for small firms have resulted in an increase in their price, thus making them attractive for construction by the private sector? Would the private sector have seized this opportunity? Would firm *i* have been seriously affected if agency *j* had not existed to provide it with advice, funding, etc. – or does the existence of funding from agency *j* merely crowd out private sector financial institutions?

To conduct a satisfactory analysis the objectives of the agency/local authority have to be clearly specified, especially if the authority sees itself as having a social function in attempting to stimulate investment and employment. An estimate of the 'policy-off' effect must be made, and comprehensive accounting of the cost of initiatives should be available. Perhaps then each local authority may be able to evaluate the effectiveness of its expenditure on economic development, and central government will be able to assess whether such expenditure is in the national interest.

## References

1.  J. D. McCallum, 'The Development of British Regional Policy', in D. McLennan and J. Parr (eds), *Regional Policy: Past Experience and New Directions* (Martin Robertson, 1979).
2.  Northern Region Strategy Team, *Strategic Plan for the Northern Region: Economic Development Policies,* vol. 2 (Newcastle-upon-Tyne, 1977). It should be noted that NRST reviewed Northern England, i.e. including Cumbria, rather than North East England.
3.  D. J. Storey, 'Do Small Firms Get Too Much Advice?', *The Bankers' Magazine,* March 1981, pp. 30–4.
4.  For example, M. M. Camina, 'Local Authorities and the Attraction of Industry', *Progress in Planning,* 3 (2) (Pergamon Press, 1974); J. F. F. Robinson, 'Local Authority Economic Initiatives: a Review',

*CES Occasional Papers,* no. 10, (London: CES, 1979); M. Boddy and S. Barrett, *Local Government and the Industrial Development Process,* Working Paper 6 (Bristol: School for Advanced Urban Studies, 1979).

5.  B. Moore, J. Rhodes and P. Tyler, 'The Impact of Regional Policy in the 1970s', *CES Review,* no. 1, 1979, pp. 67–77.
6.  C. Howick and A. Key, 'Tower Hamlets: an Inner City Profile', *CES Policy Series,* No. 9, 1979; J. F. F. Robinson, 'Trends in Employment, Labour Supply and Unemployment in Cleveland', *CES Working Note WN 535,* 1978.
7.  D. J. Storey, *Entrepreneurship and the New Firm* (Croom Helm, 1982).
8.  Coopers & Lybrand with Drivas Jones, *Provision of Small Industrial Premises* (Department of Industry, Small Firms Division, 1980).
9.  W. A. Niskanen, *Bureaucracy and Representative Government* (Aldine Press, 1971); W. Orzechowski, 'Economic Models of Bureaucracy', in T. E. Borcheding (ed.), *Budgets and Bureaucrats: the Sources of Government Growth* (Duke University Press, 1977); D. J. Storey, 'The Economics of Bureaux: the Case of the London Boroughs 1970–1976', *Applied Economics,* 12, 1980, pp. 223–34.
10.  Coopers & Lybrand Associates, *Review of Industrial Promotion Organisations* (Department of Industry, 1979).
11.  B. Moore and J. Rhodes, 'Evaluating the Effect of British Regional Economic Policy', *Economic Journal,* 83, 1973, pp. 87–110.
12.  D. J. Storey and J. F. F. Robinson, Local Authorities and the Attraction of Industry', *Local Government Studies,* vol. 7, no. 1, January–February 1981, 1981, pp. 21–37.
13.  K. Willis and P. Whisker, 'Economic Assessment of Local Authority Aid to Industry', *Planning Outlook,* 23 (2), 1981, pp. 62–6.
14.  A. McIntosh and V. Keddie, *Industry and Employment in the Inner City* (London: IFF Research Ltd and Department of the Environment Inner Cities Directorate, 1979); N. Falk, 'Finding a Place for Small Enterprise in the Inner City', in A. Evans and D. Eversley (eds), *The Inner City: Employment and Industry* (Heinemann, 1980) pp. 367–88.
15.  Coopers & Lybrand, *Review of Industrial Promotion Organisations.*
16.  *Report of the Committee of Inquiry into Small Firms,* Cmnd 4811 (HMSO, 1971).
17.  *Policy for the Inner Cities,* Cmnd 6845 (HMSO, 1977).
18.  It is not being suggested that small firms policies *are* relevant to the inner cities, but that the White Paper perceived them to be.
19.  Tyne and Wear County Structure Plan, *Report of Survey: Background Note No. 2: Economy* (Newcastle-upon-Tyne: Tyne and Wear Planning Department, 1979).
20.  Northern Region Strategy Team, *Strategic Plan for the Northern Region.*

# IV  CONCLUSIONS

# 10 The Significance of Urban Economic Development Programmes

KEN YOUNG and CHARLIE MASON

The restructuring of advanced industrial societies is producing dramatic spatial consequences in the de-industrialisation of cities and the industrialisation of fringe and rural areas. Britain, of all the European nations, has experienced this process the most acutely, although not on a scale comparable with the United States.[1] Our foremost concern in this book is not, however, with the de-industrialisation process itself, nor with the ways in which it makes itself felt at the urban level. Rather, our focus is on the responses of city governments to its least tolerable consequences. Among these are a declining fiscal base, rising welfare costs, physical obsolescence and dereliction, and the loss of industrial activity leading to high levels of unemployment in the manufacturing sector.

Of all the aspects of change, falling manufacturing employment provides the greatest single stimulus to intervention in the urban economy. As unemployment has slipped from its pre-eminent place on the national policy agenda in favour of the control of inflation it has, paradoxically, become one of the foremost concerns of local government. This 'mismatch' of concern generates a conflict of interest between central and local government, a tension which has been mentioned by several of our contributors.[2]

The formulation by local authorities of programmes for economic development is in itself no novelty. Many of the activities in which they engage are long established, despite the rhetoric of innovation in which they are often cloaked. As a group, we have tried to address the issue of how far these programmes for urban

213

economic development have brought about or arisen from changing relationships between and within governmental agencies, and between the public and the private sectors. Our overall concern has been with these changes and their consequences; in short, with the operations and role of local government in its attempts to manage the mixed economy of the city.

We want in this last chapter to refocus attention on the underlying and unstated themes which link together the several contributions within this broad overall concern. These themes emerge from our reading of the chapters as a set of questions. First, are economic development programmes intended to serve welfare or the market? Second, are the economic development activities of local government really substantive or merely symbolic? Third, are not all interventions in the urban economy swimming against the inexorable tide of metropolitan decline?

## Welfare v. the market?

The concern of national governments with economic issues has increasingly centred on questions of efficiency and competitiveness, to the extent that the welfare concerns of the 1944 White Paper on employment seem a dim memory. In their exhortations to local planning authorities successive governments have stressed the need to take local decisions in the light of national needs. The theme was notably expounded in the late 1970s in the Circular on local government and the industrial strategy and in the White Paper on the inner cities. The Circular currently in force is more explicit, as befits the climate of the early 1980s; it proclaims that 'the planning system should play a helpful part in rebuilding the economy' and should not obstruct 'the economic regeneration of the country'.[3]

Circular 22/80 is no more than the most recent and most explicit token of the national preoccupation with efficiency and competitiveness. Since the 1960s the restructuring of key industries has been actively promoted by government regardless of its spatial consequences. It is now becoming clear that the older cities have borne the brunt of restructuring and have had to meet – in both financial and human terms – the welfare costs of market goals.[4] Here surely is an ineradicable conflict of interest. Few would dispute the propriety of a national-level concern with macro-level competitiveness. Its corollary is, however, that the local interest in welfare should aim to maintain employment and income and legitimately seek to retard the process of change, if only in the hope of buying time in which to ease the transition. Even this modest local aim begs the question of transition *to what*? The rhetoric of post-industrialism paints a picture of an urban future in the tertiary, quaternary and quinary sectors, reflecting the macro-level shifts in the sectoral structure of the economy.[5] It should be clear that for most of the older industrial cities the prospect of so neat a substitution is exceedingly dim. It is a dangerous temptation to confuse macro processes with micro, and local problems with national needs.

Local authorities understandably decline to define their local problems in terms of national economic imperatives. They are naturally more sensitive to the pressures which they experience directly: to serve the welfare of their local people by stemming employment decline; to secure the fiscal base and maximise their resources; and to reduce the physical and psychological blight of industrial dereliction. The almost universal justification of such measures as are taken – whether to build small factory estates or to promote the investment image of a locality – is the relief, directly or indirectly, of unemployment. Welfare is apparently the foremost concern.

It is not surprising that the welfare consequences of urban economic decline should loom so large at the present time. Disadvantaged groups – the school leaver, the unskilled, the long-term unemployed, the redundant worker – are unable to compete in the labour market. Ethnic minorities and women, who themselves may belong to one or more of these categories, may suffer additional discrimination against their employment. At the same time, the quality of employment, the conditions of employment and the returns to employment are deteriorating.

Local authorities as 'need-meeting' agencies might be expected to give priority to tackling these consequences of restructuring and recession. Yet at the same time, due to the parallel process of decline in the urban fiscal base and new and more stringent controls on local expenditure, their ability to tackle welfare problems of this magnitude is severely eroded.[6] Nor is this all. Local authorities claim to provide no more than a welfare net of the coarsest kind.

The ultimate responsibility for the maintenance of family income lies not with them but with the national system of social security. Moreover (and for our purposes more important) a closer look at local authority programmes for employment reveals that they are *not* characteristically targeted on the needs of the most vulnerable groups. Rather, it seems, a concern for employment justifies interventions that serve welfare less directly than the needs of the market itself. Welfare concerns are on this view a symbolic rather than a substantive aspect of local economic development programmes.

**Symbol or substance?**

The intelligent citizen has long been aware that a large part of governmental activity is symbolic rather than substantive. The basic distinction is familiar to those who have never encountered Walter Bagehot, Georges Sorel, Graham Wallas or Murray Edelman. It would, however, be a gross mistake to assume that because local economic development programmes are dignified by appeals to welfare symbolism, they necessarily conceal the workings of an 'efficient' concern with market effectiveness. Rather, the very actions themselves may be symbolic, and express no more than a felt need to act and to be seen to be acting.

Faced with their immediate economic crises, local policy-makers respond to the imperative to act. The most potent argument in a novel setting is 'well, we must do something'.[7] Policy statements, new machinery and the allocation of fresh resources are almost self-justifying when they are decided upon in a climate of acute and rising public concern. There is little room for the iconoclast who asks for a firmer rationale than the comfort of 'doing something'. There are two evident problems in self-justified action. The first is that action tends to run far ahead of analysis. The second is that the political costs of monitoring and evaluating the effects of action may be seen as unacceptably high.

As the various contributors have shown, there is no shortage of action in this field and in some areas there is considerable expenditure on economic development programmes. Both have evidently increased over time, if from a rather higher initial base than is commonly supposed. There is far less evidence of this activity being directed towards clearly established problems in the local economy. Research and intelligence tends to follow action rather than to lead it. As such, it tends to be used descriptively, to quantify the problem to which policy is already addressed (and so to legitimate the policy) rather than analytically, to identify the problems to which policy might be addressed.

Local economic policies are not peculiar in this regard. Most attempts to define 'the natural history of social problems' emphasise the political and non-rational elements in the problem definition/intelligence/action relationships.[8] Particularly in areas where urgent solutions to perceived problems are sought, action comes first and research is used to underscore it. This is not a role that research and intelligence units welcome. On the other hand, their own involvement in economic affairs will sometimes prove an embarrassment as they seek to redefine the issues and pose new policy goals. Yet research and intelligence is often tangential to the main streams of policy determination, and some of the most professional and prolific research teams co-exist with executive units whose policies and practices are impervious to the counter-arguments of research. This disjuncture is perhaps especially evident where strong, freewheeling industrial development teams operate, perhaps recruited in part from the private sector.

Where there is a clear policy line it is likely to be maintained regardless of intelligence. Where there is not, research and intelligence personnel may have more opportunity to redefine the economic problem and contribute to a research-based strategy. It is, however, in just such circumstances that the gap between policy and action may be at its widest. Here we find policy waived and issues 'decided on their merits' – that is, in accordance with political and organisational power.

The second aspect of symbolic action is the deep-seated reluctance to monitor and assess the impact of economic policies. Monitoring is often dismissed as a costly and academic irrelevance. The stridency of the dismissal suggests a tacit recognition that many economic initiatives could not survive a rigorous monitoring exercise. It is still possible to encounter industrial development units who accept firms' projections of future employment growth, render financial assistance accordingly, and then provide an arithmetical justification of their activities in terms of impressively low estimates of the per capita costs of employment creation. The imperative not to monitor seems as powerful as the imperative to act, and in this respect local economic programmes share a sense of vulnerability with the far more stringently applied Department of Industry schemes.[9]

The precedence of symbol over substance also encourages policy-makers to turn a blind eye to the increasingly apparent overlap and competition of agencies and programmes. Any evaluation of the substantive impact of local schemes of assistance would have to take a wider view than the bilateral authority–firm relationship. It would have to take into account the whole pattern of financial assistance and the true opportunity–costs to the authority of any one decision to assist a firm. Such an assessment would be admittedly difficult. A major metropolitan area will possess a complex 'policy map' with possible variations in assisted area status being overlaid by variations in status under the Inner Urban Areas Act. There will be a scattering of Industrial Improvement Areas, of estates constructed by the county, the districts and the EIE, with perhaps an enterprise zone to further complicate the pattern of available assistance and place-specific costs.[10]

That firms may be able to play this network to maximum financial advantage is covertly recognised. The extent to which it occurs is impossible to assess, for the necessary confidentiality with which industrial assistance is handled provides a convenient barrier to cross-agency evaluation. It may not be too cynical to suggest that the widespread confusion and ignorance of industrialists is a stronger constraint on multiple funding than such arrangements for inter-agency co-ordination as presently exist.

Any serious attempt to articulate an economic strategy to support either welfare *or* the market and so transcend symbolic action would need to work through the multi-agency network. In so doing, it would doubtless tend towards closer scrutiny and tougher decisions on support for firms. Tougher decisions, however, imply a lower level or a slower rate of expenditure. One evident problem here is the felt need to avoid under-spend and so protect (for example) the industrial promotion budget. This is just one of the ways in which economic development programmes can become institutionalised to the extent that the symbolism of executive action takes precedence over substantive results.

## Swimming against the tide?

Even where research units chart the contours of local economic problems and industrial development officers have the expertise to assess firms' needs and growth potential, a lingering doubt remains as to the ultimate purpose of urban economic development initiatives. Most of the activities with which we have been concerned in this book are conceived in terms of, at best, regenerating and, at worst, maintaining the urban economy. What are their chances of success? There are probably few local economic policy-makers who are deaf to this question, but there are equally few who can face its implications. Most planning researchers and industrial development officers acknowledge the adverse trends in economic activity locally, nationally and even internationally. Yet their operating assumption is often a one-dimensional one, of a falling level of some desired quality – investment, employment or real income. The image is of a gradually lowering level in a static pool, the prime task being to contain the rate of leakage to an acceptable level.

The image of a receding tide better fits the contemporary experience of urban change. In broad terms, investment is relocating to urban fringe or non-urban locations in a dynamic and cumulative tide of urban de-industrialisation.[11] It is on some accounts a tide of change as powerful as that which produced the modern industrial city. It is against such a tide that urban economic programmes must swim. The overall assessment of the activities recounted in these essays is ultimately to be made against this backcloth of change, from which several factors in particular may be picked out.

One assumption of local policies for economic development is that they are applied to an industrial decision process which is itself locally based. This is less often true than is commonly supposed. The remarkable concentration of British industry, which accelerated during the late 1960s, bestows upon some large industrial cities the virtual status of a 'branch plant economy'.[12] The multi-plant national corporation and the multi-national have a significant (though not wholly determining) impact on urban economies. Historically, acquisitions and mergers have been followed by rationalisation and the contraction or closure of the less efficient plant, which, characteristically, is located in traditional urban areas.[13]

In so far as multi-plant corporations behave in this fashion they demonstrate their greater mobility and superior assessment of the relative costs of location. But all manufacturing firms face a similar pattern of locational advantages arrayed upon the spatial surface of economic organisation. The unfavourable shift in the costs and benefits of an urban location is almost universal.[14] Changes in transport technology make fringe locations more attractive. Modern production processes require spacious single-storey buildings. Labour costs, goods handling and site access problems accumulate in traditional urban locations. Latterly, Labour-controlled city councils have responded to the severity of the fiscal squeeze by increasing their rate levies, to the further deterioration of their locational attractiveness.[15]

Above all, it is the growing firms which have the strongest incentives to relocate, as they are the first to encounter the ceilings to growth that urban – and particularly inner urban – locations impose. In so doing, they effectively export growth potential and the prospects of rising incomes from the city to the fringe, or even to the shire county.[16]

Cities have experienced this cycle of firm creation, growth, move and further growth since the beginning of the industrial revolution. But two factors have in the past been seen to contain its adverse effects. The first is the persistence of inter-firm linkages, which have been thought to provide a continuing centripetal attraction, ensuring that outward moves do not continue to the point of disengagement. These linkage effects may themselves have been overestimated.[17] Moreover, increasing concentration of ownership enables large firms to enjoy an internalisation of linkages and so liberate themselves from any specific location. Second, cities have been regarded as industrial incubators, capable of replacing lost industry with few firms, some of which will have the necessary potential to generate compensatory growth. While local authority policies are increasingly targeted on this sector of the urban economy, there is a growing recognition that the industrial birth rate has fallen faster within cities than outside them, and that for many types of activity the best environment for both birth and growth is no longer to be found in the city.[18]

To a greater or lesser extent the arguments about industrial concentration, locational tendencies, linkages and birth rates apply to all of the older industrial cities. Yet there are also apparent differences *between* cities which remain even when we set London aside as a special case. Perhaps the most tantalising are those differences in the overall economic environment that produce startling differences in the entrepreneurial capacity of, say, Manchester as compared with Liverpool, or Leicester as compared with Derby.[19]

Current attempts to explain such differences centre on a complex of economic and non-economic factors which are best captured in that rather inexplicit term *milieu*. The very range of the concept draws attention to the cultural and political factors which interact with economic considerations to produce locally specific economic change. How important are the cumulative activities of local authorities in shaping these *milieux* for good or ill? While it is far too soon, given the fragmentary state of our knowledge, to answer this question, there may yet be value in posing it.

The full impact of local authority action on the urban *milieu* extends beyond the limits of the formally adopted economic development role. The urban space economy at any one point in time is a shifting (but not unstable) equilibrium of centrifugal and centripetal forces. If the weight of economic argument has shifted in favour of the former, then intangible factors – beliefs, loyalties, sentiments, preferences – may still have a powerful centripetal, pro-urban effect. Fostering those intangibles might yet prove to be a more effective means of anchoring firms against the tide of urban economic decline, and it is to that end that new roles and relationships might best be geared.

## References

1. P. Hall and D. Hay, *Growth Centres in the European Urban System* (Heinemann, 1981).
2. This is discussed further in K. Young and L. Mills, 'The Decline of Urban Economies', in R. Rose and E. Page (eds), *Fiscal Stress in the Cities* (Cambridge University Press, 1982).
3. *Development Control: Policy and Practice*, DoE Circular 22/80, para. 3.
4. D. Massey and R. Meegan, 'Industrial Restructuring vs. the Cities', *Urban Studies*, 15 (3), 1978; P. Lawless, 'The Role of Some Central

Government Agencies in Urban Economic Regeneration', *Regional Studies*, 15 (1), 1981, pp. 1–14.

5. See in particular K. Kumar, *Prophecy and Progress* (Penguin, 1978); Peter Hall (ed.), *The Inner City in Context* (Heinemann for SSRC, 1981) pp. 120–3.

6. Rose and Page, *Fiscal Stress in the Cities*.

7. Ken Young and Liz Mills, *Managing the Post-industrial City* (Heinemann, forthcoming) ch. 2.

8. Ibid; see also M. Spector and J. I. Kitsuse, *Constructing Social Problems* (Menlo Park, Calif.: Cummings, 1977).

9. Comptroller and Auditor-General, *Appropriation Accounts: vol. 2, classes iv–ix, 1979–80* (HMSO, 1981).

10. This situation is discussed further in Ken Young, 'Economic Development Incentives in Manchester, England' (forthcoming).

11. This fundamental shift is now thoroughly documented. See in particular Hall and Hay, *Growth Centres*; and S. Fothergill and G. Gudgin, *Unequal Growth* (Heinemann, 1982).

12. K. D. George, 'A Note on Changes in Industrial Concentration in the UK', *Economic Journal*, March 1975, pp. 124–7; P. Dicken, 'The Multi-plant Business Enterprise and Geographical Space: Some Issues in the Study of External Control and Regional Development', *Regional Studies*, 10, 1976 pp. 401–12.

13. W. W. Daniel, *Whatever Happened to the Workers in Woolwich?* (Political and Economic Planning, 1972); Community Development Project, *The Costs of Industrial Change* (CDP Inter-Project Team, 1977); Massey and Meegan, 'Restructuring vs the Cities'.

14. A. M. Warnes, *The Decentralisation of Employment from the Larger English Cities*, Geography Department Occasional Paper 5 (King's College, 1977); F. W. Hayden, *Factors Influencing the Location of Industry,* Research Memorandum RM 528 (Greater London Council, 1978); F. E. I. Hamilton, 'Aspects of Industrial Mobility in the British Economy', *Regional Studies,* 12, 1978, pp. 153–66.

15. Rose and Page, *Fiscal Stress in the Cities*.

16. D. E. Keeble, 'Local Industrial Linkage and Manufacturing Growth in Outer London', *Town Planning Review,* 40, 1969, pp. 163–88; Fothergill and Gudgin, *Unequal Growth*; see also the argument as to product cycles put forward in R. D. Norton and J. Rees, 'The Product Cycle and the Spatial Decentralisation of American Manufacturing', *Regional Studies*, 13 (2), 1979 pp. 141–51.

17. D. E. Keeble, 'Local Industrial Linkage'; M. Beesley, 'The Birth and Death of Industrial Establishments: Experience in the West Midlands Conurbation', *Industrial Economics*, 4, 1955, pp. 45–61; P. J. Wood, 'Industrial Location and Linkage', *Area*, 2, 1969, pp. 32–9; M. J. Taylor and P. J. Wood, 'Industrial Linkage and Local Agglomeration in the West Midlands Metal Industries', *Transactions of the Institute of British Geographers*, 59, 1973, pp. 172–54.

18. G. C. Cameron, 'Intra Urban Location and New Plant', *Papers and Proceedings of the Regional Science Association,* 31, 1973, pp. 125–

43; J. P. Firn and J. K. Swales, 'The Formation of New Manufacturing Establishments in Central Clydeside and the West Midlands Conurbations 1963–1972: a Comparative Analysis', *Regional Studies*, 12 (2), 1978, pp. 199–213; B. M. Nicholson, J. Brinkley and A. W. Evans, 'The Role of the Inner City in the Development of Manufacturing Industry', *Urban Studies*, 18 (1), 1981, pp. 57–72. For a recent re-assertion of the validity of the incubator hypothesis see J. J. Fagg, 'A Re-examination of the Incubator Hypothesis: A Case Study of Greater Leicester', *Urban Studies*, 17, 1980, pp. 35–44.

19. P. Lloyd and P. Dicken, *New Firms, Small Firms and Job Generation: the Experience of Manchester and Merseyside,* North West Industry Research Unit Working Paper 9 (School of Geography, Manchester Univerity, 1980); Fothergill and Gudgin, *Unequal Growth.*

# Notes on Contributors

**Martin Boddy** is a lecturer at the School for Advanced Urban Studies, University of Bristol, where he has worked since 1977 on DoE-funded projects on the Community Land Act and the industrial development process. His chapter arises from work carried out for the DoE, but the views expressed therein are his alone.

**D. A. Hart** is co-director of the Joint Centre for Land Development Studies of the University of Reading and the College of Estate Management. His chapter is largely based on a series of visits to German and American cities carried out as part of the Tri-national Inner City research project, sponsored by the German Marshall Fund of the United States. While the visits were made by a team of four people, the views expressed in the chapter are solely those of the author.

**Charlie Mason** is visiting research fellow at the University of Twente, Netherlands, and was formerly at the School for Advanced Urban Studies, University of Bristol, where he worked first on the SSRC-funded study of local authority economic policies, and subsequently on a study, also funded by the SSRC, of policy implementation in respect of the labour market.

**John Mawson** is lecturer in regional planning at the Centre for Urban and Regional Studies at the University of Birmingham. He wishes to acknowledge the help of all those who willingly gave up their time to discuss the formulation of local authority economic policies in West Yorkshire. Particular thanks go to David Miller, Martin Smith and Peter Thomas for their valuable comments on the first draft of his chapter.

**David J. North** and **Jamie Gough** are respectively senior lecturer in planning studies and research fellow at the Middlesex Polytechnic. The work reported here arises from a DoE-financed research project on monitoring manufacturing change in the inner city, which North co-directed. The authors are grateful to the other members of the research team, Roger Leigh and Karen Sweet-Escott, for their comments on drafts of the chapter.

**Murray Stewart** and **Jacky Underwood** are respectively professor of urban government and lecturer in urban studies at the School for Advanced Urban Studies, University of Bristol. They are currently engaged on an SSRC-financed study of inter-organisational relations in the inner city partnership and programme authorities.

**David Storey** is now senior research associate in the Centre for Urban and Regional Development Studies at Newcastle University, having previously worked in central and local government. He would like to acknowledge the help given by Stewart Cameron and Ken Willis, Directors of the Inner City Employment Project in the Town and County Planning Department at Newcastle University, who were helpful in both providing data and ideas, while a number of local government officers in the Counties of Tyne and Wear, Durham and Cleveland have discussed the issues raised in this chapter with him at length. Finance for the work on local economic development was provided primarily by the Gatsby Charitable Foundation. The Foundation's contribution is gratefully acknowledged.

**Ken Young** is senior research fellow at the Policy Studies Institute. His chapter is based on work carried out at the School for Advanced Urban Studies during 1977–9 with support from the SSRC. Charlie Mason and Liz Mills also participated in the study. The author would like to acknowledge with gratitude the unstinted co-operation of the members and officers of 'Westborough' London Borough Council.

# Further Reading

T. DAVIES, *Building Bridges: Linking Economic Regeneration to Inner City Employment Problems*, SAUS Working Paper 8 (Bristol University: SAUS, 1980).

DEPARTMENT OF THE ENVIRONMENT, *Review of Local Authority Assistance to Industry and Commerce* (DoE, July 1980).

M. M. CAMINA, *Local Authorities and the Attraction of Industry* (Pergamon, 1980).

R. HAMBLETON, *Inner Cities: Engaging the Private Sector,* SAUS Working Paper 10 (Bristol University: SAUS, 1980).

R. HAMBLETON, M. STEWART and J. UNDERWOOD, *Inner Cities Policy: Management and Resources*, SAUS Working Paper 13 (Bristol University: SAUS, 1980).

JONT UNIT FOR RESEARCH ON THE URBAN ENVIRONMMENT, *Local Authority Employment Initiatives* (University of Aston: JURUE, 1980).

N. JOHNSON and A. COCHRANE, *Economic Policy Making by Local Authorities in Britain and Western Germany* (Allen & Unwin, 1981).

P. LAWLESS, 'New Approaches to Local Authority Economic Intervention', *Local Government Studies,* Vol. 6 no. 1 (January–February 1980).

J. MAWSON (ed.), 'Special Issue on Unemployment and Economic Development', *Local Government Studies*, Vol. 7, no. 4 (July–August 1981).

J. MAWSON and A. NORTON, 'Local Action against Unemployment', *Local Government Studies,* Vol. 7, no. 5 (September–October 1981).

R. MINNS and J. THORNLEY, *State Shareholding: The Role of Local and Regional Authorities* (Macmillan, 1978).

R. MINNS and J. THORNLEY, 'Local Authority Economic Planning: A Guide to Powers and Initiatives', in G. Craig, M. Mayo and N. Sharman (eds), *Jobs and Community Action* (Routledge & Kegan Paul, 1979).

R. MULLER and A. BRUCE, 'Local Government in Pursuit of an Industrial Strategy', *Local Government Studies,* Vol. 7, no. 1 (January–February 1981).

F. ROBINSON, *Local Authority Economic Initiatives: A Review*, Centre for Environmental Studies Occasional Paper 10 (1979).

P. B. ROGERS and C. R. SMITH, 'The Local Authority's Role in Economic Development: The Tyne and Wear Act, 1976', *Regional Studies,* Vol. 11, no. 3 (1977).

D. J. STOREY and J. F. F. ROBINSON, 'Local Authorities and the Attraction of Industry: The Case of Cleveland County Council', *Local Government Studies*, Vol. 7, no. 1 (January–February 1981).

# Index

228